Heidegger: Thought and Historicity

HEIDEGGER

Thought and Historicity

Christopher Fynsk

CORNELL UNIVERSITY PRESS

Ithaca and London

Cornell University Press gratefully acknowledges a grant from the Andrew W. Mellon Foundation that aided in bringing this book to publication.

First published 1986 by Cornell University Press.

International Standard Book Number 0-8014-1879-8
Library of Congress Catalog Card Number 86-47640
Printed in the United States of America
Librarians: Library of Congress cataloging information appears
on the last page of the book.

The paper in this book is acid-free and meets the guidelines for
permanence and durability of the Committee on Production Guidelines
for Book Longevity of the Council on Library Resources.

For Greta, Arthur, and Susan

Contents

Acknowledgments   9

Abbreviations   11

Introduction   15
1. The Self and Its Witness   28
2. Nietzsche's Testimony   55
3. Difference and Self-Affirmation   104
4. The Work of Art and the Question of Man   131
5. Hölderlin's Testimony: An Eye Too Many Perhaps   174

Appendix 1. "Remembrance," by Friedrich Hölderlin   230
Appendix 2. "In lovely blueness...," by Friedrich Hölderlin 234
Index   241

Acknowledgments

The influence of Jacques Derrida, Philippe Lacoue-Labarthe, and Jean-Luc Nancy on the pages that follow is far greater than I have been able to indicate in my notes. In their separate ways, they have made this project possible. I express here my gratitude for their encouragement and for all they have offered in their teaching.

There are a number of other individuals whose friendship I cannot dissociate from the impetus that has carried me through this project. I will not try to name them all and hope only that they will find in these pages an echo of their promptings. I single out, however, René Girard, Richard Macksey, and Rodolphe Gasché, whose support has been of great importance to me, and Susan Hanson, whose patience and spirited questioning have been an unfailing source of inspiration. I dedicate this book to Susan and to my parents for their understanding and help of many years.

I also thank all those who have followed my efforts to teach Heidegger at the State University of New York at Binghamton and who have helped shape my readings with their responses; my colleagues in the Department of Comparative Literature for their warm support; Gloria Gaumer (whole time was generously paid for by the administration of SUNY Binghamton) for her careful preparation of my manuscript; Dennis Schmidt for his frequent suggestions concerning translations; and Bernhard Kendler of Cornell University Press for the attention he has given to this project. Finally, I express my appreciation to Joan Stambaugh for having shared with me portions of her forthcoming translation of *Sein und Zeit*.

Acknowledgments

A version of the first chapter appeared in *Boundary* 2 10, no. 3 (Spring 1982); I thank the editor, William Spanos, for his permission to use it in this volume. I am grateful also to Cambridge University Press for permission to reprint Hölderlin's poems "Remembrance" and "In lovely blueness...," from *Poems and Fragments*, trans. Michael Hamburger (1980), pp. 489–91 and 601–5.

CHRISTOPHER FYNSK

Abbreviations

(Unless otherwise noted, the works cited below were written by Heidegger.)

EHD   *Erläuterungen zu Hölderlins Dichtung,* 4th ed. (Frankfurt: Klostermann, 1971).

EM   *Einführung in die Metaphysik* (Tübingen: Niemeyer, 1973). *An Introduction to Metaphysics,* trans. Ralph Manheim (New York: Doubleday, 1961).

H   *Holzwege,* vol. 5 of *Gesamtausgabe* (Frankfurt: Klostermann, 1977). A translation by Albert Hofstadter of "Der Ursprung des Kunstwerkes" appears in *Poetry, Language, Thought* (New York: Harper & Row, 1971).

HH   *Hölderlins Hymnen "Germanien" und "Der Rhein,"* vol. 39 of *Gesamtausgabe* (Frankfurt: Klostermann, 1980).

N   *Nietzsche,* 2 vols. (Pfüllingen: Neske, 1961). Three of four projected volumes of a translation of *Nietzsche,* edited by David Farrell Krell, have been published by Harper & Row: vol. 1, *The Will to Power as Art* (1979), trans. Krell; vol. 2 *The Eternal Recurrence of the Same* (1984), trans. Krell; vol. 4, *Nihilism* (1982), trans. Frank A. Capuzzi.

SA   *Schellings Abhandlung über das Wesen der menschlichen Freiheit* (Tübingen: Niemeyer, 1971). *Schelling's Treatise on the Essence of Human Freedom,* trans. Joan Stambaugh (Athens: Ohio University Press, 1985).

SU   *Die Selbstbehauptung der deutschen Universität* (Breslau: Korn, 1933). A translation by Karsten Harries of this essay appears in *Review of Metaphysics* 38, no. 3 (March 1985).

SW   Hölderlin, *Sämtliche Werke,* Grosse Stuttgarter Ausgabe, ed. Friedrich Beissner (Stuttgart: W. Kohlhammer, 1946–68).

11

SZ *Sein und Zeit*, 15th ed. (Tübingen: Niemeyer, 1979). *Being and Time*, trans. John Macquarrie and Edward Robinson (New York: Harper & Row, 1962).

US *Unterwegs zur Sprache*, 3d ed. (Pfüllingen: Neske, 1959). *On the Way to Language*, trans. Peter Hertz and Joan Stambaugh (New York: Harper & Row, 1971).

VA *Vorträge und Aufsätze*, 4th ed. (Pfüllingen: Neske, 1954). A translation by Albert Hofstadter of "...dichterisch wohnet der Mensch..." appears in *Poetry, Language, Thought*.

W *Wegmarken*, vol. 9 of *Gesamtausgabe* (Frankfurt: Klostermann, 1976). A translation by David Farrell Krell of "Was ist Metaphysik?" appears in *Martin Heidegger, Basic Writings*, ed. Krell (New York: Harper & Row, 1977); this volume also contains a translation by Frank A. Capuzzi of *Brief über den Humanismus*.

WHD *Was Heisst Denken?* 2d ed. (Tübingen: Niemeyer, 1961). *What Is Called Thinking?* trans. J. Glenn Gray (New York: Harper & Row, 1968).

Heidegger: Thought and Historicity

Introduction

An admonition appears near the beginning of Heidegger's essay "Identity and Difference" which should give pause to any commentator of Heidegger's work:

> When thinking attempts to pursue something that has claimed its attention, it may happen that on the way it undergoes a change. Thus it is advisable in what follows to pay attention to the path of thought rather than to its content.[1]

These sentences suggest that we do not begin to read Heidegger until the surface intelligibility of the language is shaken and we follow not the content, a series of propositions or theses (or even a series of what may seem to be poetic figures), but the very movement of thought in its becoming-other.

Heidegger suggests to us that the claim upon thought and thought's transformation are to be understood in terms of an arrest or capture of thought by its "thing" or affair (*die Sache*). This latter, for the earlier Heidegger at least, is the finite transcendence of *Dasein*—a relation to something other than what is that makes possible any relation to beings in the world (including other human beings) and any self-relation. It makes possible the very structure of representation and therefore cannot be posed before us (*vor-gestellt*) in a theoretical or formal manner—hence Heidegger's

[1] *Identity and Difference*, trans. Joan Stambaugh (New York: Harper & Row, 1969), p. 1. This edition contains the German text.

15

effort to draw us beyond the conceptual and figurative levels of his discourse.

Of thought's transformation, we may say that the questioning relation provoked by the arrest of thought (described most frequently by Heidegger as an astonishment or perplexity—an uncanny experience of alterity that marks the presence to us of things in the world) bears not only upon the object of this questioning but also upon the act of questioning itself. Thought comes increasingly into question as it discovers ever more profoundly its initiative to have been a repetition of a determination to question. It finds in questioning that it is given to question—and no reflexive act can define absolutely the measure of its engagement in the history defined by the temporal precedence of the origin or opening of its act. To the extent that a thinking opens to that which claims it and assumes the temporal structure of its activity—assumes its finitude—it carries itself into a movement that exceeds it and carries it beyond itself.

This is an unsettling movement. It is unsettling, first, because it refuses itself to any conceptual definition or mastery and calls into question the normally secure position of the thinking subject, the position defined by the metaphysics of subjectivity in its elaboration of the structure of representation. Clearly, Heidegger did not find this situation to be an impediment for the task of thinking and even (initially) for the founding of a science. Near the end of *Kant and the Problem of Metaphysics*, he points explicitly to one consequence of assuming the finitude of metaphysical questioning:

> It remains to be considered that the working out of the innermost essence of finitude required for the establishment of metaphysics must itself always be basically finite and can never become absolute. The only conclusion one can draw from this is that reflection on finitude, *always to be renewed*, can never succeed, through a mutual playing off, or mediating equalization of standpoints in order finally and in spite of everything to give us an absolute knowledge of finitude, a knowledge that is surreptitiously posited as being "true in itself."[2]

By virtue of its inescapable temporal determination, thought can achieve no final definition of its own situation and thus cannot

<hr>

[2] *Kant and the Problem of Metaphysics*, trans. James S. Churchill (Bloomington: Indiana University Press, 1962), p. 245.

transcend the history in which it finds itself as it turns back upon that which gives it its impetus. The repetitive nature of Heidegger's course of thinking—his constant return to what he calls the "fundamental experience" of *Being and Time* (N2, 260) throughout his career—points to his own assumption of this understanding of finitude. But Heidegger suggests that, if thought cannot hold this movement in its grasp, it might hold itself in this movement in such a way as to find in it a certain measure. For the movement to which thought opens is understood by Heidegger to have a gathering and unifying character. Whether we speak in terms of the temporality of Dasein, the history of Being, or Appropriation (*Ereignis*), that which claims thought and sets it on a path that is without any assignable end also gathers it within what Heidegger terms an intimacy.

Yet there are also elements in Heidegger's thinking that problematize this fundamental assertion, just as his consistent refusal of certain dimensions of the thought of those to whom he turns in his interpretive encounters (I refer in particular to the encounters with Hölderlin and Nietzsche that I take up this book) takes on a symptomatic character. Heidegger failed to recognize in his *Kantbuch* (and, in some ways, throughout his career) just how unsettling his meditation on the finitude of Being and of thought might be. He points to this fact himself when he remarks much later (in 1956) that he has been unable to find a satisfactory answer to the problem of finitude. What was assumed affirmatively in the *Kantbuch* is now the source of a distress. I refer here to the statement in the "Addendum" to "The Origin of the Work of Art" in which Heidegger recognizes that his formulation of the role of man in art as creator and preserver remains ambiguous in his essay. He notes that, if truth is taken as the subject of the phrase by which he defines art, namely, "the setting into work of truth," then art "is conceived in terms of disclosive appropriation." He adds:

> Being, however, is a call to man and is not without man. Accordingly, art is at the same time defined as the setting into work of truth, where truth *now* is "object," and art is human creating and preserving. . . . In the heading, "the setting-into-work of truth," in which it remains undecided, but decid*able*, who does the setting or in what way it occurs, there is concealed *the relation of Being and human being*

17

[*Menschenwesen*], a relation which is unsuitably conceived even in this version—a distressing difficulty, which has been clear to me since *Being and Time*, and has since been expressed in a variety of versions. [*H*, 74/87][3]

This statement does not necessarily contradict the more assured statements in the later work concerning the place of mortals in what Heidegger calls the fourfold. But it is a sign that the relation between Being and human being is very much open to question in Heidegger's text and, necessarily with it, Heidegger's assertions concerning the gathering nature of the experience of difference (in thought's becoming-other), and thus the nature of difference itself and with it Being or Ereignis. This statement from Heidegger's "Addendum," indeed Heidegger's own methods of reading and the entire pedagogical thrust of Heidegger's project, invites us to question his path of thinking, even to repeat it in a more questioning manner. The chapters that follow represent an initial attempt to question in this way the relation between Being and human being as it is articulated in Heidegger's work of the period between 1927 and 1947 (that is, between the dates of publication of *Being and Time* and the *Letter on Humanism*).

This questioning does not take the form of an exposition of Heidegger's thought during this period; it consists, rather, in a series of individual readings that seek in each case to enter into the movement of Heidegger's thought as he refers to it in the passage from which I started. Only a most attentive reading of Heidegger's texts—one that seeks the place and function of any particular theme, figure, or statement within a larger textual disposition or configuration—leads to an experience of the dynamic quality of his thinking and to an apprehension of the strangeness or perplexity that claims his thought and gives it its movement. And such a reading is a prerequisite for a more severe textual reading that moves beyond this still phenomenologically determined apprehension of the movement of a thought and begins to follow the

---

[3]Abbreviated references indicate the page number in the German edition, followed, where available, by the page number in the English translation. In some cases, I have modified the translation for the sake of clarity or terminological consistency. I wish to thank Harper & Row for granting me this privilege in regard to their translations, in this and other works.

movement of the "letter" of the text (though the task of defining the meaning of this "moving beyond" is still very much before us).[4]

The unity of the readings that follow derives from the fact that, in seeking the dynamic element in the writings by Heidegger under consideration, I have been led to focus on the "circling" in Heidegger's thinking, whose necessity Heidegger has described as the hermeneutic circle. I analyze this movement first in *Being and Time* and attempt to describe how the circle in which Heidegger situates the questioning of Dasein in a project of Being is to be thought not in a circular fashion but rather in terms of a double movement like that which Heidegger describes elsewhere as a play of presence and absence, distance and proximity. In subsequent chapters I describe this paradoxical movement in terms of an experience of "disappropriation" that accompanies man's effort at appropriation (indissociably of history and of self); the title of Chapter 3, "Difference and Self-Affirmation," names the poles of human experience as Heidegger describes it in the essays that predate the Second World War. (By 1940, Heidegger no longer

[4] I should at least note that this movement does not lead to the impasse of restricting thought to an examination of textual phenomena in the restricted sense. The notion of finitude I attempt to elaborate in this book points to the necessary "tracing" or "inscription" of thought (just as truth must be "set into" the work, according to Heidegger's argument in "The Origin of the Work of Art"). But it should become clear that this does not dictate a kind of formalism. The movement to which I am referring is perhaps properly named deconstruction, in the sense of this term developed by Jacques Derrida. Though I have not taken up here Derrida's relation to Heidegger (in order to retain my focus on Heidegger's text, and because such a question requires an extensive, contextual analysis of Derrida's work), I hope that the reader will recognize that I am working very much in view of his thought in the latter part of this book. But I want to emphasize that this work remains somewhat short of a deconstruction in the Derridean sense (or in the sense developed more recently by Paul de Man). If I were to attempt a full deconstruction of Heidegger's text in the terms I have sought to develop in this book—out of Heidegger's own thought, therefore—I would begin by trying to fold back upon the language and structure of the text itself at least the following: Heidegger's own discussions of a work's form (in "The Origin of the Work of Art," for example), the notion of figurality that I present briefly in Chapters 4 and 5, an understanding of the performative dimension of his use of language (which I begin to develop in the last chapters), and other clues offered by Heidegger concerning his use of language, including his reference to a "fugue" articulated around the word "but" that he discovers in Hölderlin's poem "Andenken." I hope that the analyses presented in these pages will give some indication of the difficulty of the questions involved here and explain why I approach them with a certain prudence.

speaks in terms of *Selbstbehauptung* [self-affirmation], but the effort to articulate a less willful mode of creative existence in a concept such as *Gelassenheit* [releasement or letting be] still obeys the structure to which I refer.)

The hermeneutic situation described in *Being and Time* as "a remarkable 'relatedness backward or forward' of what we are asking about (Being) to the inquiry itself as a mode of being of a being" (*SZ*, 8/28), structures Heidegger's interpretation of both Nietzsche and Hölderlin. In my reading of Heidegger's *Nietzsche*, I attempt to demonstrate that, if Heidegger's encounter with Nietzsche is understood in the light of this hermeneutic situation (and it is described quite explicitly in the first volume of *Nietzsche*), then a richer interpretation emerges than the one commonly attributed to Heidegger, which consists merely in a violent resituation of Nietzsche within the history of metaphysics. I approach Heidegger's reading of Hölderlin in a similar manner, though I do so in the light of readings of *An Introduction to Metaphysics* and "The Origin of the Work of Art." The meditations on *technē* and art in these latter texts, and on what we might call the finitude of Being, lead me to a somewhat more precise formulation of the double movement of appropriation and disappropriation; thus I come to describe a creative project of Being as the tracing of the limits of Dasein whereby these limits are brought forth *as limits*, and thus as the mark of a relation to an alterity. I consider Heidegger's reading of Hölderlin, then, in relation to this description of a creative project, and by contrasting Hölderlin's understanding of the nature of the experience of difference with Heidegger's interpretation of it (as I do in the case of Nietzsche), I bring into question Heidegger's assertions concerning the gathering and founding character of a poetic project. In light of the claims Heidegger makes for poetry (*Dichtung*) and the role he assigns to Hölderlin, this questioning should give some suggestion of what Heidegger finds so distressing in the question of the relation between Being and human being.

Within the hermeneutic situation I have described, I address the problem of the constitution of identity. This problem arises first in relation to the question of *Mitsein* in *Being and Time*. One of Heidegger's fundamental theses in this volume concerns the individuating aspect of Dasein's solitary assumption of its mortality. But the reading of *Being and Time* that I offer in Chapter 1 will suggest that Dasein is not alone in being-toward-death. In his description of the originary experience to which the resoluteness of being-toward-death opens, Heidegger points furtively but consistently to an uncanny experience of the other Dasein. We might conclude from *Being and Time* that the call of Being (which first takes form in *Being and Time* as the call of conscience) first comes by way of another—strictly speaking, by way of another's presentation of the finitude of their being.

In light of this perspective on Mitsein, the nature of Heidegger's interpretive stance in relation to figures such as Nietzsche and Hölderlin calls for particular attention. In each case we may observe something like a fascination on Heidegger's part (and here I mean to refer beyond the psychological category, for fascination belongs to Dasein's originary experience of difference as it is described by Heidegger) and a corresponding violence in his interpretation. I have recourse in this context to René Girard's very rich notion of mimetic rivalry, though I seek a philosophical understanding of the grounds of this relation—an experience of the other that is more unsettling than Heidegger wishes to acknowledge. Nietzsche and Hölderlin both claim Heidegger's attention, over and above the reasons he offers for giving them privileged places in the history of Being, because their self-presentation entails something other than the withdrawal (or the reserve) that belongs to an assumption of finitude. The identity posited by them (hence, their "address") is marked by a certain instability or ambiguity, and both invite us to ask whether any measure offers itself in the assumption of finitude as Heidegger describes it. Their testimony brings into question Heidegger's assertions concerning the gathering nature of the relation between Being and human being and thus the possibility of anything like a "dwelling" as Heidegger defines it in his readings of Hölderlin.

Thus I might say that I am seeking to pose in this book the question of man—a question that might seem of preliminary and even secondary importance in relation to the thing or affair of Heidegger's thought as it takes shape along his path of thinking. For the pertinence of this question, according to most commentaries on the *Kehre*, would appear to be limited to the first steps of Heidegger's path: specifically to the foundational thinking that precedes the Kehre and thus, for example, to the final pages of

Kant and the Problem of Metaphysics, where it is said that the repetition of the Kantian effort to found metaphysics must be rooted in the question of the Dasein in man. The effort to go beyond the metaphysics of subjectivity and to elaborate a thought of difference would appear to require an abandonment of an essential reference to man.

But to this possible objection, I would offer this initial response: The overcoming of the metaphysics of subjectivity and the anthropocentrism of modern thought—in short, the overcoming of humanism—in no way implies that the question of man should lose its weight. On the contrary, when man can no longer be taken as the ground for truth, then the question of man should grow more weighty for thought *as a question.*[5] In addition, a rigorous examination of the problematic of Dasein will reveal why it must unsettle any foundational project and ultimately any project of appropriation of man's essence (any project that does not simultaneously account for the impossibility of its full accomplishment and thus open to a history that it cannot master), even if this appropriation is thought as a gathering of self in the intimacy of a response to Being.

The question of man does of course lead beyond itself. I try to show, for example, that it must be posed in relation to Heidegger's interpretation of the Greek notion of *thesis* (and his argument concerning the nature of any positing in general) as it is proposed in "The Origin of the Work of Art"—an argument that leads into the questions of language, *Technik,* etc. But if I persist in holding to the question of man as the crucial point of access to the

[5]The assertion of Philippe Lacoue-Labarthe and Jean-Luc Nancy that the question of man is not a question among others for philosophy but involves its very essence and possibility has played an important role in orienting the focus of this book. Lacoue-Labarthe and Nancy situate this question in relation to the notion of *Bestimmung* as it opens in Kant and German Idealism. In their "Ouverture" to *Les fins de l'homme: A partir du travail de Jacques Derrida,* ed. Philippe Lacoue-Labarthe and Jean-Luc Nancy (Paris: Editions Galilée, 1981), p. 13, they argue the following: "From the moment that man is no longer destined for a completion of his own essence beyond himself, but consigned to a destination whose telos can no longer be appointed or programmed—from this moment the very destination of philosophy is in question, whether it gives itself its own point of reference in the form of Knowledge or that of Wisdom. Philosophy then enters into a crisis concerning its presentation or *Darstellung* just as it is haunted by the problem of its practical effectuation. It allows itself to be opened to, or exceeded by, the problematic of its end: accomplishment, disappearance, *Überwindung,* rebeginning, etc."

"thing" of Heidegger's thought, it is because it poses itself the question of access. "Dasein" names man's situation in relation to Being, and no thought of the history or topology of Being can proceed without situating itself in relation to this topos.[6] Likewise, no reading of Heidegger's text, if it seeks to become a *repetition*, or *Auseinandersetzung*, can neglect this question of access—a question that becomes in repetition both the question of Heidegger's access which claims our interpretive attention in this relation. If we follow Heidegger in an effort to articulate something like a thought of difference, we must be wary of reassuming the all-too-comfortable place of the meditating subject of theory, a place of supposed neutrality. A thought of difference becomes no more than a repetition of the same if it repeats the ahistorical or nonsituated thinking whose place is defined by the metaphysics of subjectivity.

But in neglecting the question of man in a reading of Heidegger, there is more than the danger of failing to situate the act of questioning. Heidegger's self-criticism regarding the echoes of the metaphysics of subjectivity in his early writings, together with the evident movement in his thinking away from the existential analytic—toward a description of the epochal history of Being and finally toward a topological understanding of Being—might well lead us to conclude that the *progress* of Heidegger's thought as it moves at the limits of metaphysics and toward a nonmetaphysical thought of difference entails a resolution of the questionable element in the

[6]I affirm this while recognizing, again, that Heidegger rethinks this topos in his later work in relation to the problem of language. We are dealing here with another version of the hermeneutic circle. One cannot, finally, think the situation of Dasein without coming to grips with the problem of language, a point that can already be drawn from Heidegger's remarks on language in *Being and Time* and from his very definition of hermeneutic investigation in paragraph 7 of this work. But we cannot approach this problem in a rigorous manner without a critical examination of the earlier problematic of human finitude. The question of man must not be forgotten at any point. I might also add here for the sake of clarity that I do not mean to assert that the question of man *alone* is ever the sole way of access to the question of Being, for the question of man, as Heidegger thinks it, cannot be posed alone. It can be posed only in relation to and as the question of man's relation to Being, which implies the question of Being. Likewise, as Heidegger states most explicitly in *What Is Called Thinking?* a lecture course of 1951–52 (thus well after any dating of the Kehre), the question of Being cannot be posed except in relation to the question of man. My attention to the finitude of Dasein is meant to answer to this hermeneutic situation. But the notion of finitude, as I will attempt to demonstrate, points to the "positive necessity" (*SZ*, 310/358) that constrained Heidegger to take as his starting point an "existential analytic."

problematic of Dasein, or entails a kind of shift in perspective that reveals the problematic character of this question to have been merely a specter of metaphysics. Thus Reiner Schürmann's study of Heidegger, *Le principe d'anarchie: Heidegger et la question de l'agir*—to take a challenging recent example—argues that we should read Heidegger's text from end to beginning in order to distinguish in his thought the emerging strains of the effort that moves it through its entire trajectory and emerges fully in the latest texts: the effort to "grasp presence as pregnant with a force of plurification and dissolution."[7] Schürmann argues that Heidegger's path of thought leads him away from any reference to man as origin ("The 'origin,' henceforth, is no longer simple")[8] and finally to the effort to think without reference to man except as a component in the play of the fourfold. But just as Schürmann must overstate the "antihumanism" of Heidegger's late work in his effort to distinguish Dasein and thought, he must pass over the complexity of Heidegger's early meditation on man and fail to recognize that Dasein does not prove "simple" for Heidegger, even if he seeks in it a ground. The danger of reading in reverse order to bring forth the essential thought of difference in Heidegger is that we may lose sight of the most unsettling dimensions of his experience of difference. By crediting Heidegger's own reading of his path of thought, we might well follow him in avoiding what is "distressing" in the question of man. And by losing sight of the *question* of man, we may well lose the possibility of thinking the constitutive role of Dasein (what Schürmann designates as the "practical *a priori*") in the event of Appropriation—and thus the possibility of thinking the political import of Heidegger's thought.

In presenting as I have the thematic unity of this study, I may give the suggestion that it takes the structure of an *argument*; in fact, it proceeds in a less continuous fashion (and not always chronologically)—following the related topics of the question of man and the structure of a project of Being as a kind of *fil conducteur* (to borrow Mallarmé's phrase)[9] in a series of largely

---

[7]*Le principe d'anarchie: Heidegger et la question de l'agir* (Paris: Editions du Seuil, 1982), p. 22.

[8]Ibid., p. 67.

[9]I might translate this phrase as "guiding element." See Mallarmé's preface to "Un coup de dés," in *Oeuvres complètes* (Paris: Editions Gallimard, 1945), p. 455.

immanent readings of Heidegger's texts. The assertion I made above concerning the contextual nature of these analyses might bear some elaboration in that it marks the point at which this analysis diverges most significantly, in my opinion, from most other readings of Heidegger. I do want to claim of course that I attend to the thematic level of Heidegger's texts (I use the phrase only for heuristic purposes—the thetic content of Heidegger's writings cannot be divorced from its place in a textual configuration) in a way that differs significantly from that of other commentaries. I am convinced that an approach to Heidegger that confronts the theoretical ambiguities of the work before the *Letter on Humanism* (including the questions posed by its political dimensions) will ultimately offer a far richer reading of the entirety of his path of thinking—richer for our understanding of Heidegger and, more important, richer for the ongoing task of elaborating a thought of difference—than one that reads Heidegger for "results," as I might put it, and interprets his texts in the light of his most developed thought, screening out the more troublesome elements in the path of his thinking. This reading necessarily takes a more critical approach to the work preceding the *Letter on Humanism* than that which characterizes most efforts to proceed from the existential foundation of Heidegger's thought (Gadamer's, for example) and also points to the fact that a modern thought of difference cannot assume too easily Heidegger's later thought; the notions of the fourfold, of *es gibt*, and so forth must be situated in their history for their force to emerge.

But beyond these theoretical arguments, I consider my approach to Heidegger's *text* to be the most distinctive aspect of this interpretation. Like any text, Heidegger's body of writing is a construct that has won its apparent unity and coherence of meaning through a conflictual process of differentiation and exclusion—a process that always leaves its marks in the form of gaps, inconsistencies, aporias, etc. Like a dream, as Freud describes it, it is woven around an umbilicus that its self-reflection cannot account for. Heidegger's own description of a work, as I try to demonstrate, points to the way in which it manifests the precariousness of its limits and thus points beyond itself. I would like to suggest that Heidegger's text must be read in the light of such a concept.

Thus I have sought the openings in Heidegger's text in readings that do not draw their primary interpretive leverage from other theoretical domains (psychoanalysis, etc.) or from other perspectives on the history of thought and culture; critiques that proceed on this basis without submitting their own presuppositions to a Heideggerian form of questioning must of necessity close upon the question of Being in advance and can never come to grips with Heidegger's text. I consider my readings to be fully "Heideggerian" in this sense, but also very "suspicious" of Heidegger's text— unwilling to take it at face value, so to speak, or to be limited to what it purports to say (however obscure or difficult its meaning might seem and however important the task of explication might be). They seek instead those points where the text marks its relation to something that exceeds it and that provokes its movement. They seek to define, in other words, what gives the text its fundamentally historical character.[10] Needless to say, these readings only begin such a task.

One can undertake such a reading only on the basis of an interpretation of the text's argument, of course; though I do not carry out the kind of exposition of Heidegger's thought that characterizes most presentations of his work and though I provide relatively few evaluations of existing commentaries, I do not by any means underestimate the importance of such commentary. I consider the work of Pöggeller, Beaufret, Richardson, Marx, Harries, and others to be extremely helpful, and I hope to return on another occasion to confront some of their texts in extended analysis with a reading they have helped to make possible. But my expositions of Heidegger's thought are undertaken in order to bring my interpretation to what I have described as the limits of this thinking as I perceive them in Heidegger's text, and I direct my interpretive energies to these points. This analysis is therefore not an introduction to Heidegger, except perhaps in a sense defined by Heidegger at the beginning of *An Introduction to Metaphysics*, when he argues that the only possible introduction to his thinking is one that provokes a subsequent questioning. By seeking the historicity of the text of the thinker who has posed more powerfully than any other in this century the question of temporality, I seek the condi-

---

[10]For a development of this concept of the historicity of a thought, see Derrida's admirable essay "Violence and Metaphysics," in *Writing and Difference*, trans. Alan Bass (Chicago: University of Chicago Press, 1978), pp. 79–153.

tions for a renewed questioning. An analysis of the enabling historical background of Heidegger's thinking, a careful conceptual articulation of Heidegger's terms, and an evaluation of the philosophical merits of his arguments are all essential and important. But an Auseinandersetzung with Heidegger—a confrontation that is also the elaboration of another historical position of questioning— also requires something more, as Heidegger himself would insist. Even if the history of metaphysics comes to an end in Heidegger's thought, as he suggests and as commentators such as Schürmann and Marx are willing to assume, the historical character of this thought still demands attention: the most fundamental claim of Heidegger's text concerns its own historicity. The questioning in which a response might take form must be willing to submit this claim to the same interpretive treatment that Heidegger reserves to those who claim his own thinking. His thinking, in other words, must be situated in a movement that exceeds it, and a new understanding of this movement must be articulated. The readings that follow only begin to meet this exigency, but it defines the measure for an evaluation of their success.

1/

The Self and Its Witness

When Heidegger argues in *Being and Time* that being-with (Mitsein) is constitutive for Dasein, he breaks with a tradition that begins its inquiry concerning man by positing an isolated subject. "Being with others," Heidegger writes, "belongs to the being of Dasein that is an issue for Dasein in its very being" (*SZ*, 123/160). The existential analytic does not first posit the individual Dasein as given and then construct its relation to others and to the surrounding world. On the contrary, it seeks to define the constitution of the self within the "simple and multifold relation to others, to things and to oneself" (*N1*, 577) as this relation is founded in, but also determines, a comprehension of Being.

And yet if Heidegger succeeds in revealing through his analysis of Mitsein one limit of metaphysical thought about the subject, he seems unwilling or unable to work at this limit in a sustained manner; his analysis of Dasein in *Being and Time* leads back insistently to the solitary self. The question of the other thus forms in Heidegger's own text a kind of "inner limit" (as Heidegger might put it);[1] *Being and Time* opens the question even as it evades it. In this chapter, I will retrace this limit by considering Heidegger's few remarks on the relations between Dasein and others and by reading these remarks as they are inscribed in the paradoxical logic of the hermeneutic circle. By focusing upon the question of the other, I hope to force the analysis of Dasein at one of its most uncertain

[1]See Heidegger's concluding remarks in "Will to Power as Knowledge" (*N1*, 657).

moments and to bring forth a dimension, largely veiled in Heidegger's text, of what he describes as the uncanny opening of thought.

In *Being and Time*, Heidegger develops a definition of the self which departs from the metaphysical definitions of the subject, most manifestly from that subject of modern metaphysics posited with the *cogito sum* of Descartes. Modern metaphysics, coming to completion with Nietzsche, posits Being as being-represented (*Vorgestelltheit*) and the human subject as the foundation of this Being. The truth of Being in modern metaphysics becomes the certitude of the subject insofar as the subject is capable of representing. Heidegger seeks to unseat this subject from its central position as *subjectum* but does not renounce all effort to situate or position the subject or self; he situates it elsewhere—in relation to the "there" of Dasein—and describes the condition of possibility for Dasein's assumption of a position or stance in terms of the structure of Dasein's being as care. Thus he writes:

> Selfhood is to be found existentially only in the authentic potentiality-of-being-a-self—that is to say, in the authenticity of the being of Dasein *as care*. In terms of care the *constancy of the Self*, as the supposed persistence of the subjectum, gets its clarification. But the phenomenon of this authentic potentiality-of-being also opens our eyes for *The constancy of the Self* in the sense of its having gained a stand. *The constancy of the Self*, in the double sense of constant steadfastness, is the *authentic* counterpossibility to the non-self-constancy of irresolute falling. [SZ, 322/369]

As Dasein's being is founded in temporality, we will have occasion to define "the constancy of the self" in terms of its temporal structure. This analysis will involve considering Heidegger's concept of repetition and will lead us into the circular structure of the hermeneutic of Dasein. But before entering this circle, and in order to determine better how to enter into it (though the possibility of such decision comes into question in this analysis), we should pause over the terms of the thesis I have just quoted and consider what is at stake in the opposition set forth there.

The opposition to which I refer is the one Heidegger sets up when he posits the possibility of the constancy of the self *against* the non-self-constancy that characterizes Dasein in its state of falling (*Verfallenheit*), that is, the non-self-constancy of "being-with-one-another" in the "they" (*das Man*). The they is the nameless "who" of Dasein in its everyday existence, the they who has already defined the world before Dasein comes to it. Heidegger describes Dasein's existence in the world of the they as one of subjection, an existence in which Dasein loses its being. The most common elements of daily life pose the greatest danger:

> In utilizing public means of transportation and in making use of information services such as the newspaper, every other is like the next. This being-with-one-another dissolves one's own Dasein completely into the kind of being of "the others," in such a way, indeed, that the others, as distinguishable and explicit, disappear more and more. In this inconspicuousness and unascertainability, the real dictatorship of the "they" unfolds. We take pleasure and enjoy ourselves as *they* [*man*] take pleasure; we read, see, and judge literature and art as *they* see and judge; likewise we shrink back from the "great mass" as *they* shrink back; we find "shocking" what *they* find shocking. The "they," which is nothing definite and which all are, though not as a sum, prescribes the kind of being of everydayness. [*SZ*, 126–27/164]

The self is lost in the they, and with it the others as definite others; an infinite substitution is possible ("jeder Andere kann sie vertreten" [*SZ*, 126]) because, as Heidegger asserts in a striking phrase, "Everyone is the other, and no one is himself" (*SZ*, 128/165). Against this subjugation, Heidegger affirms the possibility of Dasein's recovering its own, proper being through the fundamentally solitary act of assuming its individual potentiality-for-being by being-toward-death. I will return to this notion; let it suffice for the moment to recall Heidegger's well-known argument that one cannot be represented by another at one's death—that Dasein dies alone, which founds the possibility of Dasein's individuality and integrity as authentically itself.[2]

The motif of individuality forms the point around which this reading of *Being and Time* will turn. The insistence with which Heidegger returns to this notion throughout *Being and Time* and, as noted by many critics, the corresponding lack of attention given to

---

[2]Heidegger writes, for example: "[Dasein's] death is the possibility of no-longer-being-able-to-be-there. If Dasein stands before itself as this possibility, it has been *fully* assigned to its most proper potentiality-of-being. When it stands before itself in this way, all its relations to any other Dasein have been undone" (*SZ*, 250/294).

Dasein's relation to the other suggest the fundamental importance of this motif. My aim is not simply to dismiss Heidegger's central affirmation concerning Dasein's autonomy or solitude, nor will I pretend to undo the knot that takes form in this text in the course of the descriptions of Dasein's relations to the other. Let me say merely that it appears necessary to displace or rearticulate Heidegger's thesis following certain indications in the text itself and at the same time to displace the "death scene" that Heidegger foregrounds in order to bring forth more what Heidegger gives us to consider as the scene of birth. It will therefore be necessary to consider further the few indications that Heidegger offers concerning Dasein's relation with the other—a relation that Heidegger designates in its primordial, existential structure as being-with.

Up to this point, we have seen that the relation of Dasein and the other, insofar as this other is the "they" of everyday existence, is a nonrelation. Either the terms of the relation are dissolved in an infinite exchangeability, or else Dasein, through its encounter with death, tears itself away from the world of the others—the world interpreted by the others—and seizes for itself another world. Does this mean that Dasein, in its authenticity, is committed to solipsism? Does Dasein, in its autonomy, lose all contact with the other? Heidegger answers that it does not; the gesture of pulling away from the world is what permits the first contact with the other, and the disclosure of Dasein's individual truth (this disclosure *is* its truth, according to the definition of truth as *alētheia* developed in paragraph 44 of *Being and Time*) is also the disclosure of the truth of the other—because, as we have seen, "being with others belongs to the being of Dasein" (*SZ*, 123/160). Dasein's understanding, its disclosure of its own being, *already* implies the understanding disclosure of the other: "Knowing oneself is grounded in being-with, which understands primordially" (*SZ*, 124/161). When Dasein discovers its being and the factical situation that is its own, it has already discovered the being of the other—Dasein has already encountered the other when it comes to assume itself as a self.

This encounter will be "shared" in what Heidegger calls "communication" (*SZ*, 162/205), but the being-with and its corresponding state of mind articulated by communication is not a form of identification, or is not an identification of a nature such that the being of Dasein that "preexists" its understanding and assumption of itself (that being *already there*, of which Dasein has a pre-understanding and toward which it proceeds in its disclosure of itself) could be confused with the being of the other. Heidegger considers the question of how Dasein comes to know the other *as other* only long enough (and his brevity is astonishing when one considers the seeming importance of such a question in the analytic of Dasein) to affirm that Dasein's relation to itself is not the basis of its understanding of the other's being. Dasein, insofar as it knows the other, does not simply project its own understanding of itself "into" the other. Here is Heidegger's argument:

> Being toward others is ontologically different from being toward things that are present-at-hand. The "other" being itself has the kind of being of Dasein. In being with and toward others, there is thus a relation of being from Dasein to Dasein. But, one might like to say, this relation is, after all, already constitutive for one's own Dasein which has an understanding of its own being and is thus related to Dasein. The relation of being to others then becomes a projection of one's own being toward oneself "into an other." The other would be a double of the self.
>
> But it is easy to see that this seemingly obvious deliberation has little ground to stand on. The presupposition that this argument draws upon—that the being of Dasein toward itself is being toward an other—is incorrect. As long as this presupposition has not proven evident in its legitimacy, it remains puzzling how the relation of Dasein to itself is thus to be disclosed to the other as other.
>
> Being toward others is not only an autonomous, irreducible relation of being; as being-with it already exists with the being of Dasein. [*SZ*, 124–25/162]

Heidegger is moving very quickly and leaving a great deal unsaid here. Yet this passage is crucial, because it is the only place in *Being and Time* where Heidegger takes up the existential nature of a difference in Dasein's relation to the other. The quick dismissal of a metaphysically laden notion of projection (however important a role it has played in the human sciences, dominated by a Cartesian notion of the subject) and the rhetorically startling evocation of its implications ("the other would be a double of the self") thus strike an odd note. Why does Heidegger approach this central problem of the difference in being-with in such an indirect manner and then leave it so rapidly? Is it possible that the notion of being-with entails equally unsettling implications and that Heidegger is screening these with his refusal of the notion of projection? This suspicion can be fully weighed only in the larger context of Heidegger's treatment of the relation between Daseins. Let me, for the moment, simply voice this suspicion, and attempt to develop somewhat further Heidegger's assertions in this passage.

We have seen that Dasein's being with others belongs to Dasein's own potential being. Dasein *is* in the way of being-with, which implies that its disclosure of itself is a codisclosure of the other. The relation of being implied here is such that the sciences of psychology designate it as "empathy" (*Einfühlung*) and take it as the ontological bridge between subjects (*SZ*, 124/162). But Heidegger insists that while being-with is the ground for any encounter with the other and belongs to the being of Dasein, the relation of being toward the other that it involves is not identifiable with Dasein's being in its being toward itself (such an identity would eliminate the otherness of the other and Dasein would lose its own fundamentally singular identity). Being toward others, Heidegger asserts, is "an autonomous, irreducible relation of being." But Heidegger must then account for the possibility of Dasein's relation to the other *as other*. The puzzle, as Heidegger says, is how Dasein's singular relation to itself is to be disclosed to the other and, of course, how Dasein is to encounter the other as other—that is, how Dasein is to discover the other's relation to itself as an instance of alterity. In Dasein's being toward the other, there must be a trace of alterity permitting an encounter that is not simply an identification. Thus, while Dasein's relation to itself and its relation to the other cannot be the same relation (or a relation of sameness), they must nevertheless be thought together, for the relation to the other must be a communication of difference.

We might therefore qualify the phrase "being toward others is an autonomous, irreducible relation of being" by suggesting that being toward others is irreducible *in each case* because Dasein relates itself to the other, or opens to the other, in or by way of its irreducible relation to itself. We might now say that being toward the other and being toward oneself are the *same* but are not the constitution or communication of a simple identity; they are the same relation insofar as being toward the other marks a difference, insofar as it is a presentation of difference (though strictly speaking, this difference is not presentable; the nature of its manifestation remains to be defined) and an encounter with difference. And insofar as Dasein opens to the other out of its irreducibly singular relation to its own being, its being for the other or its existing for the sake of others (*umwillen Anderen*) cannot be identified with the other's being for it, even if they share the same world. As Maurice Blanchot would put it, the relation of the two Daseins is dissymetrical in such a way that the distance and directionality of the passage between Dasein A and Dasein B does not coincide with that between B and A.[3] The relation of being between B and A is thus marked by an alterity, and if their relation is founded in their common world (and founds this world), this world is not an element or a unified coherent space in which one Dasein might be related to another by way of a common measure.

Heidegger's argumentation to this point in *Being and Time* hardly permits us to go any further (if even this far) in describing the differential relation between Dasein and the other. For the moment, let us retain above all the following: Dasein's relation to its own being is the ground of a radical difference in the relation of being-with. But if Heidegger at this point does not develop at greater length the existential relation of being-with and the difference that is inscribed there, we should note that the paragraphs immediately following the ones we have been reading continue to treat the subject of difference in Dasein's relations with the other. Paragraph 27 begins by introducing the concept of "distantiality":

> In taking care of what one has taken hold of with, for, or against, the others, there is constant care as to the way one differs from them, whether this difference is merely one that is to be evened out, whether one's own Dasein has lagged behind the others and wants to catch up in relation to them, whether Dasein in its priority over the others is intent upon suppressing them. Being-with-one-another is, unknown to itself, disquieted by the care about this distance. If we may express this existentially, being-with-one-another has the character of *distantiality* [*Abständigkeit*]. The more inconspicuous this kind of being is to everyday Dasein itself, all the more stubbornly and primordially does it work itself out.

[3]See his *L'entretien infini* (Paris: Gallimard, 1969), p. 104.

> But this distantiality that belongs to being-with, is such that Dasein, as everyday being-with-one-another, stands in *subjection* to others. [*SZ*, 126/163–64]

Distantiality, then, is the condition of Dasein's loss of self in the they. Dasein's anxious concern about its difference vis-à-vis the other leads it, paradoxically, into the sameness of the they. Measuring itself in terms of the other, Dasein falls into subjection to others. But this relation of being is hardly that relation without common measure that we have seen in Heidegger's description of being-with. Rather, it is a modification of this primordial possibility and makes up one of the two extreme forms that the relation with the other can take in the world constituted by being-with. Heidegger calls the mode of encountering the other in the world of everyday dealings solicitude (*Fürsorge*)—its two extreme modes are essentially "domination" and "liberation."

In domination, Dasein takes over, or attempts to take over, the place of the other. Heidegger says that in this mode, Dasein "leaps in" for the other ("sich an seine Stelle setzen, für ihn einspringen" [*SZ*, 122/158]). Distantiality is the ground of this rivalry. In the mode of liberation, Dasein concerns itself not with occupying the other's position or with acquiring the object of the other's concern but rather with freeing the other for its freedom. In the one case, Dasein relates itself to the other in terms of the work of everyday concern and everyday affairs; in the other case, it relates itself to the other in its being. But why does Dasein choose one form of solicitude and not another? Heidegger argues that the form of dominating solicitude is in fact predominant because Dasein is always falling into the world and preoccupying itself with everyday affairs. Dasein forgets its own authentic potentiality of being, forgets its own freedom, and thereby forgets the freedom of the other. It measures itself in terms of the objects of its concern and is drawn into a form of competition. When Dasein assumes its freedom, however, it discloses itself in such a way that it can disclose the other, and disclose the other as other.

To this point, then, we have seen Heidegger evoke and demarcate the possibility of a confusion of being in two forms: doubling and rivalry, each of which corresponds to a different level of analysis. At the ontological level, the possibility of the double is dismissed by assigning a radical difference to the relation with the other. The ontological relation between Daseins implies a separation. This ontological relation is in turn the foundation of the existential relations in which Dasein can exist in a liberating or dominating mode. The second possibility—the mode of rivalry in which Dasein loses its being—is founded in a distantiality, itself forgotten or dissimulated by the they. (In this way, Heidegger affirms that the harmony of the everyday world dissimulates a constant and more primordial conflict.) The menace, evoked at both levels, is a loss of identity, a dissolution of Dasein's being in the being of the other. We might well suspect that the menace is nothing other than *mimesis* as René Girard has attempted to define it.[4] Heidegger's decision in relation to it, and with the autonomy of Dasein at stake, is to turn to what we have referred to as the scene of death—the agon where Dasein, confronting death, comes into its individual being.

Let us construct this death scene, then, and let us begin there where it begins—that is, at that "birth" of Dasein (the term is Heidegger's) that is the state of anxiety. Anxiety (*Angst*) is a mode of one of the primordial *existentialia: Befindlichkeit*—"state of mind," "attunement," or, to indicate better Heidegger's use of the term, "the affective state in which one finds oneself."[5] In its *Befindlichkeit*,

---

[4]Among Girard's works, *Violence and the Sacred*, trans. Patrick Gregory (Baltimore: Johns Hopkins University Press, 1979), leads most immediately to the questions that concern me here. As I noted above, one of my indirect aims is to work toward a *philosophical* understanding of this term (even though it is a limit-term for philosophy, as evidenced at the outset of Plato's *Republic*); Girard holds resolutely and consciously to an anthropological definition.

[5]Or again, "the condition of affectability in which one finds oneself affected." The condition of affectability is also, as we will see and as the following passage reveals, the condition of repeatability. To be affected by something or someone is to experience repetition: "Only a being that finds itself attuned in accordance with the meaning of its being—that is to say, a being that in existing is as already having been, and exists in a constant mode of having been—can become affected. Ontologically such affection presupposes making-present, and indeed in such a manner that in this making-present *Dasein can be brought back to itself as something that has been*" (*SZ*, 346/396; emphasis my own). Thus, with "attunement," Heidegger attempts to develop a notion describing Dasein's access to its own origin as "thrown being" —that is, thrown being as possibility: the possibility of being *bestimmt* (determined in mode or affected) and the possibility of assuming this possibility (repetition). This access to Dasein's origin, Heidegger will call birth. By defining birth with the notions of repetition, affection, and anxiety, Heidegger approaches man's origins in a way that is astonishingly parallel to Freud's own efforts to consider the birth of

Dasein discovers its thrown being and discovers itself as the thrown being that it is and that in existing has to be. Delivered to the world, abandoned to it, Dasein finds itself powerless as regards the conditions determining the fact that it is and that it has to be as it can be. Dasein's sole power, as we will see, inheres in the possibility of resolutely assuming its thrown being, assuming it by giving itself up to—affirming and receiving—the possibility of its own annihilation. This possibility, as Dasein's most proper possibility, is disclosed as such in that particular state of mind that is anxiety.

Heidegger describes anxiety as a state in which Dasein encounters the world at hand as drained of all significance—that significance that Dasein itself projects in its being-in-the-world. Dasein thus encounters the world in an "empty mercilessness" (*SZ*, 343/393); the world is absolutely foreign to Dasein. Anxiety is therefore an experience of *Unheimlichkeit*—uncanniness or "not-being-at-home" (*SZ*, 188/233). In this moment, Heidegger says, Dasein discovers the sheer fact of existing. Unable to understand itself in terms of anything in the world, faced with what might best be termed the "withdrawal" of the world, Dasein makes the uncanny discovery of the very possibility of the significant world and of its existence in that world. Dasein is thus brought before itself as being-possible (*Möglichsein*) and brought before its freedom for assuming what Heidegger calls its "most proper potentiality of being" in its being toward this possibility.

Dasein's most proper possibility is death, the possibility of the impossibility of existence. Heidegger calls authentic being-toward this possibility "anticipation"; anticipation of the possibility of death first discloses and *makes* this possibility *possible* (*SZ*, 262/307), therein freeing Dasein for it. Dasein's freedom for death is *certainty* of the possibility of death as certain in its very uncertainty—it is Dasein's holding itself in the truth of death, holding death for true,

---

man as an individual and as a social being. Their common effort to think the origin of sociality in terms of affectability (for it is at this primordial level of being that Heidegger attempts, as we have seen, to situate being-with) deserves more attention than I can give it here. Let it suffice to point to the first published results of Philippe Lacoue-Labarthe's and Jean-Luc Nancy's reading of Freud, in "La panique politique," *Confrontations* 2 (1979): 33–57.

and, finally, holding the truth of death. For when Dasein assumes the possibility of death, its death becomes its own, in the sense of something that has been appropriated.

We glimpse here one of the oldest and greatest ruses of philosophy—an appropriation of the very event of disappropriation, an overcoming of the most radical form of otherness and negativity in the essentially tragic gesture of confronting death. Death has become a possibility. The pathos of being toward death (Heidegger calls it an "impassioned freedom toward death" [SZ, 266/311] and qualifies it elsewhere as an "unshakable joy" [SZ, 310/358]) converts the negative into the positive (and as the negative is "caught up" in the tragic gesture, we recognize the dialectical, Hegelian element in this schema), and converts innocent guilt into an affirmation of liberty and a free assumption of destiny.[6] Dasein emerges from its Angst, and from its agon with death (the words have the same root), triumphant.

But the tragic strains in this description of Dasein's assumption of its own possible annihilation can easily lead us to overlook dimensions of the experience in question. The theme of death, as I have suggested, tends to obscure the theme of birth, a second pole of experience as fundamental as the first. Let us therefore move somewhat more slowly through the exposition of the experience of anxiety and of the anticipation it gives of death in order to begin to bring forth the "bi-polar" nature of the experience in question.

The experience of being-possible, given to Dasein in anxiety, has been shown to hold in it the experience of Dasein's possible impossibility. The experience of thrownness has become the experience of death (that is, the experience of death as it is faced in life). Heidegger has not simply identified the experience of finding oneself thrown and the experience of death (though the former becomes "finding oneself thrown into death"), even if anxiety, the uncanny experience of the nonfamiliarity of what is, may perhaps seem something like such an experience. Thrownness is an experience of nothingness or "nullity," and Heidegger calls this experi-

[6]"Guilt" and "destiny" are terms that will become more clear as we proceed. For discussions of the continuity of dialectical and tragic thought, see Peter Szondi, *Versuch über das Tragische* (Frankfurt am Main: Insel Verlag, 1961), and Philippe Lacoue-Labarthe, "La césure du spéculatif," in Hölderlin, *L'Antigone de Sophocle* (Paris: Christian Bourgois Editeur, 1978), pp. 183–223.

ence "guilt"—a radical impotence regarding the conditions of the "there" in which one finds oneself thrown and a powerlessness to become anything other than what one is. In thrownness, the experience of being-possible is an experience of total powerlessness— powerlessness and fascination, or vertigo. In anxiety, "Dasein is taken back fully to its naked uncanniness, and taken with vertigo [*benommen*]" (*SZ*, 344/394). But this capture *gives* Dasein its thrownness as something possible (*SZ*, 344/394), and it gives Dasein its thrownness as something that can be repeated. It gives Dasein repeatability as something that can be taken up in a resolution (*Entschluss*) in being toward death.

But if thrownness is an experience of a kind of radical passivity, where does Dasein get the impetus to assume this thrownness in repetition? And, more simply, how is Dasein to emerge from its capture or dizziness and project itself upon its thrown being in such a way as to become free for it? Dasein's freedom is, in fact, nothing other than this passage: the assumption of its potentiality or repeatability. But how does it come about? The answer is simple, but in it lies the enigma of Dasein's circular structure. When Dasein is given its thrownness as something possible that can be repeated, it has already resolved to give itself up to this possibility. It acts upon itself, Heidegger suggests, spontaneously, out of its own being-guilty (he speaks of "letting one's most proper self take action in itself of its own accord in its being-guilty" [*SZ*, 295/342]) and thereby discloses this being-guilty as a possibility that may be acted upon. It is given repeatability as a possibility because it has already chosen this possibility—it has already made it possible. In Befindlichkeit, Dasein finds that it has already chosen what it is now given to choose.

The circularity we encounter here determines, of course, the very structure of the existential analytic, for the structure of Dasein's being *is* the foundation of the hermeneutic circle.[7] *Being and*

---

[7] In *Being and Time*, the method and mode of hermeneutic research are a function of the "object" of research: the being of existence. Research is itself a mode of existence. A circular structure is therefore inevitable: "What common sense wishes to eliminate in avoiding the 'circle,' believing that it is measuring up to the loftiest rigour of scientific investigation, is nothing less that the basic structure of care. Primordially constituted by care, Dasein is always already ahead of itself. As being, it has in every case already projected itself upon definite possibilities of its existence; and in such existentiell projections, it has, in a preontological manner, also projected

Time is an interpretive progression toward the meaning of the being of Dasein that is made possible by the fact that Dasein has already understood itself in its being. The "we" of *Being and Time* comes toward itself out of its prior discovery of itself and by projecting upon this original knowing. Returning to the structure of Dasein's existence, we see that Dasein comes toward itself as thrown by having assumed (that is, by having projected upon) its thrownness as that possible being in and from which it can most authentically be. By assuming the possibility of its eventual impossibility, Dasein brings itself most authentically into its being-possible. It repeats and discloses this being. Anxiety mounts authentically, Heidegger says (*SZ*, 344/395), in the Dasein that is resolute in respect to its own death.

Yet, as we have seen, anxiety first discloses Dasein's essence as thrown possibility and first discloses the possibility of freely assuming this essence by being toward death. Being-toward-death, then, is a repetition that brings Dasein into the very possibility of repetition. To express this "circular" paradox more tightly and in the terms of our previous question: *Dasein's coming into the fascination of thrownness is its emergence from it.* In this formulation we recognize that the structure of the hermeneutic circle already obeys the paradoxical movement that Heidegger will later unfold in his interpretation of *alētheia.* (In fact, to think Dasein's structure of being in terms of a circle is probably to remain in logical terms, however scandalous this circle might seem to logic itself. Thinking in terms of a circular movement, we tend to think in a linear fashion—we move from one point in the circle and return to that point via a linear, temporal movement. This leads to the notion that all of the moments in the circular movement are carried up into that movement [*aufgehoben,* Hegel would say]; in existential terms, such a conception would imply that, in its being-toward-death, Dasein subsumes or appropriates that more original disappropriating experience that is Dasein's encounter with its thrown possibility. We need to think this circular movement, on the contrary, as a simultaneous, open-ended movement in two

---

together something like existence and Being. Can this projecting that is essential to Dasein be denied to research, which, *like all research itself a manner of being of disclosive Dasein,* wants to develop and conceptualize the understanding of being that belongs to existence?" (*SZ*, 315/363).

opposing directions—not in terms of a circle but in terms of a paradoxical structure of simultaneous approach and withdrawal, of a casting forth that casts back.)

Again, Dasein finds the freedom to choose, is given the freedom to choose, by choosing. But if the they-self persists in demanding "How am I to choose?" before this circular exigency, this persistence is not due simply to the inertia that characterizes its way of being. Heidegger remarks, "This existentially 'possible' being toward death remains, existentielly, a fantastical demand" (*SZ*, 266/311), and he goes on to ask whether anything in Dasein's existence could present it with that authentic potentiality-of-being that it is asked to assume. He finds this attestation in conscience. Conscience is the call that reaches Dasein in its everyday existence and tears Dasein from it by summoning it (*aufrufen*) to its thrownness (which we have already described as the ground of its guilt). Conscience calls Dasein *back* to its thrownness by calling it *forth* to the possibility of assuming this thrownness. ("Der Anruf ist vorrufender Rückruf" [*SZ*, 287/333] is perhaps the clearest expression of the double movement I alluded to above.) Conscience gives Dasein to understand its thrownness, gives thrownness as a possibility.

But as the caller is Dasein in its own anxiety, the paradox through which we have just been turning reappears. Dasein can respond to the call only if it can hear it, and it can hear it only if it wants to hear it—that is, only if it already knows what it is to listen for. The call is made possible as a call of conscience by hearing (which is thus, paradoxically, "first"), just as Dasein's resolute understanding of death opens access to the very possibility of this mode of being: Dasein's guilt. The hermeneutic circle reappears because it is Dasein itself that calls and Dasein that must hear. The call "comes *from* me and yet *from beyond me and over me*"—"*'Es' ruft*" (*SZ*, 275/320), but it is Dasein itself that is heard in the immediate hearing of which Dasein is capable. Who else could it be after all?

When the caller reaches the one who is summoned, it does so with a cold assurance that is uncanny but by no means obvious. Wherein lies the basis for this assurance if not in the fact that when Dasein has been individualized down to itself in its uncanniness, it is for itself something that simply cannot be mistaken for anything else? What is it that so radically takes away from Dasein the possibility of misunderstanding itself by any sort of alibi and failing to recognize itself, if not the forsakenness with which it has been abandoned to itself? [*SZ*, 277/322]

The voice is uncanny and alien, but unmistakable. And, apparently, even if it is double. For when Dasein is listening, it is never alone. Listening opens Dasein to the other:

Listening to . . . is the existential being-open of Dasein as being-with for the other. Indeed, hearing constitutes the primary and authentic openness of Dasein for its most proper potentiality of being—as in hearing the voice of the friend that every Dasein carries with it. Dasein hears because it understands. As a being-in-the-world that understands, with the others, it is "in thrall" to *Mitdasein* and to itself; and in this thraldom it "belongs" to these. Listening to one another, in which being-with develops, can be done in several possible ways: following, going along with. [*SZ*, 163/206][8]

Who is this friend whose voice Dasein always carries with it? Clearly it is not the voice of just any other with whom Dasein might come into contact and with whom Dasein *can* come into contact by virtue of the structure of hearing. The voice of the friend is *always* there, just as Dasein itself is always there as thrown. Perhaps all we can say now in response to the question "Who?" is that when Dasein finds and assumes itself in its constancy, it finds that there is always another with it, speaking to it.

But if we are not yet in a position to say who this other is, we might consider what it tells Dasein or what Dasein hears. Heidegger says that it hears, from itself and from the other, silence. Silence is the mode of genuine disclosure: "As a mode of discoursing, reticence articulates the intelligibility of Dasein so primordially that it gives rise to genuine potentiality-for-hearing, and to a being-with-

---

[8]In its German form, the phrase "as in hearing the voice of the friend that every Dasein carries with it" might be read as saying that Dasein is open for its most proper potentiality of being—its death—in its hearing and as a hearing of the voice of its friend: "Das Hören konstituiert sogar die primäre und eigentliche Offenheit des Daseins für sein eigenstes Seinkönnen, als Hören der Stimme des Freundes, den jedes Dasein bei sich trägt" (*SZ*, 163/206).

one-another that is transparent" (SZ, 165/208). And insofar as Dasein speaks of its being, what is said is nothing other than thrown being toward death. In its silence, the voice of the friend speaks to Dasein of its death. The death of Dasein, or its own death? If death is always individual, one would have to say that the friend speaks of its own death. But at the same time, it is the witness of Dasein's death. When Dasein opens to the possibility of death, it hears the voice of its friend. Bearing witness of its own death, the friend *gives* to the other, speaks of, its possible death. And Dasein, become silent and reserved, will speak of death in its turn. Listening will become a speaking-giving, provoking and made possible by a speaking-giving that becomes a listening, and so on in an endless return.

But it is impossible to say who gives first, who is indebted to whom in this accompaniment of Dasein and its friend; for Dasein cannot hear the other unless it is ready to speak, already calling upon the call. Can one still distinguish, in this case, the acts of giving and receiving? Or are they implied, one in the other, in a kind of infinite interlacing? In terms nearer our central question: does Dasein's relation to its death necessarily imply its relation to the death of the other? The fact that Dasein is never alone in its agony leads us to suspect that the agony of Dasein is never solely its own. We know at least that Dasein, when it hears the attestation of the other, will do so in such a manner that it shares it; for hearing, according to Heidegger, is to hold as true, to hold oneself in the truth of that which is heard. Once again, it may be true that Dasein cannot be represented at its death, but Heidegger appears to suggest—in seeming contradiction with his assertion that the experience of death is strictly individual—that Dasein can understand and, thus we might say, participate in the death of the other.[9] Perhaps this should not be surprising, because the death that one can live with another is not that death in which Dasein ceases to

[9]Hearing is the condition of communication that Heidegger defines as "letting someone see with us what we have pointed out by way of giving it a definite character. Letting someone see with us shares with [*teilt . . . mit*] the other that being that has been pointed out in its definite character. That which is 'shared' is our *being toward* that sees in common what has been pointed out" (SZ, 155/197). Elsewhere, Heidegger writes: "Discourse that expresses itself is communication. Its tendency of being is aimed at bringing the hearer to participate in disclosed being toward what is talked about in the discourse" (SZ, 168/211–12).

exist altogether (in which Dasein cannot even be *alone*) but death become possibility, the death that is true, not "true" death.

Dasein's friend, then, appears in a position parallel to that of Dasein's conscience, and we may well wonder whether it is not *in* the position of Dasein's conscience, thereby supplanting Dasein itself as the caller of "Guilty!" Heidegger, in fact, remarks this possibility explicitly. Dasein, as the null basis for its null projection ("nichtiger Grund seines nichtigen Entwurfs" [*SZ*, 207/333]), is first guilty in regard to itself. But, Heidegger argues, in its being-with and on the basis of its thrown, guilty being, Dasein has *already become guilty* toward the others. What could it mean to be guilty toward an other in existential terms? Heidegger does not develop the notion of guiltiness in terms of being-with, but he gives an indication of how this might be done by giving, before his discussion of Dasein's guilt, "the formally existential idea of the 'Guilty!'" (*SZ*, 283/329). The definition is as follows: Dasein is guilty as "being-the-ground for a being that is determined by a not—that is to say, as *being-the-ground of a nullity* [*Grundsein einer Nichtigkeit*]" (*SZ*, 283/329). Being guilty toward another, then, would be being the basis of the nullity of another. Therefore, if in being-with Dasein is already guilty toward another, then Dasein is something like the cause of another's being as guilty and is thus fundamentally bound up in the other's essence. Perhaps here the term "witness" appears most appropriate, for in German, the word *zeugen* (the word used to describe the caller's act of attestation), means, in addition to "witness," "engender."

Heidegger argues, therefore, that Dasein brings the other into its being when in resolution it assumes its own being-guilty: "Dasein's resoluteness toward itself is what first makes it possible to let the others who are with it 'be' in their most proper potentiality-of-being, and to co-disclose this potentiality in the solicitude that leaps forth and liberates. The Dasein that is resolute can become the 'conscience' of others" (*SZ*, 298/344). But Dasein can bring forth the other in this way only because Dasein is already implicated, in the very foundation of its being, in the being of the other. Dasein can speak as the conscience of the other because, just as the conscience of Dasein "itself," Dasein speaks out of and as the source of the other's being. In calling, Dasein gives, or has given, Dasein to be, just as the fascination of anxiety gives to Dasein the possibility of an authentic potentiality of being. Is it possible, then, that Dasein's relation with the other is primordially one of capture? (We recall that Dasein is "in thrall" to itself and to the other in its understanding being in the world with others [*SZ*, 163/206].) And if Dasein, in the very foundation of its being, is bound to the other, how is it that assumption of this foundation constitutes individuation?

We are not yet in a position to answer this question, but we have glimpsed an aspect of what Heidegger means by the term "being-with" through this consideration of the mutual guilt or primordial indebtedness that is constitutive of Dasein's being. There remains one other motif in *Being and Time* that gives us some access to Heidegger's conception of Dasein's relation to the other—the notion of destiny. Dasein's fate (*Schicksal*), as Heidegger describes it, is essentially bound up in the destiny (*Geschick*) of a people, and Dasein discloses this fate in the resolute projection in which Dasein frees itself for its factical "there" and therein discloses its factical possibilities for existing. The more authentically Dasein projects itself upon its death, the more unambiguously are its possibilities disclosed:

> Only the anticipation of death drives out every chance and "provisional" possibility. Only being-free *for* death, gives Dasein its goal outright and pushes existence into its finitude. The finitude of existence thus seized upon tears one back out of the endless multiplicity of possibilities offering themselves as closest by . . . and brings Dasein into the simplicity of its *fate* [*Schicksal*]. [*SZ*, 384/435]

Heidegger terms this assumption of possibilities that Dasein inherits and "chooses" (*SZ*, 384/435) Dasein's "primordial historizing." But this free act, Heidegger insists, is not a solitary one. The assumption of an individual fate takes shape in a "co-historizing" that defines a community's destiny. A people's destiny is not defined by a sum of individual fates, no more than being-with can be conceived as the occurring together of several subjects, as Heidegger insists (*SZ*, 384/436); rather, destiny comes about and "becomes free" in "communication" and "struggle." We have touched upon the theme of communication in our consideration of Heidegger's notion of hearing; "struggle" is defined implicitly in the pages immediately following those pages in which Heidegger defines destiny, and I will work toward a conclusion by considering these pages.

We encounter here Heidegger's notion of interpretation as repetition. As we have seen, in existential terms, repetition is Dasein's return to itself by way of its resolute assumption of its death. Dasein returns to its thrown being by way of projecting itself upon its death. This repetition of thrownness is in turn a repetition of resolution upon the factical possibilities that have been disclosed to Dasein out of the horizon of its thrownness. Dasein gives itself its possibilities—the "current factical situation"—by "freely resolving" upon its death ("a free resolving which has not been determined beforehand but is open to the possibility of such determination" [*SZ*, 307/355]), and it *brings itself* into this situation through the redoubling of resolution that Heidegger calls "certainty." The appropriative movement of holding open in certainty what Dasein has opened to in its resolution is *"authentic resoluteness to repeat itself"* (*SZ*, 308/355; italics are Heidegger's). Dasein thus "holds" or "repeats" in its repetitive resolution its factical existence—those factical possibilities that *have been* there or that *have been* disclosed. Heidegger formulates this in other terms by saying that Dasein "hands down to itself" (*SZ*, 383/435) the possibilities that have come down to it (or, we might say, that Dasein has come down to in being thrown). In this way, Heidegger says that Dasein gives itself its fate as it takes hold of the factical possibility that it has disclosed by bringing or "pushing" (*SZ*, 384/435) existence into its finitude. The factical possibility that comes down to Dasein is, of course, a possibility that has been defined historically—and thus we encounter again a mode of being-with insofar as the possibility of existence that has been is that of a Dasein that "has been there" (*Dagewesenen*). Thus Heidegger writes:

> *Repeating is explicit handing down*—that is to say, going back into the possibilities of the Dasein that has-been-there. The authentic repetition of a possibility of existence that has been—the possibility that Dasein may choose its hero [*seinen Helden wählt*]—is grounded existentially in anticipatory resoluteness; for it is in resoluteness that one first chooses the choice that makes one free for the struggle of succession and loyalty to what can be repeated. [*SZ*, 385/437]

Dasein does not choose its hero in the sense that the hero's existence is one possibility among others that might be selected (Dasein's "choices," in this sense of the word, are given to it);[10] rather, "choice" is to be understood here in the sense of affirmation or "resolving upon." Dasein's choice, as we have seen and as these last lines indicate, originates in its primordial, free resolving, which opens it to the possibility of "loyally following" the existence that has been (this, a redoubling of resolution-choice in the sense of an active affirmation). But choosing as affirming and following is not a form of passive reception; insofar as it involves interpretation, it is also a struggle. When Dasein repeats the possibility of existence of the Dasein that has been, when it thus encounters the past Dasein's world, it does so on the basis of its own resolute existence and in the appropriative decision that Heidegger calls a "reply." In this expression we see once again that the relation to the other is structured in terms of call and response: "Arising from a resolute self-projection, repetition does not let itself be persuaded by 'what is past,' just in order that this may come back as what was once real. Rather, repetition *replies* to the possibility of the existence that has-been-there. But the reply to this possibility in a resolution is at the same time, as *in the moment*, the disavowal of what is working itself out today as the 'past'" (*SZ*, 386/437–38).

With this brief description of Dasein's "fateful" relation to the other, we are able to broaden somewhat our earlier understanding of the process of being-with as codisclosure. In repetition as fateful existence, we see how Dasein responds to the other (the Dasein that has been) in terms of the factical possibilities that constitute the existence of the world of the other, possibilities "in which fate, destiny, and world-history have been factically determined" (*SZ*, 394/446). But we also see that the relation to the other is once again founded upon a relation to the death of the other, for "faithful" disclosure of the other's existence requires an understanding of that past existence in its authenticity. ("Repetition understands the

---

[10]Karsten Harries questions this implicit assertion in "Heidegger as a Political Thinker," in *Heidegger and Modern Philosophy*, ed. Michael Murray (New Haven: Yale University Press, 1978), pp. 304–20.

Dasein that has-been-there in its authentic possibility that has-been" [*SZ*, 394/446].) Dasein's resolute repetition of its own thrownness is thus also a repetition of the other's resolute being toward death. We follow reverently the past Dasein in the same way we loyally follow ourselves and as we follow ourselves in resolute existence.[11] Again, standing with us and before us in our individual fate, there is always an other. And the other, together with ourselves, comes toward us as we progress toward it and ourselves with the same stunning force that Dasein is "struck" (*SZ*, 307/354) by its potentiality-of-being-guilty when in anticipatory resoluteness it opens to the call of conscience: "Only factically authentic historicity, as resolute fate, can disclose the history that has-been-there in such a way that in repetition the 'force' of the possible breaks into factical existence—in other words, that it comes toward that existence in its futurality" (*SZ*, 395/447).

Here, then, is Dasein's encounter with the other in all its violence: an encounter that always will have already taken place in the original codisclosure and that will have taken place in all the violence of the discovery (which Heidegger compares at one point to a theft) that will have pushed Dasein into the direction of authentic existence. We can see that the disclosure is necessarily violent, for it must counter the pull (*Zug*) of the inertia of the they; Dasein must be *torn* out of its everyday existence before it can be pushed into its authentic, finite existence by going toward its death.

Several times up to this point, we have approached the question of the origin of this movement of authentic existence, and though we have seen Heidegger assign something like a spontaneous, autochthonous birth to it, we have also seen that it is caught up in the circular structure whereby it is made possible by what it reveals. This circular structure might lead us to say simply "it happens" and thus accept this movement of freedom as a "pure fact" whose origin or impetus cannot be explained. Or we might recognize the other as providing the intervention necessary for drawing Dasein out of its subjection to the they and drawing it

---

[11]"Resoluteness constitutes the *loyalty* of existence to its own self. As resoluteness that is ready for *anxiety*, this loyalty is at the same time a possible reverence for the sole authority a free existing can have—for the repeatable possibilities of existence" (*SZ*, 391/443).

before its death.[12] The hero (a kind of model) or the friend would then be the instigator or cause of Dasein's freedom. Thus, when Dasein is led to pass under the "eyes of Death" (*SZ*, 382/434), the visage that it encounters could well be that of the one who has summoned Dasein—the other who is Dasein's cause. The scene of death would thus be a scene of recognition insofar as Dasein would already have encountered the visage that it meets here. A scene of death, but a scene of recognition—death insofar as it gives access to the more primordial experience that is an originary encounter with alterity, namely, Dasein's uncanny experience of its thrown being toward death—that having-been-thrown from which originates the call, out of which calls the other as an anonymous other (*Es ruft*).

The originary encounter, then, is somehow an experience of anxiety, fascination, and guilt—an uncanny experience[13] that yet is Dasein's first experience (and perhaps not even "first," insofar as Dasein as a self is not yet constituted or insofar as this takes place somewhere beyond the reach of the self). "What" or "who" undergoes this overwhelming, disappropriating experience of the other as the source of its "own" nullity? Clearly this question must be turned about; if the experience of guilt is an originary experience, then we must try to understand the "who" of Dasein as arising *out of* this experience and see this encounter as the birth in which Dasein is *precipitated* toward its death, and as an individual.

Thus, in going toward death—that possible death given to it as a possibility by the other—Dasein progresses at the same time to-

[12]One is tempted to say that *Being and Time* similarly *provokes* an interpretive decision by leading the reader into its circular structure and leading him to repeat the repetition that is unfolded there—which may be tantamount to saying that *Being and Time* functions precisely in the position of the other that I am attempting to describe. Let us recognize, in any case, that *Being and Time* leads us into a paradox that is apparently unresolvable. Heidegger constantly undercuts any assigning of a definite origin to the circular movement I have been describing. We have simply the fact that Dasein is called upon—enjoined—to resolve upon its own guilt (the object, but also the source of the call) and that in the structure of the call we find inscribed the possible intervention of an other. My interpretive decision is to read this intervention as a necessary one.

[13]And let me simply remark at this time what is no doubt another very important connection with Freud's research. I refer, of course, to Freud's essay "The Uncanny," in *The Standard Edition of the Complete Psychological Works of Sigmund Freud*, trans. James Strachey (London: Hogarth, 1953–57), 17:219–52.

ward the horizon of all possibility, progresses toward a repetition of the uncanny encounter with itself and with the other (*as* other, in an originary experience of difference or otherness that is not even experienced by a self). How does the other instigate this experience of fascination and guilt? In what sense is it the bearer of "nullity" and how does this become the gift of nullity as a possibility? In other words, how does the experience of fascination and originary disappropriation become an experience of appropriation and individuation? Heidegger gives no answers to these questions. On the contrary, he leads us to reconsider the mode of questioning after temporal origins and according to a linear temporal schema. First of all, by foregrounding the experience to which the encounter with death gives access, the experience that Heidegger calls "birth," we privilege one of the poles of the circular or double movement that I described above when I said that Dasein enters into the experience of vertigo or capture as it leaves it in understanding. Heidegger underscores the fact that anxiety, as any state of mind, is *accompanied by* understanding. One cannot be thought without the other. Insofar as Dasein comes to experience uncanniness and disappropriation in its self-appropriation (that resolute act of being toward death in which birth, death, and everything between are "caught up" into existence), one might be tempted to conclude that Heidegger subsumes the experience of Dasein within a tragico-dialectical structure.[14] But Heidegger also leads us to think a movement wherein the "contradictions" (appropriation/disappropriation, power/impotence, etc.) are not resolved dialectically but held together in a relation that is not one of unification. Heidegger reminds us that Dasein lives constantly with anxiety. Dasein is constantly drawn toward the experience of fascination and passivity at the same time as it is drawn (or draws itself) toward the experience of death. The mastery or "incorporation" of one's thrown being is never accomplished; or if it is accomplished

---

[14]Let us recall the structure that I have identified with these terms. Heidegger writes: "Only a being that is essentially *futural* in its being so that, free for its death and shattering itself against it, it can let itself be thrown back upon its factical there—that is to say, only a being that, as futural, is equiprimordially *having been*, can, handing down to itself the possibility it has inherited, take over its own thrownness and be *in the moment* for 'its time.' Only authentic temporality that is at the same time finite makes something like fate, that is to say, authentic historicity, possible" (*SZ*, 385/437; this paragraph appears in italics in Heidegger's text).

in some sense, that is, if Dasein is able to hold itself in the constancy of repetition and thus hold itself in its thrown being, we must conceive this in terms of a movement of constant deferral of mastery (Dasein may hold itself in its thrown being, it may never hold its thrown being). Even this formulation of authentic existence privileges the notions of liberty and decision; but we must remember that this liberty is maintained only in and through anxiety, held open by anxiety. In its repetitive affirmation of its thrown being, Dasein is constantly thrown back upon the passivity of the experience of this foundation of its existence. Thus Dasein proceeds in two directions at once—approaching the source of its being as it draws away from it toward its death. The originary encounter with itself and with the other, as the other, forms a kind of temporal horizon for Dasein in both past and future; this encounter will have never taken place and will never take place— or it will have taken place, as Blanchot would put it, in an "immemorial past" and will come about in a future always still to come.

But Heidegger accents the possibility of decision, as I have said, and Dasein emerges victorious, free to construct a monument to its agony (Heidegger speaks of " 'monumental' possibilities of human existence" [*SZ*, 396/448]), by which it preserves reverently the existence that has-been-there: its existence and that of the other. The monument will serve as a symbol of mourning and of the struggle it presupposes, a sign to memory of that immemorial past and of that future always still to come as Dasein continues forward. In this way Dasein acquires a way of recalling the repetitive understanding by which it "painfully detaches itself" (*SZ*, 397/449) from the public, fallen being of the they.

The term "monument" comes from Nietzsche, and Heidegger adopts it in alluding to the potential richness of Nietzsche's understanding of "authentic historicity." The emergence of Nietzsche's name at this point in *Being and Time* (mentioned twice before in brief allusions) does not come as a surprise. There can be no doubt that Nietzsche is present in the preceding passages in which Heidegger develops the notions of repetition and the constancy of repetition. We may confirm this assertion by turning to Heidegger's interpretation of eternal recurrence as he develops it in *Nietzsche*. For the moment, I simply note Heidegger's assertion that every encounter with the present in repetition is a confirmation and affirmation, a reconfirmation of a primordial repeating that is Dasein's being-as-having-been.

But once again, Heidegger evokes Nietzsche's name only very briefly and leaves it in order to introduce the name of Dilthey. In the lines that immediately follow the paragraph in which Heidegger alludes to the Nietzschean idea of historiography (which Heidegger has clearly appropriated in some sense, and not simply to confirm the scope of his own definition of authentic historicity, as he suggests in his reference to *The Use and Abuse of History*), Heidegger writes: "The analysis of the problem of history which we have just carried through grew out of the process of appropriating Dilthey's work" (*SZ*, 397/449). There then follows the description of another dual historical relation—Dilthey and Count Yorck—that is somewhat extraordinary because it consists in an almost constant *quotation* of Yorck. Clearly this is a monument of some kind. But to whom? And is it there to preserve something reverently or to hide something? What encounter is commemorated there? Who, exactly, is buried there?

These questions have, perhaps, no simple answer. It is true, of course, that Heidegger does not do away entirely with a notion of personal identity in his critique of the philosophical notion of the subject and that the existential analytic is inevitably determined by a given existentiell or factical situation involving something like a definable, "personal" stance on the part of its author. Heidegger had argued for such a point in his *Habilitationsschrift*,[15] and in *Being*

---

[15]In examining Heidegger's treatment of the subject of the philosophical text, Philippe Lacoue-Labarthe cites the following passage from the introduction to Heidegger's *Habilitationsschrift*: "Philosophy, like every other science, is regarded as having a cultural value. But at the same time, what is most proper to philosophy is its claim to be of worth and to function as a *value of life*. Philosophical ideas are more than a scientific material with which one might concern oneself out of personal preference and the will to further and to participate in the formation of culture. Philosophy lives at the same time in tension with the living personality; it draws from its depths and plenitude of life content and a claim to value. And for this reason there lies in general at the bottom of every philosophical conception a personal taking of position [*persönliche Stellungnahme*] of the philosopher concerned. Nietzsche captured this fact of philosophy's determination by the subject [*Subjekt*] in his implacably severe manner of thinking and in his capability of plasticity in representation with the well-known phrase 'the drive that philosophizes'" (*Die Kategorien und Bedeutungslehre des Duns Scotus*, vol. 1 of *Gesamtausgabe* [Frankfurt:

and Time he notes that the existential analytic is founded upon a "factical ideal of Dasein"—a model ontic existence that, as follows from Heidegger's argument, must be chosen by a concrete subject. The existential analytic is, in fact, an interpretive unfolding of such factical presuppositions:

> Is there not, however, a definite ontical way of taking authentic existence, a factical ideal of Dasein, underlying our ontological interpretation of Dasein's existence? That is so indeed. But not only is this fact one that must not be denied and that we are forced to grant; it must also be conceived in its *positive necessity* on the basis of the object taken as the theme of investigation. Philosophy will never seek to deny its "presuppositions," but neither may it simply admit them. It conceives them, and brings them together with that for which they are presuppositions into a more powerful unfolding. [*SZ*, 310/358][16]

This statement may appear to suggest that we may decipher a kind of factical scenario in Heidegger's text—identify Heidegger's hero, for example. But it also indicates that we cannot simply proceed from this insistence upon finite, factical existence to construct a reading of *Being and Time* founded upon biographical data. Such an interpretation would foreclose the existential dimension of Heidegger's argument and would refuse Heidegger's critique of the metaphysical subject presupposed by psychological or historiographical inquiry. Heidegger's notion of the finitude of the subject demands that while we seek to identify factically the speaking subject(s) of Heidegger's text and the subject(s) spoken for, to, or against (and this is a necessary moment in the task of interpretation), we also acknowledge Heidegger's claim that the call of the other (and its respondent) is to a certain extent anonymous, even when it can be attributed to a particular voice (to a Nietzsche, for example, or to a Hölderlin). The hero, or the friend, may be rivals, but any encounter or any agon with them is finally, or also, an encounter with what Heidegger might have called (without referring to Hegel) the spirit of history. Heidegger in-

---

Klostermann, 1978], pp. 195–96; quoted by Lacoue-Labarthe in "L'oblitération," in *Le sujet de la philosophie, Typographies I* [Paris: Aubier Flammarion, 1979], pp. 147–48).

[16]In Karsten Harries draws attention to this passage in "Heidegger as a Political Thinker," p. 308.

cludes a reference to such a "spirit" in one of his quotations from Yorck. Part of the burden of the chapters to follow will be to question how "akin to us" this spirit might be:

> "With history, what creates a spectacle and catches the eye is not the main thing. The nerves are invisible, just as the essential in general is invisible. And as it is said that 'If you were quiet, you would be strong,' the variant is also true that 'if you are quiet, you will perceive—that is, understand'" (p. 26). "And then I enjoy the silent soliloquy and commerce with the spirit of history. This spirit is one who did not appear to Faust in his study, or to Master Goethe either. They would not have flinched from it in alarm, however grave and compelling the apparition might be. For it is brotherly, akin to us in another and deeper sense than are the denizens of bush and field. These exertions are like Jacob's wrestling—a sure gain for the wrestler himself. Indeed this is what matters first of all" (p. 133). [SZ, 401/453]

2 /

Nietzsche's Testimony

In my discussion of *Being and Time* in Chapter 1, I described the encounter in which Dasein *finds* the other, and I suggested that the encounter described in that volume involves Nietzsche. *Being and Time* might in fact be described as the site of Heidegger's encounter with Nietzsche insofar as it consists in that initial casting of a historical existence that opens up the possibility of repeating a possibility of existence that has been: "The '*selection*' of what is to become a possible object for historiography *has already been hit upon* in the factical existentiell *choice* of the historicity of Dasein, in which historiography first arises, and in which alone it *is*" (*SZ*, 395/447).

Being and Time does not simply *describe* the possibility of "the factical existentiell choice of the historicity of Dasein"; it *is* such a choice, for, as we have seen, "method" and "content" overlap in the existential analytic. Therefore, if the "following" that is made possible by such an existentiell choice is a fateful necessity, then it might be said that, by writing *Being and Time*, Heidegger had to write *Nietzsche*—at least, insofar as a fate must be written.

Nietzsche, we might say, represents Heidegger's effort to *lose* Nietzsche. The engagement with that possibility of existence (or of thought) that is Nietzsche's—a repetition of the engagement marked in *Being and Time*—is undertaken for the purposes of disengagement and the demarcation of a new historical position. As Heidegger proposed in *Being and Time*, this liberating engagement takes the form of a repetition that is also an active reply. In *Nietzsche*, Heidegger terms this process "Auseinandersetzung": "Confrontation [*Auseinandersetzung*] is genuine criticism [*Kritik*]. It is the supreme way, the only way, to a true estimation of a thinker. In confrontation we undertake to follow his thinking and to trace it in its effective force, not in its weakness. To what purpose? In order that through the confrontation we ourselves may become free for the supreme exertion of thinking" (N1, 13/1, 4–5).[1]

Auseinandersetzung is a repetition that proceeds by developing, and, in developing, by situating what Heidegger calls a thinker's "fundamental metaphysical position": a stance before, and at the heart of, being in its totality. Such a position is taken in response to what Heidegger designates as "the guiding question of metaphysics," namely, What is being? The response to this question provides a determination of the truth of being as such and in its totality—it is a *project*, the nature and structure of which Heidegger first described in *Being and Time*. In *Nietzsche*, Heidegger defines such a project in the following terms: "That which we call the fundamental metaphysical position of a thinker can be defined by the manner in which one who is called to the safeguard of truth in thought undertakes the rare thing of structuring, founding, communicating and preserving truth in the anticipatory ecstatic-existential project, and so designates and prepares for humanity its place within the history of truth" (N2, 258).

To develop such a project is to allow it to emerge in its force and essential structure, to affirm it or to assume it in such a way that its inner dynamic carries or forces the repeating thinker into a distinct position. This relation is one of support,[2] but it is also one of tension and conflict, as "Auseinandersetzung" suggests. And if the process of repetition involves liberation, it also involves a kind of binding; the new position gains its tenor from its relation to the initial position. The more the thinker enters into the position of his predecessor, the firmer his own position becomes and the more

---

[1]Page references to the English translation of *Nietzsche* are provided for all of the volumes that have appeared in print. Volume 1 of the English translation, *Will to Power as Art*, translated by David Farrell Krell, appeared early enough for me to integrate it into this chapter; all other translations from *Nietzsche* are my own.

[2]Heidegger describes this relation in terms of the new position as "a fundamental position that steps out of the initial position in such a way that it does not cast aside the latter, but first allows it to rise in its uniqueness and conclusiveness, in order to erect itself *upon* it" (N1, 605).

essential the relation to the predecessor. The new position can emerge only insofar as it stands forth against a tradition.

In *Being and Time*, Heidegger describes the process of repetition as follows: "Repetition understands the Dasein that has-been-there in its authentic possibility that has-been. The 'birth' of historiography from authentic historicity then means that the primary thematization of the object of historiography projects the Dasein that has-been-there upon its most proper possibility of existence. Does historiography thus have the *possible* as its theme?" (*SZ,* 394/446). He continues on the following page, as quoted previously: "Only factically authentic historicity, as resolute fate, can disclose the history that has-been-there in such a way that in repetition the 'force' of the possible breaks into factical existence— in other words that it comes toward that existence in its futurality." To come into relation with the other, then, is to encounter the "possible" of the other's existence—and the repetition of the encounter, its interpretive unfolding, brings the repeating Dasein into its own possibility of authentic existence.

In *Nietzsche*, Heidegger describes the possible of existence as man's relation to Being as it is founded in a project of being in its totality—it is man's *situation* in the distinction of Being and what is. Man holds himself in relation to what is, Heidegger argues, only insofar as he holds himself in relation to Being, and both of these relations are born in what Heidegger calls the "ontological difference." The possible is this distinction. It is the possible *of* thought or the possible *of* existence in that it does not exist outside that history constituted by man's successive projects. But man is also the subject of the distinction in the sense that he is subject *to* the distinction—his essence resides there. The distinction is itself an Auseinandersetzung: "The distinction is more fittingly denominated with the name 'difference,' by which it is indicated that being and Being are in some way carried apart from one another, separated, but nevertheless related to one another, and this of themselves, not on the basis of an 'act' of 'distinction'" (*N2,* 209/4, 155). Using "Auseinandersetzung" to describe both the nature of the ontological difference (we will see the word used in this sense shortly) and the relation established in interpretation suggests that the ontological difference is in some way founded, not simply in the act of thought, but in the act of thought as this act is carried out in relation to another thinker. Again we find that the relation between Daseins is constitutive for the act of self-definition. The relation to Being is fundamentally historical—and it is irreducibly a relation to another Dasein.

Thus Heidegger opens *Nietzsche* by giving the name "Nietzsche" to the difference to which Nietzsche responded in his thought, expressing in this way that the difference exists only through the thought of the always singular Dasein. The gesture is, of course, depersonalizing—it is part of Heidegger's problematic insistence upon dissociating the person from the thinker (and the necessity of this dissociation in the case of Nietzsche, author of *Ecce Homo*, takes on a particular urgency for Heidegger),[3] but it underscores the fact that the history of Being is the history of Dasein.

> "Nietzsche"—the name of the thinker stands as the title for *the matter* [*die Sache*] of his thinking.
>   The matter, the case, is in itself a confrontation [*Aus-einandersetzung*]. To let our thinking enter into the matter, to prepare our thinking for it—these form the contents of the present publication.
>   ... whence the confrontation with the "Nietzsche matter" comes and whither it goes may become manifest to the reader when he himself sets off along the way the following texts have taken. [N1, 9–10/1, xv–xvi]

But the greatest difficulty of *Nietzsche* resides in the fact that the historical encounter, whose form we would expect to emerge in *Nietzsche* and out of which the interpretation itself supposedly emerges, is for the most part dissimulated by the force and insistence with which Heidegger describes the metaphysical dimension of Nietzsche's thought—that is, a rigorously determined incapacity in regard to the question of Being. What I have termed a "historical encounter" forms what Heidegger calls the "distant objective" (N2, 262) of his interpretation. It would consist in a decision *in thought*[4] —an Auseinandersetzung with Nietzsche—in which the historical decision prepared for in Nietzsche's "transitional" thought would be effected. "Decision" recovers here its meaning of separation and

---

[3] I return to this question in Chapter 4.

[4] "... granted that this thinking is initial and must still precede in the other beginning even Dichtung in the sense of poetry" (N2, 262).

distinction (from the Latin *decidere*); as we have seen, the distinction in question is between being in totality and Being. But the "distant objective" (in infinite distance from our epoch but, in another history, closest to us: "This most distant is nevertheless closer than the otherwise near and nearest, granted that historical man attends to Being and its truth" [N2, 262]) recedes from our view as Heidegger progressively foregrounds the "near objective" of his interpretation, that is, the effort to think the unity of the modern "fundamental philosophical doctrines" on the basis of the unity of Nietzsche's metaphysics, and to think this latter as the final accomplishment of Western metaphysics.

Heidegger demonstrates that Nietzsche's thought *requires decision*, in the most active sense of this phrase. But decision entails an indissociable no and yes, just as the near objective of delimiting the metaphysical horizon of Nietzsche's thought presupposes at least some anticipatory accomplishment of the distant objective, that is, the thought of an *other* history—thought must be moving beyond the domain of metaphysics in order to delimit it. Heidegger's emphasis finally falls upon the "no" in the "reply" of his repeating decision. His decision gradually hardens into the form of a critical response to what Nietzsche reveals when he brings metaphysics to its accomplishment by carrying to its extreme the metaphysical decision (prepared by Being itself in its retreat—again, metaphysics is no more than a response to this retreat; it is not the agent of its decision) in favor of the "predominance" of what is over what Heidegger calls "the sovereignty" of Being (N1, 476). Heidegger attempts to show that there is pronounced in Nietzsche's thought "the historical ground of that which occurs in the form of the Modern Times of Western history" (N1, 481). What arrives in Nietzsche's thought is "what bears and constrains history; what within being represented as objective and realized is fundamentally *that* which is" (N1, 480). What "is," in this most fundamental sense, is what Heidegger calls "the ontological dereliction of what is." Nietzsche's thought *makes visible* this fundamental event of modern history and in so doing reveals what Heidegger terms the distress of modern thought. Nietzsche's thought thus requires decision in that it stands everywhere before us as the foundation of the philosophies that vie for planetary dominance ("even if Nietzsche were no longer known by name, there would reign what his thought had to think" [N1, 479]); it calls forth the critical no, the distancing of refusal.

But this distancing must be thought affirmatively as well (though here we move to the decision that is the distant objective), since it must occur in the assumption of the possibilities that open when the foundation of the modern period is brought into evidency, circumscribed by a limit that necessarily marks the relation to an outside. As Nietzsche's thought opens onto another history (with the thought of the Eternal Return), it requires decision of a more affirmative, more adventurous kind. Nietzsche's thought requires, then, a double response; it defines the possibility of the modern forms of knowledge (the disavowal of whose philosophical foundations simply affirms the reign of metaphysics at its end or fulfillment), but it remarks at the same time (after Kant and Hölderlin in particular) the possibility and the necessity of the thought that seeks to overcome metaphysics through a questioning of its foundations.

Nietzsche thus stands in closest proximity. Perhaps too close for Heidegger in some sense,[5] for again, Heidegger's accent falls not upon the openings in Nietzsche's transitional thinking, but rather upon those aspects of his thought that bring metaphysics to its fulfillment. We have here the sign that an "anxiety of influence" or a rivalry structures Heidegger's reading of Nietzsche.[6] But it would be a mistake to read Heidegger's refusal of Nietzsche's thinking solely in terms of a dynamics of rivalry or to read the effects of this rivalry in solely negative terms. It must be recognized that the gesture of refusal is accompanied by (or entails) a form of acknowledgment. Beneath Heidegger's manifest critique of Nietzsche, a more profound and difficult interpretation is at work that far supersedes the terms of the critique.

---

[5]Heidegger states, in fact: "Nietzsche's thought and speech are still too contemporary for us. We have not yet been sufficiently separated in history; we lack the distance necessary for a mature appreciation of the thinker's strength (N1, 13/1, 4). This form of proximity probably differs from the one I refer to—but what does it mean exactly for a thinker to be "too contemporary"?

[6]"Anxiety of influence" and "rivalry" can serve only to indicate that Heidegger's identification with Nietzsche provokes a conflictual relation. The term "identification," too, must eventually be considered in relation to the forms of encounter that I described in Chapter 1. I return to this question in my discussion of Heidegger's reading of Hölderlin.

There are numerous circumstances determining Heidegger's plural (and sometimes contradictory) reading of Nietzsche. First, the reading was elaborated over a period of ten years, extending from 1936 to 1946. The hardening of the decision to which I have referred occurs, very roughly speaking, between the first and second volumes of *Nietzsche*, the second volume consisting of lectures and essays written in 1939 and after.[7] One can say that the "confrontation" takes place in the first volume and is followed by an entirely different mode of interpretation, namely, an exposition of theses whose form is certainly determined by the earlier interpretive developments but which, unlike the earlier interpretation, is carried out in a formal, critical manner, not *from out of* Nietzsche's thought (I will try to characterize this shift shortly in terms of a concept of teaching).[8] One senses that Heidegger can no longer afford the careful, more immanent explications of the first volume. But considering in even the most rapid way the historical context in which Heidegger was writing and the public role given to Nietzsche's thought, one can imagine why Heidegger should have taken an even firmer and less nuanced stance in his interpretation.

In fact, a polemical strain runs throughout the two volumes. From the outset, Heidegger's reading is directed against several interpretations, the most notable of which, perhaps, is *Nietzsche der Philosoph und der Politiker*, by Alfred Baeumler, one of the chief philosophical spokesmen for the National Socialist Party.[9] Heidegger's strategy in this case is part of a general task of criticizing—"destroying"—the forms of thought that share with Baeumler's "political" perspective a metaphysical foundation that Heidegger names

---

[7]Heidegger offers the following dates for the essays of *Nietzsche*: "The Will to Power as Art" (1936–37), "The Eternal Recurrence of the Same" (1937), "Will to Power as Knowledge" (1939), "The Eternal Return of the Same and the Will to Power" (1939), "European Nihilism" (1940), "Nietzsche's Metaphysics" (1940), "The Determination of Nihilism in the History of Being" (1944–46), "Metaphysics as History of Being" (1941), "Sketches for the History of Being as Metaphysics" (1941), "Recollection of Metaphysics" (1941). See Krell's more precise dating of the various essays in *Nietzsche*, 1:xi.

[8]Hannah Arendt notes this shift in *Willing*, vol. 2 of *The Life of the Mind* (New York: Harcourt Brace Jovanovich, 1978), p. 173. See also Krell's reference to Arendt's observation in "Analysis," in *Nietzsche*, 4:272.

[9]*Nietzsche, der Philosoph und Politiker* (Leipzig: Reclam, 1931). In the analyses of his translation of *Nietzsche*, Krell proposes an ongoing consideration of Baeumler's arguments.

"Technik." The gesture is somewhat paradoxical in that it consists in attacking the notions of scientificity active in the modern interpretations of Nietzsche in order to reveal all the more clearly the thought that founds their very possibility. But it is precisely of the essence of the modern metaphysical forms of thought (the positive and social sciences in particular) that they should dissimulate, even disavow, their own philosophical foundations. Heidegger's interpretation, on the contrary, is resolutely philosophical, and the stakes he identifies for his reading are those of the character of science itself in its most fundamental sense as the determining form and attitude of man's relation to the world. Heidegger's reading is thus political in the sense that it addresses the philosophical foundations of the modern state. Heidegger is quite clear on this point, and in several passages he points explicitly to the common interests and fundamental character of the modern sciences and the state.[10] Heidegger's description of the totalitarian character of "affirmative nihilism" in *Nietzsche* also has obvious political overtones.

Heidegger's response to the "nihilistic" elements of Nietzsche's thought hardens, then, as the meaning of Nietzsche's project (which announces, in Heidegger's reading, the fundamental event of modern history) grows more oppressive in its political realization. Again, this is not to say that Heidegger accepts the political interpretations of Nietzsche that assert a simple identification of current political reality with Nietzsche's teachings. Heidegger openly scorns these "contemporary intellectual counterfeitings" (N1, 657). In Heidegger's view, however, "Nietzsche" is in some sense responsible for the readings he has received, and Heidegger makes this part of his case against Nietzsche.[11]

---

[10]Consider, for example: "How relieving for science when it must now be told, and indeed on the basis of necessary historio-political grounds, that the people and the state need results, useful results.... Whoever happened to say one day that science could affirm its essence only by recovering it in an original *questioning* must in such a situation appear to be a fool and a destroyer of Science; for a questioning after the foundations brings an inward corrosion, for which project an effective name stands available, 'Nihilism.' But this specter has passed, calm is restored, and the students, they say, want to get back to work! The general philistinism of the spirit can begin anew" (N, 362–63/2, 103–4).

[11]This is the responsibility of a "destiny," and not that of a historical figure. When Heidegger refers to Nietzsche as a founding thinker for Modern Times, he refers

But the severity of the judgment is surely all the greater because Heidegger's own political statements of the period before the delivery of the lectures that constitute *Nietzsche* are in part "Nietzschean" in the sense he develops for this term.[12] Heidegger's thought moves from the very philosophical foundation that he seeks to lay bare and to place at a critical distance in *Nietzsche*. The complexity and unevenness of Heidegger's reading, then, derives in part from an indirect self-criticism. Heidegger seeks to absolve in *Nietzsche* an inevitable debt (signed in *Being and Time*—for if "Nietzsche" is chosen as a possibility of existence to be followed, then it is a possibility that has been followed and that has made possible the following), whose burden has grown immense by virtue of the fact that in its terms are woven Heidegger's political experiences of the early 1930s.

It would be misleading, I believe, to draw from a reading of this shift any final conclusions about the nature of Heidegger's withdrawal from the political sphere. The withdrawal is stratified in nature, moving through the various strains of Heidegger's thought in the period, including his reflections on art; it takes the form of critique (as in *Nietzsche*) but also a more questioning (and affirmative) mode as it turns back upon the (groundless) foundations of the political order. Nevertheless, the critique of the metaphysical dimension of Nietzsche's thought forms an important part of Heidegger's complex political stance, and thus we might well read the shift as a change in interpretive strategy—a shift toward

---

generally to the scientific and political domains. But in reference to Nietzsche's self-exposure in *Ecce Homo,* Heidegger extends Nietzsche's responsibility to every aspect of human existence in the modern period: "Only in *Ecce Homo* it is a matter neither of Nietzsche's biography, nor of the person of 'Herr Nietzsche'—but rather in truth of a 'fate': a matter not of the destiny of an individual but rather of the history of the age of Modern Times as a final period of the West. But to the fate of this bearer of the Western fate there also belongs the fact, it is true, that (up until now at least) everything Nietzsche sought to attain with his writings was converted into its opposite. Nietzsche, against his most inner will, also became the instigator and promotor of an intensified spiritual, corporal and intellectual auto-dissection and a setting on stage of man that ultimately and indirectly had as a consequence an abandoned exhibition of all human activity in 'sound and image' through photomontage and reportage" (N1, 473–74). In such a passage, we can perceive to what extent Heidegger sees Nietzsche as a threat—and the threat, as we see, involves mimesis. Nietzsche's histrionic behavior is the forerunner of a universal corruption. I return to this citation in Chapter 4.

[12]I develop this point further in Chapter 3.

another form of critical intervention. Let me now try to characterize this shift a bit more fully.

In the first volume, Heidegger assumes the role of teacher of Nietzsche's philosophy. This posture is implicit in the method of repetition, for Nietzsche's fundamental doctrine (the Eternal Return) must be thought "from the point of view of teaching and the teacher" (*N*1, 331/2, 75). To teach the doctrine is to incorporate it. In this regard, Heidegger quotes a remark made by Nietzsche in one of his unpublished notes: "What do we do with the *rest* of our life—we who have spent the largest part of it in the most essential ignorance? We *teach the teaching*—it is the strongest means for us to *incorporate* it within ourselves" (*N*1, 330/2, 74–75). Heidegger suggests at one point that his own effort in repetition is to incorporate Nietzsche's thought—"to let it unfold before, or better, *in* us" (*N*1, 257/2, 6). Incorporation is nothing other than the act of thinking itself insofar as it entails the assumption of a project of being in its totality:

> Incorporation [*Einverleibung*] of the thought means here: to carry out the thinking of the thought in such a way that it becomes in advance the fundamental position with regard to being in its totality and as such prevails in every individual thought. When the thought becomes the fundamental attitude of all thinking it is then first taken into possession in conformity with its essence, in-corporated. [*N*1, 332/2, 76]

Incorporation would appear, of course, to be the concept paired to, but opposing, teaching. But what Nietzsche describes with the term is a form of self-teaching or self-determination. Thought gives itself its own measure and direction in its act of thinking the Eternal Return. As we will see, Nietzsche understands thought's self-determining act of thinking being in its totality as the process of "justice." "The just," Heidegger writes, "is the uniform coherence of what is correct—'right,' *rectus*, is what is fitting to taste, what is assimilable, what goes down well, what fits—the pointing direction and that which conforms to it" (*N*1, 637).

Teaching and interpretation, then, are matters of taste. It could be instructive to examine in these terms the modalities of expulsion that are visible in the second volume of *Nietzsche*. But with the term "teaching," I wish to draw attention here to the particular form of interpretive interaction that gives form to the lectures in the first volume of *Nietzsche*. We note that teaching here, as self-determination, names a particular kind of *solitude*—it does not involve a dual relation of communication. Heidegger remarks more than once that the essential philosopher is not understood by his contemporaries; he must cease, Heidegger writes, to be his own contemporary (that is, his own interpreter). His role as a teacher can only be to educate in the sense of preparation for a later thinking of his thought, and this preparation, Heidegger suggests, takes the form of the creation of a state of distress. Only in the freedom (or autonomy) of distress can a new thought of being in its totality be received. "Distress" describes that state when being in its totality becomes questionable [*fragwürdig*]—when man no longer feels at home in the world. It is the experience of Unheimlichkeit. To teach, then, as an intersubjective act, is to bring into the experience of Unheimlichkeit—to prepare for that state in which a decision in regard to being in its totality becomes a necessary task. Heidegger remarks that in this process of preparation, "incomprehension" in itself constitutes a "formative stimulant" (N1, 404/2, 142), and he seems to suggest in this way that the frustration provoked in the interpreter (or student) by silence and indirection on the part of the teacher is itself productive.[13]

But silence and indirection are not simply pedagogical devices— they are part of the teacher's act of thought. For the essential thinker responds to an enigma, and his thought is all the more essential inasmuch as it preserves the enigmatic character of what is to be thought. The enigma, again, is "*the* enigma in which being in its totality conceals itself as 'the vision of the most solitary one' which becomes visible in 'the most solitary solitude' " (N1, 289/2, 37). Heidegger speaks of the divining of the enigma as a "leap" and insists that it is a thought of an *entirely different logic* than that of scientific calculation and reasoning (N1, 376/2, 115). *It cannot be presented in a formal manner.* Its most essential saying is in a silencing:

> The thinker inquires into being in totality as such, into the world as such. In this way he thinks always with the very first step already

[13]Heidegger describes such a pedagogical strategy in N1, 613.

beyond the world and thus at the same time back upon it. He thinks beyond the world upon that about which a world becomes world. There, where this "about which" is not constantly and audibly named, but rather silenced in the most intimate questioning, is it the most deeply and purely thought. For what is silenced is the properly preserved, and, as the most guarded, the nearest and the most real.
... The most elevated thinking consists herein, that what is properly to be said is not simply silenced, but to be said in such a way that it is named in not-saying: the saying of thinking is a keeping silent. [N1, 471/2, 207–8]

"Seduction" best describes, perhaps, the style of teaching defined by this mode of thought and its communication. Paradox, silence (an *explicit* silence), and indirection all have the effect of fascinating the interpreter and provoking an interpretive *passion* that leads him beyond himself and into the required mode of thinking. Nietzsche calls this seduction the "magic of the extreme"[14] —and in the first volume of *Nietzsche* Heidegger seeks to bring the reader to this extreme through a pedagogical practice that has many of the traits of the seductive strategy that I have briefly described. Heidegger takes a multiple approach to Nietzsche's project of thought in lengthy arguments often marked by indirectness and deferral. Nietzsche's project is *one*, Heidegger suggests, but his own argument is manifold and cannot easily be reduced to a single interpretive stance.

In the light of this stratified approach, the shift in interpretive modes between the first and second volumes is difficult to define unequivocally. When Heidegger leads the reader to the extreme of Nietzsche's thinking at various moments in his argument, he approaches the limit that makes Nietzsche, as the last Western metaphysician, a transitional thinker. He works discreetly but persistently *at the limit* in his second essay, "The Eternal Recurrence of the Same," carrying through Nietzsche's thought to the point of developing it into a "counterposition" in relation to Western metaphysics and the forerunner of a "new beginning." When in the third essay, "Will to Power as Knowledge," Heidegger circumscribes Nietzsche's thought *within* this limit, he counters and obscures his most far-reaching interpretive advances. Could this

[14]*The Will to Power*, aphorism 749, cited by Heidegger in N1, 627.

ambivalence also form part of Heidegger's pedagogical practice? The multiplication or stratification of modes of intervention must provoke in the attentive reader a productive tension. Or has Heidegger, by the end of the third essay, already spoken for those who have ears to hear? Whatever the case may be, Heidegger's shifting stance answers to the complex strategy of engaging Nietzsche in order to disengage from him and (in the argument's polemical thrust) using Nietzsche to attack the contemporary political reading of Nietzsche.

In the second volume, Heidegger no longer *teaches* in the fashion of the first volume. He adopts a manner of formal exposition that is perhaps no less challenging in its way (he situates Nietzsche's thought within a reading of the entire history of Western metaphysics), but it leaves aside, or presupposes, the *manner* of thought engaged in the first volume. It is as if Heidegger gives only the results of his previous analyses, even though one of these "results" is the demonstrated indissociability of manner and matter in the domain of thought. Heidegger's emphasis is entirely upon the metaphysical dimension of Nietzsche's thinking; he stays within the limit that emerges in the first volume and develops in a forceful fashion the lines of the modern metaphysical tradition that are drawn together in Nietzsche's determination of the character of being as Will to Power. Heidegger's strategy is explicit: only when the tradition is brought to its fulfillment and comes into full view can the transition be effected. The danger that lies in the foundations of the modern world must emerge fully—the eclipse of Being must be complete—before the glimmer of another understanding of Being can emerge. Thus Heidegger writes at the start of "Nietzsche's Metaphysics":

> The near objective of the meditation attempted here is the knowledge of the inner unity of those fundamental philosophical doctrines. For this, each of these "doctrines" must first be recognized and described separately. Their unifying ground, however, receives its determination out of the essence of metaphysics in general. Only if the commencing age manages to stand on this ground without reserve and without dissimulation will it be capable of carrying out "the struggle for planetary sovereignty" out of that highest *consciousness* that answers to the Being that bears this age and reigns everywhere in it.

The struggle for planetary sovereignty and the unfolding of the metaphysics that sustains it bring to fulfillment an age of the earth and of historical humanity; for here there are realized the most extreme possibilities of world domination and of the effort undertaken by man, to decide upon his essence purely out of himself.

However, with this accomplishment of the age of Western metaphysics, a historical fundamental position is determined at the same time in the distance, which, *after* the decision for that struggle for power over the earth itself, can no longer open and bear the domain of that struggle. The fundamental position in which the age of Western metaphysics is accomplished will then for its part be brought into a conflict of an entirely different nature. [*N2*, 261–62]

When the eclipse is complete and perceived as a shadow, Heidegger suggests, a step is already made toward another light. We might suspect that in 1940, Heidegger felt the step to be never further from being accomplished; at the same time, though, in the light of another history, he may have felt the necessity of the step to have been never more imminent. We might recall here a verse from Hölderlin's "Patmos" that Heidegger cites more than once: "Wo aber Gefahr ist, wächst / Das Rettende auch" ("But where there is danger, there grows / also what saves").

As Heidegger shifts from the mode of teaching of the first volume (a mode defined by the existential analytic, as I will show in the pages that follow) to a less "situated" (existentially speaking) formal or theoretical mode of exposition, he moves within the exigencies of the hermeneutic circle. Progress toward the distant objective is required for the accomplishment of the near objective, and this progress is made in the teaching of the first volume; but the distant objective can only emerge with the accomplishment of the near objective. Yet the gap between these two interpretive trajectories is so severe as to make it difficult for us to speak in terms of a "double approach." Rather, the shift appears to be forced by at least the two "external" factors to which I have alluded: Heidegger's ambivalent relation to Nietzsche and the political circumstances of the 1930s. While it is perhaps impossible to weigh accurately these two factors in accounting for the shift in *Nietzsche* (though surely the political factor helped to turn ambivalence into refusal, or it hastened the swerve that had to occur once Nietzsche was perceived to be *too close*), we may presume that *teaching* in the late thirties and early forties was impossible. The difficult, questioning mode of thought that characterizes the existential analytic and texts such as "The Eternal Recurrence of the Same" had lost its place. Worse (for those who follow him now), the place of this thought had been ceded in political compromise— to the extent that the evocation of "ontological distress" amid catastrophe in 1944[15] rings first as a terrible disavowal of political realities, a painful echo of Heidegger's blindness of the early thirties.

One might conclude from this general portrayal of *Nietzsche* that the second volume should be read as a kind of regression in Heidegger's reading (despite the sweep of its presentation of the history of Western metaphysics). I would suggest, rather, that we should see the second volume as unfolding within the space opened by the first volume, since the limit that Heidegger defines so rigorously and so powerfully in the second is encountered in the first as an "interior limit" of Nietzsche's thought (*N1*, 510).

One way Heidegger describes the interior limit of Nietzsche's project is to situate on either side of it that which Nietzsche consciously assumed in his thought and that which remained at a distance—the unthought of his thought. Heidegger does not ascribe this latter blind region to some personal incapacity on Nietzsche's part; rather, the unthought of his thought is that which is forgotten throughout the entire metaphysical tradition. As Heidegger explains in "Sketches for the History of Being as Metaphysics" (*N1*), the metaphysical tradition is the forgetting of the question of Being and of the space of thought opened by this question. Nietzsche's destiny as a metaphysical thinker is to think (to write) at an irrecoverable distance from the very source of his thinking. It is a tragic destiny in part because Nietzsche must experience this irrecoverable distance *as* irrecoverable. Nietzsche, the conscious subject, shatters in the effort to inhabit this distance, or so Heidegger suggests. But to inhabit this distance is already to leave the space of metaphysics—to experience the irrecoverable *as* irrecoverable is to reach a limit; a limit, again, is neither inside nor outside that

---

[15]"Perhaps the blindness before the most extreme distress of Being, in the form of the reigning absence of distress amidst all of the afflictions of being, seen in the long run from the point of view of the history of Being, is more serious than the crude adventures of a purely brutal will to violence" (*N2*, 393/4, 247).

which it delineates. As the last metaphysician, Nietzsche stands at the limit of one epoch and begins the transition to another. Thus Heidegger writes:

> The age whose accomplishment unfolds in [Nietzsche's] thought, the modern period, is an end period. This means: an age . . . in which, at some time and in some way the historical decision arises as to whether the final period will be the conclusion of Western history or the counterpart to another beginning. To pass over Nietzsche's path of thought toward the Will to Power means to look into the eyes of this historical decision. [N1, 480].

Retracing Heidegger's situation of the limit that traverses Nietzsche's thought will entail indicating where Heidegger rejoins Nietzsche in the process of repetition, both on the metaphysical side of the limit (situation, as I have suggested, involves self-situation and self-criticism) and at the point of transition where Nietzsche stands, not behind us (Heidegger's rhetoric frequently suggests that one of his aims is to surpass Nietzsche), but out ahead—always having been there in advance: "What alone must concern us is the *trace* [*Spur*] that this path of thinking toward the Will to Power has drawn in the history of Being, that is, in the still unvisited districts of future decisions" (N1, 475).

I want to suggest that the limit designated by Heidegger is the limit of *Being and Time* (the genitive both subjective and objective). As we proceed, it will become apparent that Heidegger's repetition of Nietzsche's thought is also a repetition of *Being and Time*. *Being and Time* is the limit of *Nietzsche* first in the sense that I have already noted; that is, the experience articulated there forms a kind of horizon for the interpretation of Nietzsche's thought. Heidegger opens his essay "Nietzsche's Metaphysics" with the words: "The following attempt at interpretation cannot be considered in an adequate fashion except on the basis of the fundamental experience of *Being and Time*" (N2, 260). The fundamental experience to which Heidegger alludes is described as a perplexity—a questioning—before the "unique event of Western thought": the forgetting of the question of Being as this is occasioned by the "refusal" of Being to reveal itself in its truth. This experience forms the horizon of *Nietzsche* insofar as it is a situation of distress from which emerges the necessity of developing what Heidegger designates as "the fundamental question of philosophy." The guiding question of metaphysics asks, What is being?—Western metaphysics consists in the series of responses to this question, each of which, as we noted at the start of this chapter, constitutes a "fundamental metaphysical position." Metaphysics responds to the question and in so doing turns away from the question *as* a question; it fails to develop the structure of the guiding question. Thus a fundamental metaphysical position is delimited (even enclosed) by this structure. To develop the question, as Heidegger says, is "to place oneself expressly, in the questioning of this question, within the relations that open when all is appropriated that comes to fulfillment in the questioning of the question" (N1, 457/2, 192). The development of the question reveals the question to be insufficiently radical and "fundamental question," or the question of the truth of Being. This is the question of *Being and Time*.[16] Thus the development of the guiding question (in other words, the elaboration of the question of Being) is the necessary condition for thinking the essence of a fundamental metaphysical position: the question of *Being and Time* is the horizon of *Nietzsche*.

But the limit that traverses Nietzsche's thought is also the limit of *Being and Time*, in the sense that *Being and Time* itself remains determined by a metaphysical language. Heidegger's statement on this point in his *Letter on Humanism* (W, 327–28/207–8) is well-known. But another statement concerning the metaphysical elements of *Being and Time* appears in Heidegger's essay, "European Nihilism," in the second volume of *Nietzsche*. There, while situating Nietzsche's thought within the modern metaphysics of subjectivity, Heidegger interrupts his argument to speak of the incomprehension that has met his effort to repose the question of man on the basis of his relation to Being and to repose the question of Being itself. He writes:

The reason for the incomprehension lies on the one hand in the ineradicable, self-consolidating habituation to the way of thinking of

---

[16]Heidegger writes in *Nietzsche*: "In the treatise *Being and Time*, an effort is made, on the ground of the question of the truth of Being and no longer of the truth of being, to determine the essence of man from out of his relation to Being and from out of this relation only, which essence in this treatise is designated in a rigorously delimited sense as Da-sein (N2, 194/4, 141). Heidegger uses the term "fundamental question" in paragraph 2 of *Being and Time*.

Modern Times. Man is thought as subject; all reflection on man is understood as anthropology. But on the other hand, the reason for the incomprehension lies in the effort itself, which, because it is perhaps still historically developed and not "fabricated," comes out of what has previously been, but struggles to disengage itself and thereby necessarily and constantly still refers back to the path of what has preceded it, and even calls upon it, in order to say something entirely different. Above all, however, this course breaks off at a decisive place. This breaking off is motivated by the fact that the effort (and the course entered upon) risks, against its will, becoming in its turn a consolidation of subjectivity and itself hindering the decisive steps, that is, its own sufficient description in the essential fulfillment [of the relation to Being]. [N2, 194–95/4, 141]

As we retrace Heidegger's argument concerning Nietzsche's role in bringing the modern metaphysics of subjectivity to its fulfillment, we will see one aspect of what Heidegger may be referring to in these lines, and we will then begin to glimpse how Heidegger's repetition of Nietzsche's thought is also a repetition of *Being and Time*. In *Nietzsche* (in the essays of the first volume, at least, when the essential elements of the reading are won in the process of interpretation), Heidegger casts—projects—Nietzsche's thought in the terms of the existential analytic. His situation of Nietzsche's thought within the tradition of metaphysics is thus a situation of elements of his own thinking. But as we have suggested, repeating or recasting *Being and Time* in this fashion means returning, at the same time, to the limit of this volume and reoccupying "the place of the dimension out of which *Being and Time* is experienced and indeed experienced out of the fundamental experience of the forgetting of Being."[17]

[17]"Über den Humanismus" (*W*, 328/208). One of the points that orients this reading (that Heidegger situates Nietzsche *at the limit* of metaphysics and not within it) also informs the analysis of *Nietzsche* undertaken by David Farrell Krell in his doctoral dissertation, "Nietzsche and the Task of Thinking" (Ann Arbor: University Microfilms International, 1971). Krell reaches conclusions similar to my own by reading *Nietzsche*, (as I do) in the perspective of *Being and Time*. He does not describe *Nietzsche* as a "repetition" in the manner of the existential analytic, but he takes seriously Heidegger's statement that "the fundamental experience of *Being and Time*" forms the horizon of the Nietzsche interpretation, and he reaches a similar view of the nature of the encounter. Our readings diverge in their general movement in that Krell emphasizes the continuity in Heidegger's thinking by foregrounding the presence of the thought of *Entschlossenheit* (resoluteness as a "being-open"), where-

The movement of return does not involve a simple passage to the limit: the "distant objective" of a decisive historical encounter does not issue clearly from the explication in which Heidegger places both Nietzsche's thought and elements of his own thinking back within the metaphysical tradition. There is, nevertheless, a point of critical juncture: the thought of Eternal Return. In the following pages, I would like to show how Heidegger's reading of Nietzsche's thought folds at this limit point where the most radical experiences of the two thinkers converge. At this point, the extreme distance between the two thinkers that Heidegger marks with his *critical* rhetoric becomes proximity. I shall proceed by sketching briefly the argument by which Heidegger demonstrates Nietzsche's fulfillment of the modern metaphysics of subjectivity and approach in this fashion the critical point at which Heidegger and Nietzsche meet.

As we have seen, Heidegger's claim that Nietzsche is a metaphysical thinker rests fundamentally upon his assertion that Nietzsche repeats unconditionally and definitively a decision as to the priority of what is over what Heidegger terms the sovereignty of Being. Throughout the metaphysical tradition, Being is thought on the basis of what is, as its most general determination, and in view of what is, as its reason and cause. The Will to Power, Heidegger argues, is Nietzsche's determination of the fundamental character of what is; the Will to Power names Being itself, or what is "most" being. Nietzsche thinks the Will to Power as that which creates and poses its own "values": determinations on the basis of which life assures its own stability.[18] In so doing he returns to the Platonic conception of Being (the interpretation of *physis* as Idea, in its

---

as I seek to situate this thought in its relation to the metaphysical elements in Heidegger's thinking.

[18] In the *Will to Power* (fragment 507), Nietzsche writes: "The *valuation*: 'I believe that this and this is so' as the *essence* of 'truth.' In valuations are expressed conditions of preservation and growth" (cited in N1, 546). Heidegger comments on this fragment as follows: "We can now say: truth is the essence of the true; the true is being [*das Seiende*]; being means what is taken as constant and firm. The essence of the true lies originally in such a taking-for-firm-and-sure; this taking-for is no arbitrary doing, but rather the comportment necessary for the assuring of the stability of life itself. This comportment, as a holding-for [*Dafürhalten*] and positing of a *condition* of life, has the character of a positing of value and a valuation. *Truth is in its essence a valuation*" (N1, 546–47).

essence, *agathon*) as that which in its presence and consistency conditions and renders possible a being *as* a being. Heidegger points out that Plato's interpretation of physis as Idea only prepares a notion of value. Only when the Idea becomes *perceptio* in the modern metaphysics of subjectivity (Descartes) and when Being is determined as Vorgestelltheit (condition of possibility for what is represented: Kant) can the Idea become the condition of which the subject of representation disposes and upon which it can count in its calculation as self-defined measure of everything that is.

The subject of modern metaphysics becomes the deciding instance for the determination of truth; it is the subjectum in a preeminent sense. At the beginning of modern metaphysics, subjectum, the Latin translation of the Greek *hypokeimenon*, still bears its original meaning of "that which lies at the basis" (cf. subjacent) and is initially given; any being *as* a being is conceived as a subjectum. With the advent of modern metaphysics, thought itself as representation (*das Vorstellen*)—"subjectivity"—becomes the foundation for all truth (the opening of being *as* being). Man is the founding subject for which any other entity is "ob-ject," that is, posed before vision (vorgestellt).

The essence of truth in its modern determination resides in the subject's own certitude of its capacity to represent, and this certitude resides in the fact that consciousness is essentially self-consciousness: the subject of representation poses itself in the act of posing the represented before it (though it should be stressed here that man is the subject *of* representation, for representation is itself posed, presented in representation). Heidegger writes: "All consciousness of things and of being in its totality is taken back to the self-consciousness of the human subject as the unshakable foundation of all certitude . . . all truth is founded back upon the self-certitude of the human subject" (*N*2, 129/4, 86). This Cartesian determination of certitude in turn is the foundation of the modern determination of liberty. For this certitude, as a foundation for all truth, is posed by man—self-posed and self-imposed (*liberum est quod causa sui est*): "Being-free now means that man posits, in the place of the certitude of salvation giving the measure of all truth, a similar certitude by virtue of which and in which he becomes certain of himself as the being that in this manner poses itself on the basis of itself" (*N*2, 143/4, 97). Modern man defines himself, then, as self-determining—certain of himself as the being able to pose himself as such. Certitude here, as the foundation of liberty, is endlessly self-reflexive.[19]

Nietzsche attacks the notions of the self and the subject as inventions of logic and rejects subjectivity as an illusion (N2, 186/4, 133), but he embraces subjectivity in its metaphysical sense by determining the Will to Power as the unconditioned subjectum. Nietzsche thinks the will not in terms of conscious spirit as in the Hegelian metaphysics of absolute subjectivity but on the basis of the body and its corporating drives. He thereby inverts the metaphysical conception of man wherein the *rationalitas* defines the essence of the *animal rationale*; the *animalitas* becomes determinant in Nietzsche's definition of man. However, Heidegger argues, this overcoming is simply an exhaustion of the final possibilities of the metaphysical tradition and therefore an accomplishment (*Vollendung*) of modern metaphysics.

Heidegger reminds us that the determination of Being as will is not new; it leads back immediately to Schopenhauer and, more fundamentally, to Schelling and Hegel. (Schelling argues in his *Treatise on the Essence of Human Freedom* that Being is fundamentally will, and Hegel thinks spirit in terms of conscious will.) Both Schelling and Hegel expressly take up Leibnitz's own

[19]Heidegger indicates this as well in his summary of the way in which man provides the measure of the truth of being: "For Descartes, man is the measure of all being in the sense of his presumption to extend the act of representation to self-assuring certitude" (N2, 191/4, 137). The unsettled and unsettling quality of the will is evoked less abstractly when he says of liberty: "Mere unboundedness and arbitrariness is always only the dark side of freedom, the luminous side is the claim to something necessary as what binds and supports" (N2, 143/4, 98). Unlike most of Descartes's commentators, Heidegger recognizes here that liberty does involve indifference, yet he is faithful to Descartes in arguing that this indifference is not, for Descartes, the most important aspect of this liberty (though it is essential, properly speaking); rather, the "luminous side" of liberty is certitude, which Heidegger describes as this "demand" for something necessary that "binds and supports." The designation of this demand as the "luminous side" of certitude, however, is not without some irony; Heidegger describes this demand as the "secret spur" (N2, 145/4, 99) that drives the man of "Modern Times" to constantly renewed efforts to secure his own assurance of his mastery in an anxious positing and repositing of binding forms (among which Heidegger cites the classical structure of humanism, nationalism, and the power of a nation, class, people, or race, the *Weltgeist*, and the notion of the type as defined by Nietzsche). Heidegger shows that certitude is never certain of itself; rather, it consists of a demand that redoubles with any act that might satisfy it.

notion of the essence of Being as the unity in thought of perception and *appetitus*, a unity whose fundamental character resides in force (*vis*). As the unity of perceptio and appetitus, thought is a placing before, and a relating to, the self; it is representation as Vor-stellen, as we have seen.[20]

In the Nietzschean notion of will as the essence of life, this notion of representation emerges fully. Here the *sich-vorstellen* is stressed, the *sich-hervorbringen* (producing before the self) in the sense of a positing and establishing—a representation or ex-posing in the structure of a form ("Dar-stellens im Gestell einer Gestalt"). Life accomplishes itself in this praxis, a securing and stabilizing of its own process of becoming within a fixed horizon of possibilities. Life's positing of its own conditions of possibility and its holding itself in its possibilities, its holding-for-true, is nothing other than the essence of knowledge that Nietzsche thus terms a *poetizing* (poetic in the original sense of *poiēsis*) *command*. It is a free act of self-definition:

> Original commanding and the ability to command always only originate in *freedom*, indeed it is itself a fundamental form of authentic being-free. Freedom—in the simple and deep sense in which Kant conceived its essence—is in itself to poetize [*Dichten*]: the groundless grounding of a ground in such a manner that it [freedom] gives to itself the law of its essence. Commanding means nothing other than this.

[20]I am moving rapidly, throughout this passage, over topics treated at great length in the second volume of *Nietzsche* and also in Heidegger's subsequent statements on Nietzsche. (There are many references to Nietzsche in the work published after *Nietzsche;* the most significant of these appear in "Nietzsche's Word, 'God Is Dead'" [*H*, 209–67], "The Overcoming of Metaphysics" [*VA*, 67–95], "Who Is Nietzsche's Zarathoustra?" [*VA*, 97–122], and *What Is Called Thinking?*) In my brevity here I do not wish to minimize the value of these discussions, for again, Heidegger presents throughout his readings of Nietzsche a most powerful interpretation of the history of metaphysics in terms of the history of Being. My primary concern, however, is to sketch the structure of Heidegger's encounter with Nietzsche, not to give a full account of Heidegger's rich exposition of Nietzschean themes. Also, as this book focuses on publications preceding the *Letter on Humanism*, I have elected not to present the arguments of the subsequent essays. I might note in addition that the readings of Nietzsche presented after *Nietzsche* move entirely within ground sketched in volume 2 of this work. The reading of Nietzsche contained in *What Is Called Thinking?* represents an exception, in that it might be said to recover to some extent the kind of "situated" questioning that I find in the first volume of *Nietzsche*.

The double indication concerning the imperative and poetic [*Befehls-und Dichtungs-*] character of knowledge points to a unique, simple and hidden essential ground of holding-for-true and of truth. [*N1*, 611]

Heidegger's reference to Kant in this last quotation points to his argument that Nietzsche's notion of the poetizing essence of the will (as well as the conception of the essence of absolute reason in the metaphysics of German Idealism) is founded upon the Kantian understanding of the essence of reason as transcendantal imagination.[21] We recognize also the modern metaphysical (and Kantian) notion of liberty as a self-legislation (Nietzsche will define this as justice), and we see again that the foundation of this liberty, as of truth (in the sense of holding for true), inheres in the reflexive essence of the poetizing command. Heidegger restates this notion in the following lines:

Directed toward the commanding and poetic character of cognition, we have been provided with a view upon a particular necessity governing in the essence of knowledge that alone founds why and in what manner truth as holding-for-true is a necessary *value*. The necessity—the "must" of commanding and poetizing—springs out of freedom. To the essence of freedom belongs the with-oneself [*Bei-sich-selbst-sein*], the fact that a being of a free kind can come suddenly upon itself, that it can consent to itself in its possibilities. [*N1*, 614]

In the reflexive nature of the Will of Power, Heidegger finds the source of Nietzsche's notion of the Eternal Return of the Same. Will is in its essence "open" to itself: it has the character, Heidegger says, "of an opening-holding-open" (*N1*, 63/1, 51). In willing, the

---

[21]Compare also: "Kant's thought announces, however, only what must be said on the soil of modern metaphysics concerning the essence of reason. Reason, according to the modern experience, comes to have the same meaning as the subjectivity of the human subject and signifies: the representation, certain of itself, of being in its property of being, that is, here, *objectivity*. Representation must now be certain of itself, because it now becomes the subjective posing-before-itself [*Vor-stellen*] of objects that reposes purely upon itself. In self-certitude reason assures itself that it secures what is encountered with its determination of objectivity and thereby poses itself within the sphere of everywhere calculable security. Reason then becomes more expressly than ever that faculty that imagines and forms to *itself* everything that is being. It becomes simply imagination as understood in this fashion" (*N1*, 584–85).

willed, the one who wills, and the will itself are revealed, just as in the structure of representation as it comes to expression in the Cartesian definition *cogito est cogito me cogitare*, where the represented, the representer, and the act of representation itself come to presence ("representation poses itself in that opening that it measures as representation . . . : representation is a representation of itself with that which is represented" [N2, 157/4, 109–10]). Will maintains itself in a constant opening to itself, a constant appearing to itself that is a reiterated act of self-position. Nietzsche thinks this as will's assumption of its own power, a self-authorization that carries will beyond itself. Will constantly surpasses itself in self-affirmation; will's affirmative act opens upon itself and reiterates itself. If we describe this affirmative act as a "yes," then we might say that there is always a yes inscribed in the yes, that the yes is always in the process of doubling itself in its affirmation of an affirmation (the structure is implicit in the phrase "will to will"). The affirmation is in itself divided and always in excess of itself. Heidegger thus says that the essence of the Will to Power resides in its own heightening or intensification—in its essence, it is an Eternal Return of the Same. The eternal recurrence of the will's intensification of itself, its constant affirmation of itself in its repeated return into its own essence (Selbstbehauptung) gives the will its character of constant presence, the fundamental trait of the metaphysical determination of Being.

I began this overview of Heidegger's description of Nietzsche's accomplishment of the modern metaphysics of subjectivity (and thereby of Western metaphysics in its totality) with the suggestion that Heidegger's argument reflects critically upon elements of his own project in *Being and Time*. We are perhaps now in a position to glimpse how the process of "appropriation," in which Dasein assumes its thrown being and in which is founded the "constancy" of the self, resembles fundamentally the repetitive movement of the Will to Power that founds the certitude of the subject of this will. In both cases, of course, existence involves an ecstatic "coming into one's own" in the phenomenon of Entschlossenheit. The same circular structure prevails wherein existence becomes capable of itself (Nietzsche would think this in terms of self-authorization) by opening to itself. Heidegger calls this capability the "certainty" of existence. In both cases—as in Descartes—truth (in *Being and*

Time, the truth of existence) and freedom are founded in certitude (*Gewissheit*). The following passage from *Being and Time* should make the connection evident:

> With the phenomenon of resoluteness [*Entschlossenheit*] we were led to the primordial *truth* of existence. As resolute, Dasein is revealed to itself in its current factical potentiality of being, and in such a way that Dasein itself *is* this revealing and being-revealed. To any truth, there belongs a corresponding holding-for-true [*Für-wahr-halten*]. The explicit appropriation of what is disclosed or discovered is *being*-certain [*Gewisssein*]. The primordial truth of existence demands an equiprimordial being-certain in which one holds oneself in what resoluteness discloses. It *gives* itself the current factical situation, and *brings* itself into that situation. . . . *What, then, does the certainty belonging to such resoluteness signify?* This certainty must maintain itself in what is disclosed by the resolution. But this means that it simply cannot *become rigid* as regards the situation, but must understand that the resolution, in accordance with its own meaning as a disclosure, must be *held open* and free for the current factical possibility. The certainty of the resolution means that one *holds oneself free* for the possibility of *taking it back*, a possibility that is always factically necessary. This holding-for-true in resoluteness (as the truth of existence) by no means, however, lets us fall back into irresoluteness. On the contrary, this holding-for-true, as a resolute holding-oneself-free for taking back, is the *authentic resoluteness to repeat itself*. . . . The holding-for-true that belongs to resoluteness tends, in accordance with its meaning, to hold itself free *constantly*—that is, to hold itself free for Dasein's *whole* potentiality of being. [*SZ*, 307–8/355–56]

The resolve of authentic existence resolves constantly upon itself—it is, in its essence, constantly open. It thus has the same structure as the Will to Power, which, as we saw, is in its essence resolve, and has the character of an "opening-holding-open." Dasein's hold over itself in its truth, as Heidegger describes it here, its "certainty," consists in its constant holding open of that openness that is the truth of existence: the disclosedness of the world. Such constancy, as we noted in the preceding chapter, derives from the repetitive structure of existence. Dasein's state of mind gives it access to its "there" or the world and brings it before its being-in-the-world as thrown possibility. At the same time, Dasein's uncanny experience of its own "guilty" essence presents Dasein with the possibility of assuming or *repeating* this essence. Heidegger thus says that anxiety brings us back to "repeatability." We saw that the passage from the fascination of anxiety to the resolute assumption of existence is already effected when Dasein comes into the experience of anxiety. Dasein's resolution upon its thrown possibility in its authentic being toward death is what opens it to its thrown possibility: the experience of repeatability is experienced in repetition.

How does the experience of repetition differ from the fundamental experience of Nietzsche's thought—the experience of eternal recurrence, or the Eternal Return? The repetition in *Nietzsche* of terms used in *Being and Time*, such as "resoluteness" (Entschlossenheit) and "holding for true" as a holding in the truth of existence, points to the proximity of the two experiences. But if Nietzsche's thought of repetition is guided by a will to certitude founded in the reflexive character of representation as it is determined in the metaphysics of subjectivity, is Heidegger's description of the repetitive structure of existence then simply a recasting of this fundamentally metaphysical determination of the subjectum? Is the constancy and steadfastness of the Self ("Die Ständigkeit des Selbst im Doppelsinne der beständigen Standfestigkeit" [*SZ*, 322]), whose possibility Heidegger seeks to found in *Being and Time*, another form of the metaphysical determination of Being as the "constancy of presence"? Heidegger's remark in *Nietzsche* to the effect that the existential analytic was interrupted because it "risked, despite itself, to become a consolidation of subjectivity" would seem to support such a hypothesis.

The reading of *Being and Time* that I presented in Chapter 1, however, demonstrated that this interpretation of the volume finds its confirmation only in a certain triumphal strain of the text, namely, in that strain of the argumentation where the repetitive assumption of Dasein's essence as thrown possibility becomes self-affirmation (Selbstbehauptung) in the form of self-appropriation. I attempted to show that repetition in *Being and Time* is the repetition of difference (not the repetition or the return of the same—unless "same" is used here in a Heideggerian sense to designate the ontological difference). Dasein's return to the foundation of its existence in the repetitive movement of resolve is a return to the "there" whose "nothing," experienced in uncanniness, is the veil of Being itself as an absence of foundation, an abyss. Dasein returns constantly in its understanding to this un-founded foundation that opens in its comprehension of Being.

The foundation to which Dasein constantly opens in its repeti-tion of its essence is thus itself a kind of opening: repetition is a constant return to the limit or the boundaries of that site that is "pitched" in Dasein's relation to Being and that delimits Dasein's very being. On the groundless foundation of "the finitude that is in it" (a foundation that is won in Auseinandersetzung), Dasein discloses beings in their truth. Disclosure, "holding for true" as it is described in the passage just quoted, is grounded in truth thought as alētheia.

In this conception of truth, Heidegger suggests, knowledge is defined on the basis of the essence of truth, whereas in modern metaphysical thought (and thus in Nietzsche), the opposite is the case: truth is defined on the basis of a determination of knowledge:

> As soon as in Modern Times the *verum* becomes *certum*, truth becomes certitude, the truth holding-for-true, the question concerning the essence of truth in the determination of the essence of cognition shifts toward the question of what and how certitude is: wherein consists the being-certain-of-oneself, what indubitability means, wherein absolutely unshakable cognition is founded. On the contrary, and inversely, where truth first constitutes the space in which knowledge may move, the determination of the essence of knowledge is rooted in the inception of the concept of truth. . . . for the initial Greek thought— though for only a moment of history and only in a first start—the essence of cognition is determined out of the essence of truth. [N1, 550–51]

However, this simple opposition proves problematic in the case of Nietzsche. For Nietzsche, too, as we will see, repetition is a return to an "open foundation" that is a kind of abyss, and hence "disappropriating." If Nietzsche and Heidegger thus rejoin the metaphysical tradition in a certain affirmative dimension of their projects, they both point at the same time to a more radical experience of truth and of knowing. Their common orientation will become visible as we consider Heidegger's description of Nietzsche's notion of truth.

Nietzsche's understanding of truth, as we have seen, is also that of a "holding for true." This determination of truth is founded in

Nietzsche's conception of knowing as that praxis wherein a living thing secures its constancy in the midst of the chaos of becoming through its projection of the conditions of its own existence. The praxis of knowing, emerging from life's "practical need," a need for schematizing, is a perception (or perspective) that projects the conditions of perceptibility and delimits a horizon of possibilities for the living thing. Knowledge is thus essentially a projection of a space of the *same*, the horizon of unity of the categories of representation. It is, in its essence, the determination of what it means to *be*. Heidegger thus terms Nietzsche's notion of praxis the "accomplishment" of life—it is life's own process of bringing itself to stand, its bringing itself to presence as something firmly established: "To represent some thing, to think reasonably is *the* praxis of life, the original securing of stability for itself. To bring something objectifiable to stand and to grasp in representation, thus 'concept-formation,' is not an unusual, special occupation of a theoretical understanding, nothing foreign to life, but rather a fundamental law of the human accomplishment of life as such" (N1, 581).

Nietzsche's determination of the essence of truth derives from this conception of the foundation of human knowledge and consists in a "holding-for-true," that is, a "taking-as-being" (N1, 616). But insofar as the truth constituted in the imperative "holding-for-true" of representation consists in a fixation of the chaos of becoming that is life itself, the truth, for Nietzsche, is not in accord with what is properly real. The truth is thus essentially in error; it is an appearance (*Anschein*), an illusion, even if it is necessary to the living being insofar as it is a condition of existence. (Heidegger frequently cites this line from aphorism 493 of *The Will to Power*: "Truth is the kind of error without which a certain species of life could not live.")

But the definition of truth as "error," as a representation "inadequate" to the essence of life, is possible only if one presupposes the possibility of adequation or accord. Thus there reigns in Nietzsche's thinking, according to Heidegger, the very notion of the essence of truth that is determinant throughout the metaphysical tradition, namely, truth as *homoiōsis* (which Heidegger renders as "accord" [*Einstimmung*]). This latter notion, Heidegger argues, determines, and finds its extreme expression in, Nietzsche's conception of art. Whereas the praxis of knowing establishes truth as an appearance (Anschein) of stable identity in the midst of the flux of becoming, art is the establishment of the appearance (*Aufschein*) of becoming *as* becoming in the process of "transfiguration" (*Verklärung*).[22] What becomes, of course, is life, or the Will to Power in its creative movement of "poetizing command." Life itself brings itself to appear in a stable form (in truth) and in its essential manner of becoming (in art). Both truth and art are thus founded in the creative, "perspectival" essence of life that Heidegger defines as *das Scheinen*. But while truth is an essential condition of life's process of self-conservation and self-affirmation (life must conserve itself in order to affirm itself and carry itself beyond itself) and thus of relative value to life, it is of less value than art, which is more "intensifying." Art produces an appearance of life in its productive character—it brings to appearance, or "brings to show" (*zum sich Zeigen bringen*) life's own nature as a "bringing forward into appearance." Art is more intensifying insofar as it affirms life in its affirmative essence, redoubling its poetizing command. As Heidegger puts it, it wills to bring waxing life itself (the Will to Power) to power. In this sense, it is the highest exercise of the Will to Power itself. It poses life in the "clarity of Being," Heidegger says, and establishes this clarity as the "heightening" or intensification of life.

Since the intensification of life, its manner of being, is nothing other than eternal recurrence, art entails the revelation of what Nietzsche attempts to think with his notion of the Eternal Return. The Eternal Return is the "supreme figure" of the Will to Power:

> It [the thought of the Eternal Return] is true because it is just in that it brings the essence of the Will to Power to appearance [*Erscheinung*] in its highest figure. The Will to Power as the fundamental character of being justifies the Eternal Return of the Same as the "appearance" [*Schein*] in whose radiance the highest triumph of the Will to Power radiates. In this victory appears the accomplished essence of the Will to Power itself. [N2, 328]

In the perspective of the essence of truth as homoiōsis (thought by Nietzsche, as we see in this last quotation, with a notion of

---

[22]See, in particular, N1, 247–51/1, 215–18 for Heidegger's remarks on appearance (*Schein*).

"justice"), the Eternal Return as revealed in art is itself a truth posed by the Will to Power. Heidegger expresses this explicitly when he writes:

> The thinking of the most difficult thought is a believing, a holding-oneself in the true. Truth, for Nietzsche, means always the true, and for him the true signifies: being, what becomes fixed as constant, such that the living thing secures its constancy within the compass of and through this fixed being itself. Believing as fixing is assuring oneself of constancy.
>
> *The thought* of the Eternal Return of the Same fixes *how* the essence of the world *is* as the chaos of the necessity of a constant becoming. [N1, 391–92/2, 129]

Here again we see that art and truth are founded in the same reality: the perspectival *Scheinen* of the Will to Power. Both are figures, "mere appearances" (*Schein*), posed as conditions of constancy. There is, however, a certain ambiguity in this term "constancy" (thus an ambiguity in truth itself), which is in turn founded in an essential ambiguity in the term "Schein." The constancy of truth is a fixed figure of becoming that is transfigured in art (the movement implied by the prefix "trans" must be noted here) to become an af-firmed appearance (*fest-gemacht*, made firm—but we might also understand in this an affirmation of appearance as appearance), a figure of the constancy of becoming. The becoming of truth in which art and truth find their essential unity is described by Heidegger as follows:

> Being [*das Seiende*] and what becomes are united in the fundamental thought that what becomes is insofar as it *comes to be*, and *is becoming* in creation. But this coming-into-being becomes a being-in-becoming in the constant becoming of what has become firm as the liberating transfiguration in the passage from a fixed to an affirmed state. [N1, 465–66/2, 200–201][23]

---

[23]The German original reads: "Das Seiende und das Werdende sind zusammengeschlossen in dem Grundgedanken, dass das Werdende ist, indem es *seiend wird* und *werdend ist* im Schaffen. Dieses Seiendwerden aber wird zum werdenden Seienden im ständigen Werden des Festgewordenen als eines Erstarrten zum Festgemachten als der befreienden Verklärung" (N1, 465–66).

The smoothness of the passage described here (and the smoothness of this passage which has distinctly Hegelian overtones) betrays somewhat the conflictual nature of the movement involved. Elsewhere Heidegger describes the process as follows:

> In order for the real (the living creature) to *be* real, it must on the one hand ensconce itself within a particular horizon, thus perduring in the illusion of truth. But in order for the real to *remain* real, it must on the other hand simultaneously transfigure itself by going beyond itself, surpassing itself in the scintillation of what is created in art—and that means it has to advance against the truth. While truth and art are proper to the essence of reality with equal originality, they must diverge from one another and go counter to one another. [N1, 250/1, 217]

Schein has a double meaning: appearance as fixation in the form of Anschein and appearance as Aufschein, which also entails fixation (the work of art is *Gestalthaftes*, or something structural) but in which there appears *becoming becoming becoming* through the shining appearance of new and higher possibilities. But in this double meaning, Schein in fact bears a "tearing rupture." In it is played out the conflict between art and truth of which Nietzsche writes: "Very early in my life I took the question of the relation of *art* to *truth* seriously: and even now I stand in holy dread in the face of this discordance" (quoted in N1, 167/1, 142). The fateful character of the word "Schein" carries in it the "interior abyss" (N1, 480) of the process of truth. And just as Nietzsche, according to Heidegger, cannot master the "fateful" character of Schein (N1, 248/1, 215), he is unable to surmount this abyss in the essence of truth.

The discord between art and truth, which is the place of the revelation of an abyss, defines for Nietzsche the tragic character of existence. The tragic, Heidegger writes, "is a position of the will and therewith of knowledge in regard to being in its totality whose fundamental law lies in struggle as such" (N1, 317/2, 61). The conflict consists, as we have seen, in the transfigurative movement wherein art *turns against* truth. The discord thus resides in art itself. Art, says Heidegger, "is the most genuine and profound will to semblance, namely, to the scintillation of what transfigures, in which the supreme lawfulness of Dasein becomes visible" (N1, 249/1, 216). Transfiguration, as we have seen, is the appearing of the Will to Power's "semblant" essence; in it, life's intensifying essence comes to appear as the Eternal Return. Tragedy, Heidegger argues, the highest form of art for Nietzsche, begins with the thought of the Eternal Return: "With the thinking of the thought of the Return, the tragic as such becomes the fundamental character of being. From the historical point of view, it is the beginning of 'the tragic age of Europe'" (N1, 279/2, 28).

As we work through aspects of Heidegger's reading of Nietzsche's thought of the Eternal Return, it should become clearer how this notion constitutes the "interior abyss" in Nietzsche's determination of the essence of truth (the reciprocal play of art and truth in justice). And it will become clear how Nietzsche's recognition of the abyss already leads him away from the metaphysics of subjectivity that, in Heidegger's reading, comes to fulfillment in Nietzsche's philosophy. For Nietzsche's precarious stance in relation to that "opening" that is revealed in the ambiguity of the word "Schein" involves a relation to truth (and a determination of truth) profoundly different from that defined in the metaphysics of subjectivity. The stance is precarious because it involves perhaps no more than Nietzsche's failure to "master" the ambiguity of Schein, the tenor of the stance being defined by the resistance of the thought of the Eternal Return—its concealment and refusal to thought. But this incapacity on Nietzsche's part can be read in a more affirmative fashion as Nietzsche's opening in thought (and *of* thought) to another, more original determination of truth—truth as alētheia.[24]

[24]Heidegger does in fact argue that Nietzsche's thought recovers (in a kind of echoing or *après-coup* effect) the Greek interpretation of truth as alētheia, but he denies to Nietzsche any consciousness of this return, arguing that this is a recovery of alētheia as thought by metaphysics. In "Nietzsche's Metaphysics" Heidegger summarizes the argument concerning Nietzsche's determination of the essence of truth as justice in the terms that we have seen up to this point, but he redefines what he describes as the discord between art and truth by determining each of these in relation to a different determination of truth—or rather, in relation to the originally dual nature of truth: "There emerges in what Nietzsche names truth and interprets as 'error,' adequation to being as the guiding determination of the essence of truth. In the same way, the interpretation of art in the sense of transfiguring appearance unknowingly calls upon the inaugural opening and bringing-into-the-open (unconcealment) as a guiding determination. Adequation and unconcealment, *adaequatio* and *alētheia*, govern in Nietzsche's concept of truth as the undying, though nevertheless entirely unheard echo of the metaphysical essence of truth" (N2, 318).

Heidegger goes on to recall in this passage his argument concerning the forget-

To define the precariousness of Nietzsche's stance in regard to truth, we should follow Heidegger's own focus on the *situation* of the thinking subject implied by Nietzsche's fundamental metaphysical position. Let me reiterate the basis of Heidegger's judgment concerning the metaphysical character of this position. We have seen in Heidegger's argument that the Will to Power, in its innermost essence, wills *itself* in its surpassing of itself. In this self-affirmation lies the unconditioned essence of subjectivity, for which man is the preeminent subject. Will's self-affirmation (its reflexivity) is the foundation of man's certitude as the subject who is foundation and measure of the truth of being as such, the foundation of truth. The original essence of truth ("the letting-appear as unconcealment of the concealed: unconcealedness" [N2, 324]), alētheia, appears in its modern, distorted form as representation:

> This re-presentation, however, has its full essence in that it brings itself to presence before itself in the open measured and stamped out by itself alone. In this way the essence of Being as subjectivity determines itself. It demands as representation the representative [*Repräsentanten*] who each time, in that he represents, brings being itself in its Being, that is in presence [*Präsenz, parousia*], to appearance such that it *is* being. [N2, 324]

Here the original process of truth ("the inaugural opening and bringing-into-the-open," as we have seen) is reduced to the process of truth as accord, homoiōsis. The Will to Power as the fundamental character of being appears to itself as an Eternal Return. The determination of the process of truth as a self-production is a return to the initial thought of Being as physis (N1, 656), but as

---

ting of a more original notion of truth. The essence of truth as alētheia is forgotten with the determination of truth as homoiōsis and *adaequatio*. This oblivion with regard to the "opening and concealing character of truth" forgets itself in turn with the Cartesian definition of the certitude of consciousness. But this forgetting of the essence of truth does not constitute its annihilation; on the contrary, it governs in the understanding of truth in a perverted and disguised form and "brings the metaphysics of unconditioned and accomplished subjectivity to place itself, from its hidden beginning, in the most extreme counter-essence of the initial determination of truth" (N1, 319). The "counter-essence" of the initial determination of truth as alētheia emerges in Nietzsche, Heidegger argues, in the "simple unity" of the Will to Power, in which truth (as error) assures to power its consistency for its constant intensification in art.

a final sealing of the metaphysical determination of truth, that is, a final sealing of the forgetting of Being:

> This last project of the property of being is further than ever from the thought of truth in the sense of the essence of alētheia, whose arrival-in-essence is born by Being which lets this essence come into the state of belonging to the beginning. "Truth" has hardened in Nietzsche's thought in its now insipid essence in the sense of accord with being in its totality, in such a way that out of this accord with being the free voice of Being can never become audible. [*N*2, 11–12]

In the domain defined by this forgetting of Being, man assumes the role of the preeminent subject—foundation and measure of the truth of what is. Man's self-determination in the metaphysics of subjectivity is, as we have seen, the basis for the determination of the essence of truth. Herein lies the foundation of the anthropomorphic nature of Western science, its projection of human criteria and laws into the universe that it pretends to describe. Nietzsche, of course, made the exposure of the humanizing tendencies of metaphysically prompted thinking—its projection onto the "chaos of becoming" of human notions such as form, causality, intention, and corresponding evaluative judgments such as beauty or wisdom—one of the fundamental aims of his thought. The term "chaos," suggests Heidegger, is adopted by Nietzsche in order to prevent a "humanization" of being in its totality; it functions, as in a negative theology, as a refusal to attribute characteristics to it. But Nietzsche's will to "dehumanize" (which is also a will to "dedivinization") is accompanied by the recognition that man's interpretation of the world cannot be accomplished from any perspective other than his own and from any place other than his position in the midst of being. Thus Nietzsche, Heidegger argues, is at the same time the foremost proponent of a "humanization" of the world—recognizing the necessity of man's anthropomorphic bias and affirming this bias absolutely, though in such a way as to resituate this perspective within the perspectival character of being itself. Heidegger argues that this very determination of Being, however, is fundamentally metaphysical and a final confirmation of the metaphysics of subjectivity. Despite Nietzsche's will to dehumanization, he instigates and legitimates a final campaign of absolute domination by man over what is. Man is installed again, and absolutely, as the arbiter of truth.

Yet as Heidegger describes this situation of man in Nietzsche's project of dehumanization, a different kind of position becomes visible. Nietzsche, he says, assumes fully man's perspectival character and recognizes that any possibility of limiting or even escaping humanization in the interpretation of the world can come only with an initial determination of man's essence and of his situation in the world. The determination of being in its totality must in some way entail a situation of the perspective from which it is accomplished. But the hermeneutic difficulties are evident; the interpretation of man's position in the world requires, presupposes, an interpretation of the world. And how is man to bring his perspectival character into perspective?

Heidegger argues, however, that Nietzsche is able to maintain together both a will to humanization (an assumption of man's perspectival character) and a will to dehumanization or renaturalization of man and the world. For the interpretation of the world as it is accomplished in a project of being in its totality *is* a project of self-localization or self-situation, and it can be such a project only inasmuch as this self-localization is achieved. This argument is one of the key elements in Heidegger's reading. It is also, perhaps, the point at which the greatest interpretive forcing occurs (let us call it "forcing" for want of a better word—it is not necessarily a violation), for at this point Heidegger reads Nietzsche's thought as a *project* of Being and casts the hermeneutical situation first described in *Being and Time*. Heidegger's constant focus in *Nietzsche* on the question of man and the problem of humanization reflects this interpretive intervention; his constant reiteration of the fact that self-determination necessarily accompanies a conception of being in its totality as well as the attendant argument that the manner of thinking in Nietzsche's fundamental thought is indissociable from (determined by and determining) the object of this thinking (what is to be thought) together betray the fact that Heidegger is working through hermeneutical exigencies addressed in paragraph 2 of *Being and Time*.[25] He writes in that paragraph, we recall: "In the

[25]One of the difficult implications of this hermeneutic approach is that it poses the necessity of following the manner of thinking determined by the notion of Being

question of the meaning of Being there is no 'circular reasoning' but rather a remarkable 'relatedness backward or forward' of what we are asking about (Being) to the inquiry itself as a mode of being of a being. The essential way in which the inquiry is affected by what is asked about belongs to the most proper meaning of the question of Being" (*SZ*, 8/28).

Casting Nietzsche's project of thought in this way, Heidegger opens the possibility of redefining Nietzsche's decision as regards the relation of knowledge and truth (the nature of truth in modern metaphysics, we recall, is determined by the essence of knowledge, whereas in early Greek thought an inverse relation prevailed). Heidegger's interpretive intervention entails making us consider dehumanization not so much in terms of a renaturalization where man restores nature to its essence and situates his own creative activity within this nature (in the sense of grounding man's activity within the self-production of physis) but rather in terms of a radical redefinition of man's situation in the world and point of view.

Nietzsche's project of Being, Heidegger says, is simultaneously a self-determination and a perspective upon being in its totality. The conception of being is a conception *by* man and is thus related to man, but it occurs only insofar as man is engaged, in the midst of being, in his historical situation, the *there* of his existence. Such engagement, Heidegger argues, occurs as the assumption of the temporality of eternal recurrence in and as the willed moment of decision. "Transposing oneself into the temporality of one's own action and one's own decision in looking toward what is given as a task [overcoming nihilism] and in looking back upon what one has received" (*N1*, 446/2, 182) defines the *manner* of Nietzsche's thought in the conception of being in its totality. As such a thought, in such a manner, Nietzsche's thought recoils upon itself (or provokes the recoil of what is thought) in such a way as to catch itself up with that which is thought: "In this thought, *what* is to be thought

---

that is projected in it. It requires a thinking that situates itself in the movement of what is to be thought. Heidegger asserts, then, that the interpreter must himself experience the Eternal Return if he is to penetrate to the inner dynamic of this thinking. Once again we touch upon the performative dimension of Heidegger's argumentation (in my reading of *Being and Time*, I suggested that the existential analytic not only describes the structure of existence but is *cast* in such a structure) and the necessity of repetition.

strikes back upon the one who is thinking by the *manner* in which it is to be thought; and this again only in order to bring him into what is to be thought" (*N*1, 447/2, 183). The structure of the "counterblow" belongs to Nietzsche's thought insofar as it is a project of being in its totality:

> That, in general, what is to be thought in the thinking of the thought of the Eternal Recurrence of the Same strikes back upon the thinker and brings him into what is thought does not lie primarily in the fact that the Eternal Recurrence of the Same is thought, but rather in the fact that this thought thinks being in its totality. Such a thought is termed a "metaphysical" thought. Because the thought of the Return is *the* metaphysical thought of Nietzsche, there exists this relation of the recoil that engages and the recoiling engagement. [*N*1, 448/2, 184]

The thought of eternal recurrence is a questioning that encounters its own ground—of the same repetitive structure as the act of thinking described in *Being and Time*, in which resolution opens to its own possibility, which comes upon it violently. In *Being and Time*, as we have seen, repetition opens to repeatability. Here in *Nietzsche*, the will to repeat, as we will see, also opens to the experience of repetition, which is at once disappropriating and enabling.[26]

---

[26]As Heidegger notes in the opening pages of *An Introduction to Metaphysics*, the structure I am focusing upon here is the *general structure* of the act of thinking being in its totality. Heidegger develops the structure of the recoil of thought in this text in terms of the event of questioning in which the question poses itself, "Why are there beings rather than nothing?" It is a "fundamental question," Heidegger says, in that it occurs in man's transcendence of being in its totality and opens the whole of being as such, placing *itself* in question as itself part of the whole (thus transcendent and immanent—in an "internal distance" from what is questioned). I quote here at length because, again, the structure of the questioning defined here is homologous with the structure within which Heidegger casts Nietzsche's project of thinking. "But whenever being as a whole enters into this question, a privileged, unique relation arises between it and the act of questioning. For through this questioning, being as a whole is for the first time opened up *as such* with a view to its possible ground, and in the act of questioning it is kept open. . . . The question 'why' may be said to confront being as a whole, to break out of it, though never completely. But that is exactly why the act of questioning is privileged. Because it confronts being as whole, but does not break loose from it, the content of the question reacts upon the questioning itself. Why the why? What is the ground of this question 'why' which presumes to ask after the ground of being as a whole?" The "event" of this questioning presents itself, at least superficially, in the form of repetition. Thought

We may develop the structure of this event by following Heidegger's discussion in the third essay of *Nietzsche*, "Will to Power as Knowledge." The structure of the counterblow, we see there, belongs to the act of thought insofar as thinking is a manifestation of Will to Power. Thought opens to its source in the act of self-determination because it is founded in the Will to Power's self-disclosing movement. The will, as we have seen, is an "opening holding-open" wherein both the will and the one who wills are disclosed; this structure, we noted, characterizes the act of representation as it emerges in the metaphysics of subjectivity. But in the process of questioning Nietzsche's conception of knowing (and in the effort to confirm his argument that Nietzsche "thinks absolutely in the sense of Modern Times" by determining the essence of truth on the basis of a determination of the essence of knowledge), Heidegger suggests that this structure of representation may be "opened out." This latter possibility, we may presume, is what in Heidegger's view generates the disquiet in all great metaphysical thinkers who are driven to meditate on the act of thought (*N*1, 496) and what makes the effort to reflect upon knowledge and the foundation of its essence a historical task (*N*1, 553). The effort to reflect upon knowing, Heidegger says, is in no way absurd, because knowing is in itself reflexive and holds in it the possibility of man's self-situation:

> The representation of being as such is not a process that simply runs its course, so to speak, in man, but a comportment in which man

---

more profoundly, it retains this character, as we see in every description of ecstatic existence; it is thought here by Heidegger as a "leap":

"At first sight the question 'Why the why?' looks like a frivolous repetition ad infinitum of the same interrogative formulation, like an empty and unwarranted brooding over words. . . .

"But if we decline to be taken in by surface appearances we shall see that this question 'why,' this question as to being as such in its entirety, goes beyond any mere playing with words, provided we possess sufficient intellectual energy to make the question actually recoil into its 'why'—for it will not do so of its own accord. In so doing we find out that this privileged question 'why' has its ground in a leap through which man thrusts away all the previous security, whether real or imagined, of his life. The question is asked only in this leap; it *is* the leap; without it there is no asking. What 'leap' means here will be elucidated later. . . . Here it may suffice to say that the leap in this questioning opens up its own source—with this leap the question arrives at its own ground. We call such a leap, which opens up its own source, the original source or origin [*Ur-sprung*], the finding of one's own ground" (*EM*, 3–4/4–6). We might say that the *reverberation* of the "folding" question is Heidegger's experience of eternal recurrence.

stands in such a way that standing-in this comportment exposes him in the open of this relation and thus com-ports his human-being. Thus one finds that in the representing comportment toward being, man already comports himself each time also with regard to himself, with or without "theory," with or without reflection upon himself. [N1, 522]

Even more significantly, Heidegger continues, the opening of the relation in which man is exposed is itself out in the open; the relation of cognition is open to cognition—it is in its essence re-cognition:

> Knowing [*das Erkennen*] is always already known as such; to want to know knowing is nothing absurd, but rather a design of a highly decisive character, for everything rests upon the fact that in the effort of bringing out explicitly the essence of knowledge, knowing be experienced as it has already been known, before any meditation upon it and as it lies open according to its proper essence. . . . [Knowing] is *in itself* and never subsequently reflective [*besinnlich*], and by virtue of this reflectiveness stands always already in the clarity of its own essence.
>
> To know knowing in its essence means, correctly understood, to go back to its already open, though not yet developed, essential foundation. [N1, 552–53]

The possibility of thought's *becoming other*—its dehumanization— depends upon the nature of thought's "open foundation" and the nature of the experience of repetition that occurs as thought opens upon itself. Let us reconsider Heidegger's description of Nietzsche's determination of the act of thought in the light of this last question.

For Nietzsche, in Heidegger's interpretation, thought's self-opening occurs in the act of "imperative poetic transfiguration," by which thought assimilates chaos in a perspectival horizon and poses in this act of self-legislation a figure of its own truth. Thought gives itself a horizon of possibilities in its project of a determination of being and opens upon this horizon—carries itself into it—thus carrying itself "over and beyond itself" and into its own essence. Thought holds what is projects for true, and holds itself in its own truth: "The *thought* of the Eternal Return of the Same *fixes how* the essence of the world as the chaos of the necessity of constant becoming *is*. The thinking of this thought holds itself in being in its totality *in such a way* that the Eternal Return of the Same, as the Being determining all that is, holds true for it" (N1, 392/2, 129). The thinking subject, as he engages himself in the thought of the Eternal Return, becomes the site for the revelation of the truth of being in its totality. In this act is accomplished the "localization" of his being. It is a self-determination (and self-situation) in the sense that it is an assumption of the initial determination posed in thought, a repetition of and return to its "open foundation." Thought's open foundation, Heidegger argues, is opened in thought's originally creative act.

But "creation," here, cannot mean "conception" in the sense we normally give to this term—that is, in the sense of authorship. Heidegger's description of the thinking of the Eternal Return points rather to a kind of "opening" to this determination that comes from outside the reach of the subject's conscious power and that is itself open in the sense of a "possible" for thought (N1, 392–93/2, 129–30). In the *Gay Science*, as Heidegger observes, Nietzsche describes the thought as coming to him through the agency of a "demon" ("sliding into your most solitary solitude" [N1, 270/2, 19])who poses it in the mode of a possibility. Nietzsche's description of the event of the thought in *Ecce Homo* (an event occurring at a specific time and place) also points to the thought as something that *befalls* the thinker. Heidegger makes it clear that Nietzsche is subject to the thought, not its subject: "In reality, the thought of the Eternal Return of the Same means a convulsion of all being. The sphere of vision in which the thinker looks is no longer the horizon of his 'personal experiences': it is something other than himself that has passed under and over him and is henceforth there, something that no longer belongs to him as its thinker, but remains that to which he merely attends" (N1, 264/2, 13). Heidegger also constantly underscores the independent character of the thought by referring to the project of being in its totality in which it is posed with a seemingly redundant phrase, "the thinking of the thought of the Eternal Return."

The act of thought that establishes a relation to being in its totality, then, is "open" in that it defines a foundation to which any act of knowing returns. But it is open, too, in the sense that its act of founding is an opening to something that determines it. Again, we have seen in the structure of the Will to Power a movement like the one described here, whereby the act of willing opens to the "attack" of will that comes upon the subject as if from outside and beyond him. But this attack is of the subject's own essence, and in this sense it is a repetitive movement of founding that simply reaffirms the infinitude of the will as the essence of what is. Indeed, in Heidegger's description of the thought of the Eternal Return in the second volume of *Nietzsche*, the will itself poses the thought of the Return as its own "obstacle" and condition. If man is the preeminent subject of the Will to Power, then this unconditional accomplishment of the will's essence would be an absolute humanization of being in its totality. But as we will see in Heidegger's description of the thinking of the Eternal Return, the thinker is carried *beyond* what is and into an encounter with the nothing of Being in the experience of Unheimlichkeit.

Thus, if the Will to Power constitutes the foundation of any thinking act in Nietzsche's philosophy, then its openness, as experienced in the thought of the Eternal Return, points to its determined character. The experience of the Eternal Return is an experience of the finitude of the will, and as a project of being in its totality, it is dehumanizing. This conclusion forces itself upon us as we consider further how man is situated by this project and where he must be situated in order to think it.

> The possibility remains that the accomplishment of the determination of the essence of man remains always and necessarily the affair of man and is thus human, but that the determination itself, its truth, raises man outside and beyond himself, and thereby dehumanizes him and also attributes another essence to the *human* accomplishment of the determination of the essence of man. The question of who man is must first be experienced as a necessary question, and for this the distress of this question must break in upon man with all its power and in every form. [N1, 361/2, 102]

The question of man becomes *necessary* when the question itself is experienced as distressful, when man is least assured of himself and when posing the question is of the utmost consequence. Then, Heidegger suggests, the project of self-determination can become something other than human in its essence (and in the quotation above we recognize still the movement of the Will to Power: "its truth raises man outside and beyond himself"). But when is man ever unsure of himself—man, who is by definition in the metaphysics of subjectivity one who is certain of himself and of his capacity to represent? The determination of being in its totality and the accompanying determination of man must come into question (become fragwürdig, "question-worthy") and thereby lose their determining power in order for such a metaphysical distress to arise—a metaphysical need for a new determination of man's essence.

Nietzsche, of course, recognized such a situation and termed it "nihilism": "What Hegel asserted concerning art—that it had lost its power to be the definitive fashioner and preserver of the absolute—Nietzsche recognized to be the case with the 'highest values,' religion, morality, and philosophy: the lack of creative force and cohesion in grounding man's historical existence upon being in its totality" (N1, 108/1, 90). With the term "nihilism," Nietzsche names the collapse, the devalorization of the "highest values"—Nietzsche's term for the founding conditions of existence, whether these be located in existence (with notions such as finality and meaning, or unity) or in a true world beyond this world. The consciousness of the devalorization of the supreme values entails the recognition that life *leads to nothing* (hence the *nihil* of nihilism) and is born in either a weak pessimism (an impotence before the historical movement of collapse) or a strong pessimism that affirms the collapse and seeks analytically its conditions in order to overcome it. In the categories of reason that have been used to interpret the world and that have been fallaciously projected into it, strong pessimism recognizes man's "hyperbolical naïveté," his blind attribution of himself as meaning and measure of the worth of things in the world. Strong pessimism recognizes this world projected by man to be a fiction and seeks in this fictioning the condition of the values that have reigned throughout the metaphysical tradition, thereby seeking the condition of a transvaluation of these values in a different relation to their source.

Pessimism issues in "incomplete nihilism" if the values that have collapsed are replaced simply with new values (such as progress) that occupy the same places as the old. Strong pessimism becomes "extreme nihilism" when the consequences of the recognition that values are solely the product of a will to truth are carried to the point of acknowledging that there is no truth in itself. Extreme nihilism, in turn, is *passive* when the recognition that there is no truth in itself is accepted as meaning that there is no truth and is *active* when the recognition provokes a search for the source of truth. And it is classic or ecstatic when the Will to Power is recognized as the foundation of the possibility of truth.

The doublings we see here (weak/strong pessimism, active/passive nihilism) point to the fact that the thought of nihilism marks a turning point, a place of passage. The divisions express different attitudes or postures of the will before the crisis in thinking that occurs at the extreme point in that history that Nietzsche designates as the devaluation of values—the point at which the world appears as nothing more than appearance (and even the term "appearance" comes into question, since there is no longer a "truth" to define it against) and as an appearance that leads to nothing beyond itself. Nietzsche, Heidegger says, accomplishes the passage beyond nihilism by fully assuming its essence.[27] The thought comes to Nietzsche only because he carries nihilism to its extreme limits; he stands not outside this historical movement as a spectator, but assumes it as his own history, as his own destiny. Heidegger describes this limit-situation as one of "solitude"—a situation and a moment in which the thinker stands

[27]Nietzsche represents this passage in *Beyond Good and Evil* as it is effected in strong pessimism (aphorism 56, quoted in N1, 320/64–65). It issues, as we see, in the ecstatic nihilism of the thought of the Eternal Return: "Whoever has endeavored with some enigmatic longing, as I have, to think pessimism through to its depths and to liberate it from the half-Christian, half-German narrowness and simplicity in which it has finally presented itself to our century, namely, in the form of Schopenhauer's philosophy; whoever has really, with an Asiatic and supra-Asiatic eye, looked into, down into the most world-denying of all possible ways of thinking—beyond good and evil and no longer, like the Buddha and Schopenhauer, under the spell and delusion of morality—may just thereby, without really meaning to do so, have opened his eyes to the opposite ideal: the ideal of the most high-spirited, alive, and world-affirming human being who has not only come to terms and learned to get along with whatever was and is, but who wants to have *what was and is* repeated into all eternity, shouting insatiably *da capo*—not only to himself but to the whole play and spectacle, and not only to a spectacle but at bottom to him who needs precisely this spectacle—and who makes it necessary because again and again he needs himself—and makes himself necessary—What? And this wouldn't be—*circulus vitiosus deus*?" (trans. Walter Kaufmann [New York: Random House, 1966], p. 68). Note that the event of reversal, the dawning of the "inverse ideal," is not unlike the turn that occurs in *Being and Time* as the assumption of death leads into a disappropriating experience that turns into the *possibility* of authentic existence.

in "the most essential relations of his historical existence, in the midst of being in its totality" (*N*1, 275/2, 24). We recognize this "historical existence" as that possibility of authentic existence described in *Being and Time*. Heidegger's evocation of this notion is quite explicit:

> The "most solitary solitude" lies before and beyond any distinction of the "I" from the "you," and of the I and the you from the "we," of the individual from the community. In this most solitary solitude there is nothing of a singularization as separation; it is that singularization that we must conceive as *appropriation* [*Vereigentlichung*], where man comes into his own in his self. The self, authenticity [*Eigentlichkeit*] is not the "I," it is *that Da-sein* in which the relation of the I to the you and of the I to the we and of the we to the you is founded, and from which these relations first and alone may be mastered and must be mastered if they are to become a force. In being a self, there is posed for decision the weight of things and man, the balance with which they are weighed, and who the weigher is." [*N*1, 275–76/2, 24–25]

As we see, the solitude of historical existence is decision in the form of the appropriation of the possibility of existence (or Dasein). And, as Heidegger argued in *Being and Time*, the essence of history is encountered in a decision upon history. When the thought of the Eternal Return enters into Zarathoustra's most extreme solitude, it comes as a creative "counterthought" (*N*1, 434/2, 172) in which the history of nihilism is posed as such for the purpose of surmounting it. Stepping into the destiny that is nihilism is the condition of the emergence of the creative thought that poses nihilism as a history and accomplishes its overcoming; but the thinking of the thought is what makes possible the historical stance that is the assumption of this destiny. The paradox, again, is the one I described in my reading of *Being and Time*. The thought of the Eternal Return comes as a possibility in a decision upon that possibility.

The thought of the Eternal Return comes to Nietzsche as a project of being in its totality in which the most extreme experience of nihilism—that existence should be without finality and without meaning—achieves figuration. Inasmuch as the thought of the Eternal Return emerges in the domain of nihilism and poses this historical movement as such, Heidegger says that it has a nihilistic foundation. As the thought of nihilism, it is "terrifying"—it threatens to paralyze the will. As Nietzsche states, the will would prefer to will nothing rather than not to will at all; the horror of nonwilling "is the fundamental fact of human will" (*N*2, 65/4, 31). The thought of the Eternal Return, therefore, as the thought of the essence of nihilism, is the equivalent of the encounter with death; once again we find one of the essential elements of the existential analytic: "In the most solitary solitude just the worst and most dangerous menace is let loose upon ourselves and our task, and cannot be turned upon other things and men; it must pass through us, not to be set aside, but rather, out of the authentic knowledge belonging to the highest wisdom, recognized as belonging to solitude" (*N*1, 300–301/2, 47).

Heidegger's charge that Nietzsche's response to the crisis of nihilism is metaphysical (and thus an evasion of the crisis) rests upon his claim that Nietzsche fails to think precisely the essence of the nihil that determines this experience of the "nothing" of what is. Nietzsche, Heidegger argues, passes over the crisis in nihilism in his will to ground the play of appearance in the perspectival essence of the Will to Power, and he thereby reconfirms the anthropomorphic basis of modern metaphysics. But the passage in question—Nietzsche's affirmative countermovement in relation to nihilism—is effected in his thought of the Eternal Return, and in the description we have just seen of the menace that it bears, we have a clear indication that Nietzsche's "step beyond" nihilism actually carries him back into that experience that Heidegger describes as a thinking encounter with the essence of the nothing. As a project of being in its totality, in fact, the thought of the Eternal Return *necessarily* carries the thinker into the domain of the opening of Being;[28] if this thought is terrifying, it is because Nietzsche confronts the nothingness of this opening.

The thought of the Eternal Return, emerging in solitude, threatens to be paralyzing because it can suggest that no action can make a difference; everything that can be has already been and will be again as such throughout eternity—nothing has more meaning

---

[28]"That this chaos in its totality should be an Eternal Return of the Same first becomes the strangest and most fearful thought once the view is attained and taken seriously that the thinking of this thought must have the essential nature of a metaphysical project. The truth of being as such in its totality is then alone determined by the Being of being itself" (*N*2, 289).

than anything else, everything comes back to the same. But, as Heidegger puts it, an abyss separates this understanding of the thought from the affirmation that says that everything comes back to the same, and therefore nothing is indifferent. The thought of the Eternal Return draws the line, so to speak, between these two forms of understanding (and the line is nothing other than the historical limit of nihilism)—it poses both as a possibility: "This thought thinks being in such a way that it is from out of being in its totality that the constant challenge comes to us; whether we want merely to let ourselves be carried along or whether we want to be creators" (N1, 437/2, 174). But the posing of the possibility to become creative is itself a creative act, already an overcoming of the lapse of creative will that is nihilism. Again, the thought of the Eternal Return is the thought of the essence of nihilism, which essence can only be encountered insofar as this thought overcomes nihilism. The thinking of the thought of the Eternal Return *is* the passage across the abyss between the nihilistic foundation of this thought and its creative assumption. It is this passage *in both directions at once* insofar as the thinker is brought repeatedly and ever more profoundly into the terrifying character of what is thought in the thought. The entry into the essence of nihilism is the departure from it. Heidegger expresses this when he writes:

> With the development of Nietzsche's philosophy there grows at the same time the depth of the vision of the essence and of the power of nihilism; the distress and the necessity of its overcoming intensify.
>
> This means also: the concept of nihilism can only be thought in a simultaneous appropriation of the fundamental thought, the counter-thought, of Nietzsche's philosophy. Therefore, the inverse holds true: the fundamental thought, that is, the teaching of the Eternal Return, is to be conceived only out of the experience of nihilism and out of the knowledge of its essence. [N1, 435/2, 173]

The surmounting of nihilism is an ever more intense confrontation with its essence—an ever more profound solitude and historical self-situation. But however terrifying the encounter with this historical fate may be, it is an encounter with the source or the "possible" of thought. Affirming the essence of nihilism in its terrible necessity, the "gay science" draws from it a greater force. Heidegger describes the repetitive or circular dynamic of intensification here as the "weight" of the thought of the Eternal Return (the description of the encounter with the demon in the *Gay Science* bears the title "the greatest weight"). The gravity of the thought brings the thinker into his historical situation, just as Dasein is "pushed" into the finitude of its existence (*SZ*, 384/435). "The thought of the Eternal Return is to be a defining weight, that is, determining, for the task of standing-in-the-midst of being in its totality" (*N*1, 273/2, 22). But as in *Being and Time* (and let us not forget Zarathoustra's levity), the push into existence entails also an ecstatic movement (is occasioned by this ecstatic movement): "It poses us in the midst of being and therewith it exposes us outside" (*N*1, 274/2, 23). As a thought of being in its totality, "it must be thought into the innermost plenitude of being, thought out to the most extreme limit of being in its totality, and thought through the most solitary solitude of man" (*N*1, 276/2, 25). What is this "outside"? Elsewhere Heidegger writes of the manner of thought required to think the thought of the Eternal Return: "The divining of this riddle must venture out into the open of what is concealed, into the untrodden and trackless, into the unconcealedness (alētheia) of this most concealed, into the truth" (*N*1, 290/2, 37). What is this divining, then, other than the revelation of the meaning of Being— truth as alētheia?: " 'Meaning' denominates, according to *Being and Time*, the domain of the project [*Entwurfsbereich*] and properly intends (according to the one question concerning the 'meaning of Being') the clearing of Being that opens and founds itself in the projecting. This projecting, however, is what in the thrown project occurs as the essencing of truth" (*N*2, 20).

When the thinker becomes the site of the revelation of the truth of being in its totality (the site of eternal recurrence), he then stands in the distinction between Being and what is, and in relation to Being. He stands in that space that Heidegger calls "the same": "The distinction between Being and what is proves to be that same out of which all metaphysics issues, but that it also immediately evades in its arising, that same that it leaves as such behind it and outside its district" (*N*2, 208/4, 154). The *matter* of Nietzsche's thought—his understanding of being in its totality as this is founded in his relation to Being—lies "beneath" or "behind" the domain of metaphysics. *Amor fati* names Nietzsche's will to occupy this unheimlich space, the "there" of his existence. Heidegger defines this passion as "the transfiguring will that wills belonging to the most being of being" (N1, 471/2, 207). But the will to reach back in thought to the world as such carries the thinker beyond what is and back to that "around which the world becomes world" (N1, 471/2, 207). Nietzsche names this movement of thought, and also that which it thinks, *circulus vitiosus deus*. The naming is a silencing, for the essential reasons we have seen. Heidegger forgets this silence when he denies to Nietzsche the step beyond metaphysics and the thought of the question of Being. Yet he writes also at the end of his essay "The Eternal Recurrence of the Same": "For that which is withheld is what is properly guarded and as the most guarded that which is closest and most real. What for the common understanding appears as 'atheism' and must appear as such is fundamentally the opposite. And in the same way: there where nothingness and death are dealt with, Being and only this is most profoundly thought" (N1, 471/2, 207–8).

Bringing Western metaphysics to its fulfillment, Nietzsche's thought, says Heidegger, reaches back to the beginning of Western thought and closes the circle described by this manner of thinking. This is to say, in relation to Heidegger's own conception of the repetitive movement of philosophy (that is, in relation to the "hermeneutic circle"), that Nietzsche's project suspends the turn of thought, its return to its source in the "open foundation" of Dasein. Yet Heidegger recognizes, too, that there is a *hyperbolical* movement in Nietzsche's thinking that prevents Nietzsche from closing the circle of his own project of thought. In Nietzsche's successive attempts to found or center his thinking in one of his three "fundamental positions" (founded respectively on the notions of the Eternal Return, the Will to Power, and the Transvaluation of all Values), he encounters in each case the problem of philosophy's *exorbitant* nature:

> And it was nothing else than the question of the center [*Mitte*] that genuinely "maltreated" Nietzsche. Of course it was not the extrinsic question of finding a suitable connection or link among the handwritten materials available; it was, without Nietzsche's coming to know of it or stumbling across it, the question of philosophy's self-grounding. It concerns the fact that whatever philosophy is, and however it may exist at any given time, it defines itself solely on its own terms; but also that such self-determination is possible only inasmuch as philoso-

phy always has already grounded itself. Its proper essence turns ever toward itself, and the more original a philosophy is, the more purely it soars in turning about itself, and therefore the further the "circumference of its circle presses outward to the brink of nothingness." [N1, 24/1, 6]

But the negative characterization of Nietzsche's experience of the hyperbolical movement of thought is not sufficient; again, as Heidegger tells us, Nietzsche named this movement: circulus vitiosus deus. Heidegger is curiously circumspect in his explication of this name, as of the name that it points to: Dionysus—as if the celebration of this name in the "feast of thought" for which the interpretation prepares would carry the interpretive movement beyond and outside itself, disrupting its *"Heimischsein"* (N1, 15/1, 6). Though Heidegger's reading points in the direction of the unheimlich essence of the god (that which is terrifying in the thought of the Eternal Return), Heidegger also renders Nietzsche's stance finally *heimisch* in relation to this determination of Being. This will become more apparent as we consider Heidegger's remarks on Nietzsche's aesthetic thinking in relation to "The Origin of the Work of Art." My purpose here has been to bring forth the two readings (or two of the readings) at work in *Nietzsche* and to suggest how the contradiction between them centers in the "tragic" discord that Nietzsche situates in the turn of art against truth. The turn of art, as we have seen, opens out of the "encircling" element of metaphysical thinking that Heidegger finds in Nietzsche. In my subsequent consideration of *Nietzsche*, I will focus more specifically on this turn and will seek to determine how Heidegger appropriates it within his own "tragic style."

3/

Difference and Self-Affirmation

Heidegger opens the published version of his 1936 lectures on Schelling's *Treatise on the Essence of Human Freedom* with a brief description of the political climate in which Schelling conceived his treatise. He remarks that in 1809 Prussia was beginning to emerge from the domination of Napoleon—the domination of a particular "political representation" of the world—and sought its form as a "state of the spirit" where culture (*Bildung*) was recognized as a founding force. Clearly, Heidegger sees the Germany of 1936 as moving in the opposite direction. Napoleon's famous words to Goethe thus have a particular resonance: "[Tragedies] belonged to a darker period. What do we want with fate now? Politics is fate! Come to Paris. . . . There is a larger view of the world there" (*SA*, 1/11). The "profound nontruth" of this statement, remarks Heidegger, was about to emerge in 1809, and he writes in response: "No, spirit is fate, and fate is spirit. The essence of spirit, however, is freedom" (*SA*, 2/11).

Throughout Heidegger's writings of the thirties, this same note is sounded: fate is spirit, and its fate is tragic. With the same conviction, Heidegger writes in *Nietzsche* that the "passion for reflection" that is proper to Western man is the condition for his salvation (*Rettung*) (*N1*, 533) and in *An Introduction to Metaphysics*, identifies Oedipus as the representative hero for the Western Dasein: "We must see him as the embodiment of Greek Dasein, who most radically and wildly asserts its fundamental passion, the passion for disclosure of Being" (*EM*, 81/107). Hölderlin, he says, captured this insight in his phrase "King Oedipus has an eye too many perhaps" in his poem "In lovely blueness. . . ." "This eye too many," Heidegger writes, "is the fundamental condition for all great questioning and knowledge, and their only metaphysical ground" (*EM*, 81/107).

In his *Rektoratsrede* (rectoral address) of 1933, "The Self-Affirmation of the German University," Heidegger calls on the members of the university to repeat the original emergence of Greek philosophy, which is, he says, "the beginning of our spiritual-historical being" (*SU*, 8/471). To repeat this beginning is to will the essence of science and thus to recover "the passion to remain close to and hard pressed by what is as such" (*SU*, 9–10/472). Such repetition, he argues, is the condition of self-affirmation or self-appropriation in a "world of spirit." But in Heidegger's description of the tragic essence of science in his Rektoratsrede and more fully in *An Introduction to Metaphysics* we may glimpse a more complex configuration in the process of world-building than the rhetoric of the rectoral address suggests. In a similar manner, we may find throughout Heidegger's writings of the thirties evidence of the precariousness of his claim for the possibility of a gathered self-appropriation in a creative project of Being. Heidegger seeks in these works (always in relation to the project of *Being and Time*) what we might call a "tragic style";[1] but in his effort to elaborate in this way a founded and unifying mode of being, he excludes or elides the unsettling dimensions of Dasein's self-affirmation in the nearness of Being.

My aim in this chapter is to define the configuration of Selbstbehauptung that Heidegger seeks in tragic experience and to open Heidegger's description of this configuration (always a relation of appropriation and disappropriation) to its more disruptive possibilities. Heidegger's consistent focus on the gathering traits of the relation of Being and human being requires, in my view, a counterbalancing emphasis on his own description of the destabilizing

---

[1] I draw this term from Heidegger's reference to a "hidden stylistic law of the historical determination of the German people" (N1, 124/1, 104) to which Hölderlin, with his description of the conflict of holy passion and sober representation, and Nietzsche, with his description of the conflict of the Dionysian and the Apollonian, together point. I return to this quotation in Chapter 4.

sources of change. I will seek a general critical model in the context of politics by turning briefly to Heidegger's Rektoratsrede and then to *An Introduction to Metaphysics*.

In "The Self-Affirmation of the German University," Heidegger claims for the university a guiding role in the shaping of the "state of the spirit." But Heidegger's definition of this role answers to a "political conception of the world" by reason of its very philosophical, or rather, metaphysical, thrust. Heidegger's address reiterates the essential tie between philosophy and politics established at philosophy's beginnings (Heidegger's concluding citation of Plato is telling in this regard) and renewed in the metaphysics of subjectivity. In his *Letter on Humanism*, Heidegger points to the metaphysical aspect of the modern political movements in terms that might well implicate his own address of 1933 and his embracing of National Socialism:

> Every nationalism is in metaphysical terms an anthropologism and as such a subjectivism. Nationalism is not surmounted through simple internationalism, only expanded and raised to a system. Nationalism is thereby brought and carried up into the *humanitas* as little as is individualism through collectivism without history. This latter is the subjectivity of man in totality. It accomplishes its unconditioned self-affirmation [*Selbstbehauptung*]. [*W*, 341–42/221]

But even in Heidegger's retreat from political involvement after the episode of the rectorship in 1933, that is, after what appears to be a recognition of the nature of the German National Socialist movement in its philosophical dimensions and its political reality, Heidegger continues to assert in terms that are essentially those of his Rektoratsrede—in the same tragic schema—a fundamental role for science (as philosophy) in the configuration of the German destiny. In *An Introduction to Metaphysics*, delivered at the University of Freiburg in Breisgau in the summer semester of 1935, Heidegger cites both his inaugural address of 1929 ("What Is Metaphysics?")[2] and "The Self-Affirmation of the German University" to describe the fragmentation of the German university resulting from the "misinterpretation" of spirit as intelligence in the modern conception of science. The

2"Was ist Metaphysik?" *W*, 1–19.

"progressive" practical conception of knowledge and the "reactionary" interpretation of science as a cultural value complement one another, he argues, and even merge in the "technical organization of the universities" (*EM*, 37/49). In opposition to this misinterpretation of the spirit, Heidegger quotes from his Rektoratsrede and says:

"Spirit is neither empty cleverness nor the irresponsible play of the wit, nor the boundless work of dismemberment carried on by the practical intelligence, much less is it world reason; no, spirit is fundamental, knowing resolve toward the essence of Being" (*Rektoratsrede*, p. 13). Spirit is the empowering of the powers of being as such and as a whole. Where spirit prevails, being as such becomes always and at all times more being. Thus the inquiry into being as such and as a whole, the asking of the question of Being, is one of the essential and fundamental conditions for an awakening of the spirit and hence for an original world of historical Dasein. It is indispensable if the peril of world darkening is to be forestalled and if our nation in the center of the Western world is to take on its historical mission. [*EM*, 37–38/49–50]

In *An Introduction to Metaphysics*, as in "The Self-Affirmation of the German University," Heidegger maintains, as we see, that science, as philosophy, consists in the production of a world, this latter designated as the foundation of political reality. He thus maintains the equation of theory and practice asserted in "The Self-Affirmation of the German University," in which *theōria* is described, following the Greek understanding of philosophy at its beginnings, as the highest modality of *energeia*, the "being at work" of man—"the highest realization of authentic praxis": "For the Greeks, science is not a 'cultural good' but the innermost determining center of all that binds human being to people and state [*volklich-staatlichen Daseins*]. Science, for them, is also not a mere means of bringing the unconscious to consciousness, but the power that hones and embraces being-there [*Dasein*] in its entirety" (*SU*, 10/473).

As an activity of "world-building," "science" in this context, as in *Nietzsche* and, indeed, throughout Heidegger's writings of the late twenties and thirties, refers to a mode of ex-istence, man's fundamental relation to what is in its truth: the finite transcendence of Dasein. In transcending, Heidegger says, Dasein projects before itself a world as an initial sketch of the possibilities for its relation to what is. It projects this sketch, a delimitation of being and a determination of the *how* of Dasein's relation to it, from the midst of being, that is, from an "affective situation" in which Dasein is penetrated by the tonality of what is, traversed and seized by it. The finitude of Dasein's project derives from this fundamental determination. But the paradoxical logic of finitude appears in the fact that Dasein can only be seized by what is (and thus grounded there) as being-in-the-world, that is, as transcending.

The project of the world cast in Dasein's transcendence is a sketch in the sense of a prefiguration or preimage for what is, cast in a creative act: " 'Dasein transcends' means that in the essence of its being it is *world-forming*, and indeed 'forming' [*bildend*] in the manifold sense that it lets world happen and through the world provides itself with an original view (form) which does not grasp explicitly, yet serves as a model for, all of manifest being, to which belongs each time Dasein itself" (*W,* 157). Dasein's world-forming offers in this way the occasion for the manifestation of what is. But the world cast in a project is also that from which Dasein comes to itself as a self (*W,* 157). Transcending toward the world and thus being in the world, Dasein's selfhood temporalizes. This selfhood is in turn the condition of a "my-self" (revealing itself always in relation to a "your-self") or a "we" (standing in relation to a "you"). Selfhood, as Heidegger argues in *Vom Wesen des Grundes,* is neutral (*W,* 158) in relation to "being-me" or "being-you" and sexually undetermined;[3] and it is, as we have seen in *Being and Time,* multiple in its identity. Dasein's historizing or occurrence (*Geschehen*) as self is always a cohistorizing: "But if fateful Dasein, as being in the world, exists essentially in being-with others, its historizing is a cohistorizing and is determined as *destiny* [*Geschick*]. With this term, we designate the occurrence of a community, of a people" (*SZ,* 384/436).

Transcending toward a world, then, Dasein comes to itself in a community, in a people. Heidegger thus proceeds rapidly in "The Self-Affirmation of the German University," though appropriately

[3] I leave this assertion unexamined here. For an approach to the question of sexuality in Heidegger's work, one may consult a recent essay by Jacques Derrida, "Geschlecht, différence sexuelle, différence ontologique," in the volume of *Les cahiers de l'herne* devoted to Heidegger (Paris: Editions de l'Herne, 1983), pp. 419–30, as well as his work on Blanchot, collected recently in *Parages* (Paris: Galilée, 1986).

in his terms, to designate science as "the most intimately determining center of their [the Greeks'] entire existence as a people in a state" (*SU*, 10) and in *An Introduction to Metaphysics*, to name the *polis* as the "there" of existence: "*Polis* is usually translated as city or city-state. This does not capture the full meaning. Polis means, rather, the place, the there, wherein and as which historical Dasein is. The polis is the place of history, the there *in* which, *out of* which, and *for* which history happens" (*EM*, 117/152).

Again, Heidegger is founding political existence in Dasein's metaphysical essence, that is to say, its transcendence. The gesture is entirely consistent with his project of a fundamental ontology, and thus it is not surprising that the core of Heidegger's assertions in "The Self-Affirmation of the German University" should reappear in subsequent contexts, despite the disastrous political engagements of 1933. However offensive Heidegger's rhetoric may be in "The Self-Affirmation of the German University,"[4] his argument follows strictly, if not fully, the terms of his philosophical thought. And although we may be tempted to dismiss his statement quickly or to ignore it, we cannot easily discount Heidegger's effort to address the problem of the specialization and fragmentation of knowledge in the disciplines of the university. The philosophical compromise (which is also part of the political compromise) lies, I would argue, in Heidegger's failure to carry through his foundational thinking: to define self-affirmation in relation to a foundation or ground that he describes elsewhere as an *Ab-grund* (abyss)—to expose fully, in other words, the finitude of Dasein. Carrying through the thought of finitude perhaps undoes Heidegger's own *founding* design, as I mean to suggest in this and the next two chapters. But even without taking the analysis this far, we may see that Heidegger's notion of Dasein's finite transcendence should prevent him from calling the members of the university to assume their destiny as a collective subject—the self-appropriating subject of their history, "a people that knows itself in its state" (*SU*, 7/471).

An Introduction to Metaphysics, for example, betrays a caution that would have made the exhortations of "The Self-Affirmation of the German University" impossible. Heidegger offers in this text a

---

[4]I refer in particular to Heidegger's use of phrases such as "*erd- und bluthaften Kräfte*," translated by Harries as "strengths . . . tied to earth and blood" (*SU*, 13/475), but also to the exhortative and sometimes martial quality of his tone.

more circumspect view of the founding role of philosophy. He leaves undefined the ontic (and first political) conditions that determine its founding function, questioning simply the causal conception of such a function: "Philosophy can never *directly* supply the energies and create the opportunities and methods that bring about a historical change" (*EM*, 8/10). He asserts this first because philosophy is "always the concern of the few" (*EM*, 8/10)—a qualification, perhaps, of his assertion in the *Rektoratsrede* that science should ground a general movement as the body of students and the body of teachers find their essences respectively in the essence of science (though Heidegger reserves in his Rektoratsrede a special role for the "leaders").

But if philosophy is the concern of the few, it is because it is "ambiguous" in its essence (*EM*, 7/9)—it complicates existence and "embarrasses" [*erschweren*] Dasein by rendering to beings their "weight" and, as we will see, their enigmatic, uncanny character. In the Rektoratsrede, Heidegger only alludes to the ambiguity of philosophy, and upon the effective exclusion of this ambiguity, he pretends to put before his public a *choice* regarding science and the historical way of existence that it defines. However, as Heidegger demonstrated in *Being and Time* and as he suggests in *An Introduction to Metaphysics*, such a choice (essentially a self-affirmation) is possible only on the basis of, and in constant confrontation with, the ambiguity to which philosophy opens. In *An Introduction to Metaphysics*, the unsettling aspects of philosophy's role of "breaking the paths and opening the perspectives of the knowledge that sets the standards and hierarchies..., the knowledge that kindles, threatens, and necessitates all inquiry and assessment" (*EM*, 8/10), are still somewhat muted. But, operating with the same tragic schema as in the Rektoratsreder, Heidegger allows us to read the concept of self-affirmation in terms other than those of the production of the metaphysical subject—as individual, group, or nation. I will demonstrate this in the following pages by describing briefly Heidegger's argument in his Rektoratsrede and then by considering the development of its logic in *An Introduction to Metaphysics*.

I would like to recognize before proceeding, however, that to read "The Self-Affirmation of the German University," even briefly, is to raise the question of Heidegger's political activity of 1933. I have chosen to consider within this space some of the philosophical dimensions of this activity and to leave unassessed the way in which this activity, undertaken in the name of philosophy and within the framework of the politics of the university, answers to its historical context.[5] I spoke of Heidegger's compromises in his Rektoratsrede; these compromises (both political and philosophical) can be fully understood only within their sociopolitical context. "Compromise" is in fact a misleading word, since it suggests some measure of philosophical purity or authenticity against which Heidegger's actions might be judged. Philosophy, however, does not exist outside its sociopolitical context. Heidegger's own thought of finitude points to the necessity of thinking philosophy's inscription within the sphere of social institutions; it suggests that the

[5]Although I will not attempt to analyze Heidegger's political activity of 1933, it may be appropriate to describe briefly the nature of Heidegger's involvement in national politics. According to Heidegger's own account given in an interview held in September 1966 with Rudolf Augstein and Georg Wolff of *Der Spiegel* and printed in *Der Spiegel*, no. 23, May 31, 1976, his activity included the following moments. In April 1933 Heidegger was elected rector of the University of Freiburg after his predecessor was relieved of his duties for refusing to allow the Association of German Students (Deutscher Studentenbund) to post their demand that all Jewish students and professors be removed from the university. Heidegger refused to accede to the same request by the Studentenbund and met resistance from the National Socialists on a number of similar issues during his tenure. He resigned in February 1934 after refusing to bow to political pressure in the choice of deans for the schools of law and medicine. Heidegger's official tenure as rector of the University of Freiburg was thus ten months. Heidegger explains that his decision to assume the rectorship was prompted by his sense that it was possible to tap the still remaining "constructive forces" (*Der Spiegel*, p. 193) of the current social movement—a movement of whose "inner truth and greatness" he speaks in *An Introduction to Metaphysics* (*EM*, 152/199)—and to resist in this way the effort to politicize the university in the name of the practical utility of science for the state. Heidegger's gesture was therefore a complex one—his *Rektoratsrede* both an affirmation and critique. But his political actions were based upon sincere belief in the possibilities of the National Socialist movement and answer to what can only be termed a very conservative political inclination. In addition to the *Spiegel* interview (translated by Maria P. Alter and John D. Caputo in *Philosophy Today*, Winter 1976, pp. 267–84), one may consult Heidegger's 1945 essay "The Rectorate 1933/34—Facts and Thoughts," translated by Karsten Harries and published with a translation of the rectoral address in the *Review of Metaphysics* 38, no. 3 (March 1985): 467–502. (Harries translates the title of the rectoral address as "The Self-Assertion of the German University.") Of numerous references available on the subject of Heidegger's politics, three discussions of "The Self-Affirmation of the German University" in particular should be noted here: Karsten Harries, "Heidegger as a Political Thinker"; Gérard Granel, "Pourquoi avons-nous publié cela?" in *De l'université* (Paris: Trans-Europ-Repress, 1982), pp. 99–143; Lacoue-Labarthe, "La transcendance finit dans la politique," in *Rejouer le politique* (Paris: Editions Galilée, 1981), the first collective publication of the *Centre de recherches philosophiques sur le politique*. This essay by

practice of philosophy can never be disinterested.[6] But the notion of finitude also suggests that philosophy's sociopolitical interests are exceeded, even disrupted, by its hyperbolical return to its own uncertain foundations in language—the foundation of any form of human production (compare *H,* 62/74).

Our first task in evaluating and criticizing Heidegger's political activity of 1933 is to develop the implications of Heidegger's notion of the finitude of the various forms of discourse and production: to account philosophically for the necessary insertion of philosophical discourse within a play of interests that inevitably exceeds its power to make those interests *its own,* but also to describe why philosophy cannot be wholly of its time, even as it assumes the responsibility of its history. I can only sketch the terms of this latter argument at this time, but its general lines are relatively clear.

To develop the concept of philosophy's "practical finitude"[7] is to

---

Lacoue-Labarthe might be read in the context of his contributions to *Les fins de l'homme,* ed. Lacoue-Labarthe and Nancy, including "Au nom de . . ." (with which my argument in this chapter runs parallel at certain points) and his response to my paper "Activité philosophique/pratique politique" presented in the seminar on politics (*Les fins de l'homme,* pp. 487–500).

[6]I am concerned in this chapter with other aspects of the limits of Dasein's freedom, but I think we should not lose sight of this dimension of the finitude of existence. As Heidegger explains in *Being and Time,* Dasein situates itself always within its factical situation and projects upon this situation: "The authentic existentiell understanding is so far from extricating itself from the way of interpreting *Dasein* which has come down to us, that in each case it is in terms of this interpretation, against it, and yet again for it, that it seizes the chosen possibility in the resolution" (*SZ,* 383/435). Let us recall also the sentences quoted by Karsten Harries regarding the impossibility of divorcing philosophical inquiry from the concrete stance of the thinker within his or her ontic circumstances: "Is there not, however, a definite ontical way of taking authentic existence, a factical ideal of *Dasein,* underlying our ontological interpretation of *Dasein*'s existence? That is so indeed. But not only is this fact one that must not be denied and that we are forced to grant; it must also be conceived in its *positive necessity*" (*SZ,* 310/358). As Harries observes, fundamental ontology cannot be pure. Again, this is not a weakness but a "positive necessity" deriving from Heidegger's very notion of the finitude of existence and related to his notion of the finitude of Being that needs or requires Dasein in order to come about in its truth. The unconcealment of Being, as Heidegger suggests in "The Origin of the Work of Art" (the focus of Chapter 4), can occur only *from within the world* opened in Dasein's finite project and as it is "set up" in a being. Thus, if philosophy contributes to the founding of a polis that is not in its essence political in the ontic sense but the historical foundation of political existence, it nevertheless elaborates this site from within a factical situation determined by a sociopolitical reality.

[7]I borrow this term from Gérard Granel, who uses it in his essay "Appel à ceux

explore the way in which philosophy, even when it is most actively engaged, stands in a relation of disjunction with the sphere of political or practical interests. Its thinking (or writing) practice disrupts the relation of theory and practice as it has been defined throughout the metaphysical tradition. If philosophy is part of the struggle for a world (in a Platonic sense, following the epigraph to *Being and Time*, and in a political sense), it does not posit this world—represent it—as an object or a work to be produced. It is something more than a *theoretical* practice—that is, a practice that would consist in producing an objective representation of a field of conflicting interests, and even representing (as a *delegate* or as a *voice*) a given position. As Heidegger argues in "The Age of the World View,"[8] the concept of philosophy as a "representing production" belongs to the metaphysical epoch that Heidegger terms "Modern Times" and that lies under "the domination of subjectivity"; it belongs to what Heidegger calls in the *Letter on Humanism*, the dictatorship of publicity: "the metaphysically conditioned establishment and authorization of the openness of beings in their unconditioned objectification" (*W*, 317/197). Philosophy must move upon the "scene of representation"—it cannot simply escape the structure of representation, just as it cannot pretend to be free of practical or political interests (nor should it want to, I would argue); but in its effort to mark the limits of that structure (the limits of the metaphysics of subjectivity itself, which define modern history), it seeks to give itself up to the radical possibilities of language that positive discourses must close upon in order to assure their *ideal* mastery over a domain of what is. Philosophy seeks the "event" of history itself, the dispossessing sources of historical change—it seeks to produce difference. In this way it is *unzeitgemässe*.

The significance of the terms of this last statement will emerge only in the course of the discussion that follows. But I want to argue that it is against such a philosophical background that we

---

qui ont affaire avec l'université en vue d'en préparer une autre," in *De l'université* (Paris: Editions Trans-Europ-Repress, 1982), pp. 75–96.

[8]"Die Zeit des Weltbildes," in *Holzwege*, translated by Marjorie Grene as "The Age of the World View," in *Martin Heidegger and the Question of Literature: Toward a Postmodern Literary Hermeneutics*, ed. William V. Spanos (Bloomington: Indiana University Press, 1976), pp. 1–15.

may effectively assess Heidegger's political activity of the thirties, including both his membership in the National Socialist Party and his subsequent, active withdrawal from national politics. Any critique of this activity that fails to take the full measure of this philosophical context (that is, Heidegger's questioning of the nature of the political domain itself) is of questionable pertinence, since it stands in the shadow of Heidegger's own critique of the modern, technical, "political conception of the world." This proviso holds, of course, for any assessment of the political thrust of Heidegger's thought in general. An analysis of the political import of Heidegger's text must at some moment move at the level at which Heidegger pitches his own questioning—that is to say, it must proceed at the level of the question of Being. To do so is not to surrender in advance to a metaphysical hegemony over political thought; it is to question the limits of both philosophy and politics and to seek to repose the questions of political existence.

"The Self-Affirmation of the German University" opens with a strikingly involuted statement defining for the students and teachers of the university the necessity of self-affirmation (Selbstbehauptung). The essential character of the university, Heidegger observes, resides in its autonomy, its self-legislation. Autonomy (Selbstverwaltung) means, Heidegger says, "to set our own task, to determine ourselves the way and manner in which it is to be realized, so that thus we shall be what we ought to be" (*SU*, 6/470). But self-legislation presupposes that the students and teachers know *who* they are, thus it presupposes constant self-examination or self-meditation (*Selbstbesinnung*). This latter is possible, however, only in the act of willing the essence of the university that is defined for the future. The affirmation that accompanies self-legislation is a self-affirmation that renders self-meditation possible. Students and teachers may come to themselves, Heidegger suggests, only in willing themselves in the act of projecting the essence of the university.

There emerges from this spiral of philosophical exigency Heidegger's fundamental assertion that the university can attain the "clarity, rank, and power of its essence" only insofar as the teaching body and the body of students situate themselves in relation to the "spiritual mission" that determines German destiny and gives it the mark of its history. This act of self-situation entails essentially an assumption (or willing) of a scientific manner of being. To will the essence of science and thus "the spiritual-historical mission of the German people" (*SU,* 7/471) is to will to stand forth ("discovered") in a questioning that is a constant opening to the essence of what is. "Decision"—the assuming of this stance in the "knowing resolve" that is spirit—constantly calls for renewed decision, for it is always a further opening or exposure to the question-worthy character of Being. To will the essence of science, Heidegger says, creates for a people its "world of spirit," which is "a world of the innermost and most extreme danger" (*SU,* 13/474).

The decision that opens a world calls for decision in the sense of preservation of the powers of the earth (or physis) that are disclosed to it, but it calls for decision also in that no decision in regard to the essence of Being can hold or preserve this essence fully. There is always an unmastered depth that is disclosed in spirit's creative activity and that requires a further creative response. A decision in regard to Being is always marked by its own finitude (I return below to the nature of this marking). A creator—and here Heidegger speaks of Dasein as a people—is thus constantly posed the alternative of renewed creation or the cultivation of what is already disclosed and the "decadence" that necessarily ensues with the abandonment of the founding relation of an opening to truth.

The repetitive nature of a relation to Being in its truth is defined by Heidegger in the Rektoratsrede in terms of a martial rhythm of reiterated choice between grandeur and decadence: "A spiritual world . . . necessitates that the constant decision between the will to greatness and a letting things happen that means decline, will be the law presiding over the march that our people has begun into its future history" (*SU,* 13–14/475). The Rektoratsrede itself sets the rhythm of this choice. The paragraphs immediately preceding the end, for example, reiterate it as follows:

> Do we, or do we not, will the essence of the German university? It is up to us whether, and to what extent, we concern ourselves with self-examination and self-affirmation not just casually, but penetrating to their very foundations, or whether—with the best of intentions—

we only change old arrangements and add new ones. No one will keep us from doing this.

But no one will even ask us whether we do or do not will, when the spiritual strength of the West fails and the joints of the world no longer hold, when this moribund semblance of a culture caves in and drags all that remains strong into confusion and lets it suffocate in madness.

Whether this will happen or not depends alone on whether or not we, as a historical-spiritual people, still and once again will ourselves. Every individual participates in this decision, even he, and especially he, who evades it.

But we do will that our people should fulfill its historical mission.

We do will ourselves. For the young and the youngest strength of the people, which already reaches beyond us, *has* by now decided the matter. [*SU,* 21–22/480]

The last line (referring first to the students, as a previous paragraph reveals) is more than an affirmative, self-confirming rhetorical turn toward a conclusion; it is *required* by the rhetoric of self-legitimation and self-affirmation. For, following the logic of repetition as we have seen it thus far, the decision must *have taken* place in order for it to take place—that is, in order for the choice to be first posed as a possibility. Dasein must have opened to its history in order to project upon it and affirm it (though, following the logic of the hermeneutic circle, it only truly enters this history in projecting). To take up the terms of *Being and Time,* Dasein projects only in response to a call. (In *Being and Time,* this is the overwhelming call of conscience that comes not in exhortation but as an assault or striking throw; here it is the call of Being in its history.) The yes or no, either-or alternative that Heidegger poses to his audience is a false one, since the alternative does not emerge except *in* the event of call and response—here, questioning in a scientific mode in relation to the challenge of the modern destiny of "dereliction" that Heidegger designates with Nietzsche's phrase "God is dead." At this moment, Heidegger says, science becomes "the fundamental happening of our spiritual being as part of a people" (*SU,* 12/474). Heidegger's "spiritual direction," as he calls it in the opening paragraph of his Rektoratsrede, cannot lie in exhortation, and the will of resolve of which he speaks cannot be reduced to a will *to* resolve—at least not if we are to follow

Heidegger in his effort to distinguish the openness of Entschlossenheit from the arbitrary *Willkür* of willful determination. Part of the offensiveness of Heidegger's discourse lies in his willful confusion of these last two concepts; one question that this discourse raises for us lies in the possibility that these are at some point indistinguishable from one another.

But the question on which I wish to focus here concerns the problem of will and resolve only inasmuch as these are related to the possibility of self-appropriation in the resolved stance of scientific questioning. To approach this question, let us return to Heidegger's description of the tragic character of this questioning.

Heidegger states that the willing of the essence of science is a willing to situate ourselves "under the power of the *beginning* of our spiritual-historical being" (*SU*, 8/471). This beginning, Heidegger says, lies in Greek philosophy, of which he brings forth two essential properties. The second of these properties concerns the practical essence of theory (theōria): theory, as we have seen, was understood by the Greeks as "the highest realization of authentic praxis." The first property concerns the tragic essence of science. Heidegger illustrates it with the words of Prometheus: "Knowing, however, is far weaker than necessity" (*SU*, 9/472). Heidegger glosses these words as follows: All knowing about things has always already been delivered up to overpowering fate and fails before it. Just because of this, knowing must develop its highest defiance; called forth by such defiance, all the power of the hiddenness of what is must first arise for knowing really to fail. Just in this way what is opens itself in its unfathomable inalterability and lends knowing its truth (*SU*, 9/472).

These are potentially somber words. But Heidegger does not really explicate them; to do so would carry him into the unsettling character of the "event" that defines the tragic character of existence. In *An Introduction to Metaphysics*, however, he does undertake this development in the terms of tragedy that are those of the Rektoratsrede. *An Introduction to Metaphysics* provides also a more complete view of the nature of Selbstbehauptung.

In *An Introduction to Metaphysics*, Heidegger describes the event of world-building in terms of the unconcealment of beings as the Greeks understood it with the term "physis." Physis "struggles to become itself" as a world; in a world, "being first comes about as

117

being" (*EM*, 47/62). Heidegger defines this struggle in terms of the originary conflict called *polemos* by Heraclitus; he translates this term as Auseinandersetzung. It is conflict not in a human sense, Heidegger observes; rather, it is the conflict that "first caused the realm of being to separate into opposites [*im Gegeneinander auseinandertreten*]; it first gave rise to position and order and rank. In such separation there open cleavages, intervals, distances and joints [*Fugen*]. In the conflict a world comes about" (*EM*, 47/62). Heidegger further defines this polemos as *logos*: the contending that separates also binds and gathers.

Man is *situated* in the original struggle. Heidegger cites in this respect Heraclitus's fragment 53: "Conflict is for all (that is present) the creator (that lets emerge), but (also) for all the dominant preserver. For it lets some appear as gods, others as men; it sets forth some as slaves, others however as free" (*EM*, 47/61–62). Conflict *gives rise to* the contending parties—in it, they first come to be. The conflict "first projects and develops what had hitherto been unheard of, unsaid and unthought. The battle is then sustained by the creators, poets, thinkers, statesmen" (*EM*, 47/62). The "creators" carry out the original conflict, that original separation that occurs first in the essence of language as logos:

> Against the overpowering power they set the barrier of their work, and in their work they capture the world thus opened up. It is with these works that the elemental power, the *physis* first comes to stand in what is present. Only now does being become being as such. This happening of world is history in the authentic sense. Not only does conflict as such give rise to being, it also preserves being in its constancy. Where struggle ceases, being does not vanish, but the world turns away. Being [*das Seiende*] is no longer asserted [*behauptet*] (i.e. preserved as such).... What is accomplished is no longer that which is impressed into limits [*in Grenzen geschlagene*] (i.e. placed in its form [*in seine Gestalt Gestellte*]). [*EM*, 47–48/62]

Man effectively redoubles the originary conflict with his own energeia. Heidegger defines this human initiative, drawn forth within the space of conflict, in terms of man's apprehension (*Vernehmung*, corresponding to the Greek *noein*) of what is. In apprehension, man "contends" with what is—apprehension is both a receiving and a questioning or interrogation, as Heidegger suggests when he likens it to questioning a witness (*EM*, 105/138). It is a receptive attitude toward that which shows itself, but it is not receptive in a passive sense: "When troops prepare to receive the enemy, it is in the hope of stopping him at the very least, of bringing him to stand. This receptive bringing-to-stand is meant in *noein*" (*EM*, 105/138).[9]

As man brings being to stand in its essential limits (that is, as he carries out the delimitation of what is), he brings himself to stand. Man *shows* in the conflict of world-building in both transitive and intransitive senses. "According to Heraclitus what man is, is first manifested . . . in polemos, in the separation of gods and men, in the irruption of Being itself" (*EM*, 107/140). But he "shows" only insofar as he shows what is in his assumption of the conflict and brings it to appearance in the work. In these terms we must understand the notion of self-affirmation. Among the points summarizing his argument concerning the determination of the essence of man, Heidegger lists the following:

4. Only where being discloses itself in questioning does history happen and with it that being of *man* by virtue of which he ventures to set himself apart from being as such and contend with it [*Auseinandersetzung*].
5. This questioning contending first brings man back to the being that he himself is and must be.
6. Man first comes to himself and is a self as a questioning-historical being. Man's selfhood means this: he must transform the Being that discloses itself to him into history and bring himself to stand in it. [*EM*, 109–10/143]

But the turn by which man turns against what is, as he turns back to himself, remains fundamentally a mystery. Heidegger terms it "the happening of strangeness [*die geschehende Unheimlichkeit*]" (*EM*, 121/158). To define this term, Heidegger draws upon the first chorus from the *Antigone* of Sophocles, which names, in his reading, the uncanny character of the Greek Dasein (exemplary, we should remember, for the Western Dasein in general).

In Sophocles' description, Heidegger argues, man's confronta-

[9]The aggressiveness revealed in these metaphors is instructive with regard to Heidegger's early conception of Entschlossenheit. Heidegger will later understand this kind of relation to what is in terms of the violence of Technik.

tion with being is traversed or *measured (durchmisst)* by the term *deinon (das Unheimliche)* in its very ambiguity: "The Greek word *deinon* is ambiguous in that uncanny ambiguity [*unheimlichen Zweideutigkeit*] with which the saying of the Greeks traverses the contending separations [*Aus-einander-setzungen*] of Being" (*EM,* 114/149). The word "deinon" itself is "uncanny" in that it refers first to physis, which, as the "overpowering power," is the "terrible" and inspires panic or *Angst* as well as "the collected silent awe that vibrates with its own rhythm" (*EM,* 114–15/149). But "deinon" refers also to the powerful in the sense of one who disposes of power and is violent. Man gathers the overpowering power and brings it to appearance; he essentially turns the power against itself, and as such he is *to deinotaton,* "the most powerful": "violent in the midst of the overpowering" (*EM,* 115/150).

Heidegger further explicates this opposition between man and being as the confrontation between *technē* and *dikē.* Heidegger translates "dikē" as *Fug*: "Here we understand *Fug* first in the sense of joint and framework [*Fug und Gefüge*]; then as decree, dispensation, a directive that the overpowering imposes on its reign; finally as the governing structure [*das fügende Gefüge*] which compels adaptation and compliance. . . . Being, physis, as power, is basic and original togetherness: logos, it is governing order: dikē" (*EM,* 123/160). Physis, as "governing order," disposes (*verfügt*) of technē in their confrontation. "Technē" Heidegger defines as "knowledge": the transcendent "looking out beyond what is given at any time" (*EM,* 122/159), by which the Being of what is is disclosed and realized—opened and held open—in the work as a being. Technē, Heidegger says, provides the basic trait of deinon in the sense of "the violent." Heidegger does not develop here the interdependence of physis as dikē and technē as he does in his lectures on Hölderlin and in "The Origin of the Work of Art"; however, he argues that the reciprocal confrontation *is* only insofar as it is gathered by the realization of Dasein as "to deinotaton": "The reciprocal confrontation *is.* It is only insofar as the strangest thing of all, being-human, occurs, insofar as man is present as history" (*EM,* 123/161). (Here we see how "deinon" traverses but also measures and gathers the contending elements; one of the two meanings of "deinon" folds or doubles in such a way as to mark the difference between physis and technē and to found the conflictual relation.)

Man is deinon in that he moves in the violent action of "machination" (*mechanoen*) that Heidegger defines in terms of technē, but man is the strangest or most uncanny (to deinotaton), in that in his opening of paths in all the realms of being, he is constantly "issueless": "he becomes the strangest of all beings because, without issue on all paths, he is cast out of every relation to the familiar and befallen by *atē*, ruin, catastrophe" (*EM*, 116/152). Man is "issueless," Heidegger says, not simply because he encounters obstacles, nor even (though this is Heidegger's first definition of "issuelessness") because man becomes mired in his own paths as he loses hold of that opening to Being in which the truth of his knowing is founded. Man is "without issue on all paths" (*pantoporos aporos*) because his violent and venturesome way-making must shatter against death, "this strange and uncanny thing that banishes us once and for all from every thing in which we are at home" (*EM*, 121/158). "It is not only when he comes to die, but always and essentially that man is without issue [*Ausweglos*] in the face of death. Insofar as man *is*, he stands in the issuelessness of death. Thus Da-sein is the happening of strangeness" (*EM*, 121/158).

The basic trait (*Grundzug*) of the human essence, Heidegger says, is to be the strangest of all, to deinotaton—within it, "all other traits must find their place" (*EM*, 116/151). The "basic trait" of deinotaton, lies, in turn, in the interrelation of the two meanings of "deinon." As man ventures to master being in technē, he constantly stands before the possibility of death. To stand before death is fundamentally to stand in the possibility of disaster— downfall into the placeless and issueless (*EM*, 124/162), the event of Unheimlichkeit itself. Disaster is not simply the result of failure: both victory and defeat, Heidegger says, are menaced by disaster (*EM*, 123/161): "Disaster [*Verderb*] and the possibility of disaster do not arise only at the end, when a single act of power fails, when the violent one makes a false move; no, this disaster is fundamental, it *governs* and *waits* [my emphasis] in the conflict between violence and the overpowering. Violence against the preponderant power of Being *must* shatter against Being, if Being rules in its essence, as physis, as emerging power" (*EM*, 124/162).

Disaster, then, is not only possible, it is necessary. Man is driven to assume his essence as Dasein in technē by Being that *requires* a place of disclosure: "The Da-sein of historical man means: to be posed as the breach into which the preponderant power of Being bursts in its appearing, in order that this breach itself should shatter against Being" (*EM*, 124/163). This shattering in disaster is also described by Heidegger as an *Untergang* that is "the deepest and broadest affirmation [*Ja*] of the overpowering" (*EM*, 125/163)—and surely we must hear Nietzsche in this line. Being is *affirmed* in the very *shattering* (*Zerbrechen*) of the wrought work.

But how should we understand terms such as "disaster" (Untergang and Verderb) or "shattering," or even the experience of Unheimlichkeit as "placeless confusion"? We might refer, of course, to *Being and Time*, in which the theme of Unheimlichkeit first emerges, particularly inasmuch as disaster is defined in *An Introduction to Metaphysics* as "standing in the issuelessness of death," an obvious reference to the notion of being-thrown-toward-death. It is clear that Heidegger has carried the theme of death as it appears in the chorus of *Antigone* (that is, death in the sense of a "loss of life" resulting from the creative violence by which man discloses what is) into a reflection consonant with his argument in *Being and Time*, wherein the experience of mortality is seen to open upon the more originary experience of thrownness. But the role of the concept of death in the argument of *An Introduction to Metaphysics* is no less ambiguous than it is in the existential analytic, as I want to demonstrate shortly. We might turn more profitably to Heidegger's 1929 address "What Is Metaphysics?" (cited as I noted, in *An Introduction to Metaphysics*), in which the experience of Unheimlichkeit is treated in terms of the encounter with the nothing rather than in terms of an encounter with death.

In "What Is Metaphysics?" Heidegger focuses on the event in which Dasein is driven, in need (*Not*), into "the freedom of undertaking technē" (*EM*, 130/170). Dasein's transcendence, Heidegger writes, lies in its retaining itself, its "standing within" the *Nichtung* that is the essence of the nothing. Heidegger describes this movement of Nichtung, which belongs to the very Being of what is, as the repulsion (*Abweisung*) of nothing that expels (*verweisen*) being in is totality (*W*, 114/105). Heidegger says that this event in Being presses upon Dasein in Angst; opening to this primordial event, Dasein experiences being in its totality as "sliding" from it. Opening to the movement of Nichtung, or rather thrown by it (the throw opens the space in which Dasein will come to stand), Dasein retreats before what is—a movement that is not a flight, Heidegger says, but rather a "fascinated repose" (*W*, 114/105). Heidegger is describing, of course, the event that in Chapter 1 I termed the "withdrawal of the world." In this movement, Dasein can first encounter the world as such. By virtue of its encounter with the nothing (experienced as nothing more than this withdrawal of being in its totality), Dasein can first undergo the uncanny experience that there *is* something rather than nothing. This "rather than nothing," Heidegger says, is the initial condition that renders possible the manifestation of what is in general.

Dasein's transcendence of being in its totality in its fascinated retention within the movement of Nichtung is the condition of its questioning relation to what is, as well as its relation to itself: "Without the original manifestness of the nothing, there would be no being of the self and no freedom" (*W*, 115/106). But this transcendence is not at the disposition of man's will. "Our finitude," Heidegger writes, "is such that we are precisely incapable of bringing ourselves originally before the nothing through our own determination or will" (*W*, 118/108). Anxiety appears only at rare moments. We bear our being-thrown (*Geworfenheit*) in the movement of Nichtung—the *primordial foundation of any negation*—most immediately (that is, in nearest proximity to its abyss) in nonlogical modes of comportment. "More abyssal than the simple adequacy of thought's negation is the harshness of transgression and the bite of execration. More responsible is the pain of failing and the mercilessness of forbidding" (*W*, 117/107). But if the human essence is penetrated throughout by the throw of Nichtung, this abyssal foundation is revealed only rarely in anxiety. As Heidegger argued in *Being and Time*, anxiety is constantly with us but is normally repressed. And our opening to anxiety is not within our power. Anxiety is most steady in the *audacious* Dasein, Heidegger says—this is the audacity to which he calls his public in the rectoral address—but audacity only arises out of that "greatness" that is Dasein's opening to Being, and thus out of Nichtung.

We do not enter into the presence of the nothing by our will, then, nor can this encounter be fully mastered or appropriated: "So abyssally does the finitizing [*Verendlichung*] dig into Dasein, that the most authentic and deep finitude [*Endlichkeit*] refuses itself to our freedom" (*W*, 118/108). As Heidegger argued in *Being and Time*, we cannot bring our own thrownness fully into our power. The opening of Being in Nichtung that Dasein is called upon to hold open exceeds its mastery. Thus, the more essentially Dasein opens to this abyssal movement that founds its transcending essence, the more it encounters the limits of its power—its fundamental *determination*. The transcending essence of man being meta-physics itself ("Metaphysics is the fundamental happening in Dasein. It is Dasein itself" [*W*, 122/112]), Heidegger writes: "Because the truth of metaphysics resides in this abyssal foundation, it has in its nearest vicinity the constantly waiting possibility of the most profound error" (*W*, 122/112).

Herein lies the essence of what Heidegger, in *An Introduction to Metaphysics*, identifies as the constant possibility of disaster. The encounter with the overpowering power as it opens in Nichtung drives Dasein into the freedom of undertaking technē; but as we noted earlier, this effort at mastery must come up against its own limits—it *traces its own limits*. The basic trait of the human essence is to be "the strangest of all," to deinotaton, inasmuch as man stands always in the possibility of disaster. All other traits must find their place within this trait, which, as we now see, marks the limit of man as that being that undertakes technē. "To deinotaton" names the *finitude* in man, whose occurrence (the *Verendlichung* of *Endlichkeit*) marks, and is marked in, the reciprocal confrontation of technē and dikē.

The figures of writing (tracing, trait, marking) are meant to point here to the theme of the "rift-design" (as Hofstadter translates "Riss"), to which Heidegger refers only in passing in *An Introduction to Metaphysics* (*EM*, 123/161) and which he develops further in "The Origin of the Work of Art." I return to this notion in Chapter 4, but I shall anticipate my discussion by remarking simply that the Riss is named as the gathering trait of the conflict of world and earth that is set into (traced in) the work of art and brought to appear there as the event of the opening of truth. If, as we see here, this trait must also mark the possibility of disaster in the confrontation of world and earth (of dikē and technē, in *An Introduction to Metaphysics*), then we must conclude that the work of art bears the trace of the limits of man's creative endeavors. The work must bear the trace of man's finitude as a kind of pointer that signals an unmastered, abyssal depth: the opening of the finitude that conditions his creative activity. The work marks man's Untergang and is thus itself necessarily a fragment, the result of a "shattering."

We might translate Verendlichung as a "making-finite," but the term also bears in it *verenden* (to die or perish). In the analysis of *Being and Time*, I pointed to this originary event (following Heidegger) as the birth of Dasein and sought to emphasize in this way the abyssal foundation of being-toward-death. In *An Introduction to Metaphysics*, as we have seen, disaster, "the happening of strangeness," is defined at one moment as "standing in the issuelessness of death." Death is "the limit beyond all limits" (*EM*, 121/158). But as in *Being and Time*, the notion of death is potentially misleading—it leads Heidegger, at least, to define Dasein's possible act of violence against itself and the choice of "not-being-there" as "the highest recognition" of Being (*EM*, 135/177) and thus, if we follow the logic of self-affirmation in Auseinandersetzung, the highest affirmation of Dasein in its creative freedom. Heidegger calls it "the supreme victory over Being" (*EM*, 136/178).

Yet we might wonder whether the valorization of this negative manifestation of man's freedom and the "negativity" of the terms that seem to point to this end term of the logic of tragedy do not mask dimensions of the event that is being described. Verendlichung does indeed define man's mortality. But by thinking man's relation to this condition of his creative being (and of his thought in general) in terms of an experience of "disaster" or "shattering," and by developing the notion of freedom in terms of the possibility of a violent denial of being-there,[10] Heidegger marks negatively an

[10]I should note here that I am inclined to interpret this *Gewalt-tat*, or "supreme act of violence" (*EM*, 135/177), as an act of suicide. This interpretation strikes me as probable not only because it is difficult to conceive of the "repression" to which Heidegger is referring in other terms but also because the theme of suicide is so easily developed from the notion of tragedy that appears to inform Heidegger's argument. I refer here to the interpretation of tragedy carried out in German Idealism, and I would point in particular to the tenth letter of Schelling's *Letters on Dogmatism and Criticism* (translated by Fritz Marti in F. W. J. Schelling, *The Unconditional in Human Knowledge: Four Early Essays (1794–1796)* [Lewisburg: Bucknell University Press, 1980], pp. 192–93), a text that has received attention from Peter Szondi and Philippe Lacoue-Labarthe (see Lacoue-Labarthe, "La césure du spéculatif," in *Hölderlin, L'Antigone de Sophocle*, ed. Philippe Lacoue-Labarthe [Paris: Christian Bourgois, 1978], pp. 196–97, and Szondi, *Versuch über das Tragische*). Schelling offers in this letter a model for what is virtually a dialectical resolution of the contradiction between objective necessity and subjective freedom. He places the emphasis upon the initiative of the tragic subject and argues that Greek art allows its tragic hero the possibility of expiating a crime that is the work of destiny. By letting its tragic hero *provoke* his own defeat by struggling against necessity and by showing the hero punished for a crime that is any case inevitable, Greek art, Schelling argues,

experience that is perhaps not fundamentally negative. For Heidegger asks us to consider in "What Is Metaphysics?" that the foundation of negation is not negative—particularly inasmuch as we can conceive of negation only with difficulty in other than speculative, metaphysical terms. Further, when Heidegger speaks in 1933 of the "danger" that teachers are called upon to assume at "the most advanced posts in the danger of constant world-uncertainty . . . in the essential nearness to the hard-pressing insistence of all things" (SU, 14/475), there is a confusion of ontic and ontological categories that can do little more than feed a political and philosophical paranoia. Hölderlin and Nietzsche, of course, both testify to a danger that lies in man's relation to the Being of what is, but they also point to positive dimensions of this determining condition of man's relation to his mortality, and both speak of a more joyous assumption of man's finitude.[11] Heidegger himself seems to offer the possibility of thinking a different "tonality" of being when, in the *Letter on Humanism* (and throughout his later work), he turns to the theme of possibility and employs the notion of "giving" to define Being's throw or destining of man.

---

recognizes human liberty. But the initiative of the tragic subject is, of course, a fatal one; as a resolution of the fundamental speculative contradiction, it amounts to "speculative suicide." Hence Schelling adopts the strategy described explicitly by Bataille in his famous article on Hegel, "Hegel, la mort et le sacrifice" (*Deucalion* 5 [1955]: 21–43); that is to say, he proposes it as a spectacle: "It could not become a system of action, for such a system would presuppose a race of titans, without which it would doubtless result in the greatest ruin of mankind." This remark might well give us pause when we consider that a schema very much like Schelling's (where freedom is affirmed in the very loss of freedom) appears to be at work in Heidegger's own Rektoratsrede and active throughout his descriptions of a free assumption of destiny, resulting, in the privileged cases, in the fragmentation of an *oeuvre* (Schelling) and/or madness (Nietzsche and Hölderlin). Schelling, Nietzsche, and Hölderlin are all, to a certain extent, sacrificial victims. I might add that the theme of suicide may well mark itself negatively in Heidegger's argument in his very silence concerning Hölderlin's interpretation of tragedy. (Heidegger's silence in *An Introduction to Metaphysics* concerning Hölderlin's work on *Antigone* and *Oedipus the King* is indeed remarkable.) Hölderlin, of course, meditated extensively on his own notion of a "speculative suicide" in his efforts to write *The Death of Empedocles*, and although the strange repression to which Heidegger refers with his "Gewalt-tat" is probably not identifiable with Empedocles' act of self-sacrifice, Hölderlin's meditation on this act of suicide could not have been absent from Heidegger's own reflection on the tragic essence of Dasein.

[11]Nietzsche's notion of "gaiety" is fairly well known. But consider also Hölderlin's epigram "Sophocles": "Many sought in vain to say joyfully the most joyful / Here finally, here in mourning, it pronounces itself to me" (SW1.1, 305).

Putting it simply, there are different ways of bearing finitude. If I question the negative accent in the tragic ethos that Heidegger invokes in his Rektoratsrede and *An Introduction to Metaphysics*, it is because this accent seems not only to dissimulate other tones or styles but also to circumscribe the conditions of the experience in question. By resorting to the theme of suicide, Heidegger seems to avert the more unsettling logic of finitude. To name suicide the ultimate affirmation of Dasein is perhaps to reiterate negatively the idea of limitation; Dasein's space of possibility for action is strictly defined and always determined by what is—Dasein's only escape from this determination is death. But this exception still accords to Dasein a negative, but unmediated, relation to itself. Heidegger seems to note the impossibility of such a relation when he says: "But for Dasein such refusal of openness toward being means to renounce its essence, which demands: emerge from being or never enter into Dasein" (*EM*, 135/177). But he does not follow out the paradox. The problem is that Dasein must first *be* its essence in order to renounce it, and to be its essence, Dasein must offer a site to Being—such offering is the condition of any form of recognition. Unless we allow that Dasein offers a site to Being in Dasein's very death, or rather *dying*—that pure moment of passage (and to escape what seems a morbid path of reflection, we might begin with Mallarmé's "Cantique de Saint-Jean," the third section of "Hérodiade")—we must consider the act of suicide merely one possibility of action among others rendered possible by Dasein's elaboration of its finitude. As in *Being and Time*, this particular possibility of being toward what is (that is, denying to Being a site in which to manifest itself) is rendered possible by the experience of Unheimlichkeit as disaster. The possibility of not-being-there is "the possibility of breaking the preponderant power of Being by a supreme act of violence against itself. Dasein has this possibility not as an empty evasion; no, insofar as it is, Dasein *is* this possibility, for as Dasein it must, in every act of violence, shatter against Being" (*Em*, 135/177). Can Dasein's passing (at) its limit in suicide be thought together with the freedom of Dasein's standing before its limits in creation? This would indeed be a dark version of self-affirmation; the remarking of Dasein as possibility, the pure manifestation of the condition of its freedom, would immediately efface this possibility.

But as I have suggested, to render suicide a work of art would appear to circumvent the finitude of Being as Heidegger attempts to think it in his meditation on art as technē. He names art in *An Introduction to Metaphysics* "das seiende Sein": that which brings Being to stand in its appearing, that which "stabilizes it in a being" (*EM*, 122/159). In "The Origin of the Work of Art" he develops this notion at length, arguing that the openness of beings that first opens in the throw of Nichtung must be *set up* in a work *in order to occur*. The Open that is the clearing or lighting of Being opens only *from within* the delimited sphere of beings that it traces out; only as it is set into the defining bounds of what is does the world open. The opening of the truth of Being in poiēsis, Heidegger argues, must be thought in relation to the Greek "thesis":

> The openness of this Open, that is truth, can be what it is, namely *this* openness, only if and as long as it establishes itself within its Open. Hence there must always be some being in this Open, something that is, in which the openness takes its stand and attains its constancy. In taking possession thus of the Open, the openness holds open the Open and sustains it. Setting and taking possession are here everywhere drawn from the Greek sense of thesis, which means a setting up in the unconcealed. [*H*, 48/61]

I discuss this description of the "work" that occurs in art in the next chapter. My point here is simply to observe that freedom must be thought within this "event" of the determination of the truth of Being in technē. Heidegger designates man's freedom negatively with his designation of the choice of "not being there" as Dasein's highest affirmation, and in so doing he turns away from the finite freedom that manifests itself in the process of technē. Freedom *is* only inasmuch as it is elaborated—it exists only in man's creative practice, in the conflict of dikē and technē. Freedom is not a trait that Dasein *has* or that is simply given to it; rather, freedom is an event. It is the foundation of, and yet emerges in (here again we encounter a version of the hermeneutic circle), man's creative activity. We may understand freedom, then, as the possibility of standing before and at one's limits: "going under" or "standing in the possibility of disaster" belong essentially to this freedom.

The limits in question here, to return to the question of politics with which I began, are those of the polis. These limits are set each time history happens, each time that a people, from the possibilities of its language, undertakes the task of creation. There is no self-subsistent foundation of human activity; the foundation is cast in each form of creative practice. In *each form:* Heidegger names five ways in which truth "sets itself to work," including art, in "The Origin of the Work of Art," and suggests that all of them find their single possibility in language (*H,* 49/62). Does language, which "alone brings what is, as something that is, into the Open for the first time" (*H,* 61/73), define *one* possibility of being? Does it create the possibility of *one* unified world in the happening of the saying "in which a people's world historically arises for it" (*H,* 61/74) if this happening can only occur in the finite forms that set forth a world? A correlate of this question: Do each of these forms of elaboration in which history first happens belong to the *same* history? Or is the configuration of truth that occurs in each case different from any other configuration, defining its own temporal conditions and thus its own history? If there is no self-subsistent foundation for the forms of human activity, then we must ask whether the difference (what Heidegger terms the ontological difference) fashioned in each form of creative practice does not differ from itself in the general space of a culture, in which case the meaning of the term "general" becomes particularly problematic.[12]

In the texts that I have considered thus far, Heidegger does not answer these questions in any satisfactory manner, but they emerge as questions once we recognize that the limits drawn in each founding act have a precarious, finite nature. The finitude of Dasein, as we have seen, exceeds its determining or form-making power. To address the question of the nature of the public space fashioned in the forms of practice, we must define more precisely the nature

[12]The question of the possibility of a *general* movement of reflection taking account of multiplicity and fragmentation is, of course, one of the central problems of the project of deconstruction and less easily dismissed than it is in the general reception of the deconstructive project. Granel addresses the problem forcefully in his "Liminaire" in *Traditionis traditio* (Paris: Gallimard, 1972). A rereading of Derrida's *Of Grammatology,* trans. Gayatri Chakravorty Spivak (Baltimore: Johns Hopkins University Press, 1976), is instructive in the light of this question. The problem toward which I am working here—that of the unity of the world fashioned in the various creative practices—is posed also by Harries at the end of his essay "Heidegger as a Political Thinker" (though in quite different terms).

of the "open foundation" of these practices—the open foundation that art manifests as it brings the limits of human activity to appear as limits. We need to define the way in which this "open foundation," the finitude of Dasein, either gathers the forms of human production into a space of the same (gathered, unified) or, as the experiences of Nietzsche and Hölderlin seem to suggest, is the condition of their discontinuity and essential multiplicity.

4/

The Work of Art and
the Question of Man

The assertive accents in Heidegger's description of Selbstbehauptung in his writings of the early thirties are of a piece with the
subsequent, more muted claims for the possibility of achieving a
gathered, unified being in the poetic project. In each case, the
description of the constitution of identity entails what might be
termed a disavowal of dimensions of the tragic experience; while
the possibility of "disaster" is constantly marked in some way, the
unsettling implications of this *governing* possibility are evaded.

I will attempt to demonstrate in Chapter 5 how this claim holds
true for Heidegger's readings of Hölderlin. But before approaching
these readings, I would like to consider Heidegger's most general
and, in some ways, most challenging statement on art and Dichtung,
"The Origin of the Work of Art." In this essay, Heidegger argues,
as I want to show, that the work of art achieves an identity
founded in difference. He elaborates the notion of finitude in a
remarkably dense and problematic form: dense because of the
severity of the "circular" logic that is at work, problematic because,
as Heidegger himself observes, the use of the Greek notion of
"thesis" leads to formulations that overlap later descriptions of
modern technology and because the problem of the relation of
Being and human being remains "unsuitably conceived" (H, 74/87).

In this chapter, I will focus primarily on what I take to be the
heart of Heidegger's essay—his formal articulation of the relation

of identity and difference in art—and I will attempt to define on this basis the second difficulty observed by him in his "Addendum."[1] In so doing, I will also return to Heidegger's reading of Nietzsche (specifically, his reading of Nietzsche's concept of art), both in order to reiterate the general lines of what Heidegger seeks in a "tragic style" and in order to consider this notion in the light of Nietzsche's *Ecce Homo*, a text that foregrounds precisely the relation of Being and human being.

I might reach most quickly the cluster of questions that have shaped my reading of Heidegger thus far by noting that "The Origin of the Work of Art" provides something of an answer to a problem that oriented my approach to *Being and Time*. In that volume, as we saw, Heidegger addresses the question of access to the problematic of Dasein by asking how it is that we can leave the everyday view of the world and come to project ourselves upon our mortality in such a way as to encounter the very source of our thrown being—our original openness to Being. The problem, in

---

[1]With this restricted focus, I will leave untreated here Heidegger's extensive response to the entire tradition of philosophical reflection on art. This critical dimension of Heidegger's essay is largely implicit. The readings of Kant (the reworking of the Kantian understanding of form and the sublime) and Nietzsche (most significant, the use of a notion of will in the context of the discussion of the finitude of truth) are not openly identified. Only in the case of Hegel does Heidegger designate (though still indirectly) the terms of his confrontation. He provides in his Epilogue three sentences from what he names "the most comprehensive reflection on the nature of art that the West possesses... Hegel's *Vorlesungen über die Ästhetik*" (*H*, 68/79): (1) "Art no longer counts for us as the highest manner in which truth obtains existence for itself"; (2) "One may well hope that art will continue to advance and perfect itself, but its form has ceased to be the highest need of the spirit"; and (3) "In all these relationships art is and remains for us, on the side of its highest vocation, something past" (*H*, 68/80). Heidegger answers each of Hegel's points by arguing that art is one of the most distinctive possibilities by which truth may occur in the midst of beings and that art is for truth an *exigency*, inasmuch as truth has an "impulse" [*Zug*] toward the work of art and wills to be established in art. (*H*, 50/62). He adds finally that art is untimely, an origin in historical existence that opens a past, a present, and a future and whose becoming (*H*, 66/78) Heidegger's meditation can only prepare. Numerous other points should be mentioned here, including the fact that Heidegger takes as his point of departure and orientation precisely what Hegel takes to be the limit of art, namely, its material determination. But on this point, as with each of the others, we should recognize that Heidegger is contending not just with Hegel but with the entire tradition of Western thought on art. Heidegger is addressing himself in this essay to the fundamental concepts of aesthetics, beginning with the distinction of matter and form as it is coupled with the subject/object relation.

short, concerns our thinking entry into the hermeneutic circle. I argued that Heidegger points persistently, though in a somewhat veiled manner, to the intersubjective encounter as the precipitating event for Dasein. This confrontation, I argued, takes the form of the apprehension of another Dasein's relation to an alterity—its finitude.

Heidegger suggests that this "scene of primal instruction"[2] may occur in an encounter between two Daseins somehow present to one another, or it may occur through the address of one Dasein to another by way of some form of record or monument. Heidegger argues, in this latter respect, that any existential project is also a history that takes the form of an active interpretation—a kind of counterinterpretation—of a possibility of existence that has been, an existence that presents itself as a kind of model to Dasein.

"The Origin of the Work of Art" proposes a formal account of how such a historical address could occur—or how, in general, a work of human creation can have the effect of arresting our attention (as Heidegger is manifestly arrested by the texts of Hölderlin and Nietzsche) and opening us to a configuration of truth that, if assumed, "transforms our accustomed ties to world and to earth" (*H*, 54/66). It suggests how a work of art might offer itself in such a way as to open the very possibility of seeing or, perhaps more rigorously (as I shall argue in Chapter 5), reading it—and thus it suggests how the work might "create" its preserver in an originary fashion, just as the gift of mortality (the friend's testimony of its mortality, the presentation of its finitude as I argued in Chapter 1) is constitutive for what Heidegger terms *Existenz*.

[2]I use this phrase with reference to Harold Bloom's descriptions of the nature of poetic tradition in the series of books that begins with *The Anxiety of Influence: A Theory of Poetry* (New York: Oxford University Press, 1973). In his latest work, *Agon: Towards a Theory of Revisionism* (New York: Oxford University Press, 1982), Bloom sketches a notion of creative succession that captures nicely what I take to be Heidegger's understanding of the origins of creativity: "Psychoanalytic explanations of 'creativity' tend to discount or repress two particular aspects of the genealogy of aesthetics: first that the creative or Sublime 'moment' is a negative moment; second, that this moment tends to rise out of an encounter with someone else's prior moment of negation, which in turn goes back to an anterior moment, and so on" (*Agon*, p. 98). But Bloom understands this "negative moment" only in terms of subjectivity, and he fails to give a *formal* account of the work of difference (as Heidegger attempts to do in "The Origin of the Work of Art"). Heidegger points to ways in which Bloom's very powerful sense of poetic tradition might be developed within a philosophical reflection.

Heidegger says relatively little in this essay concerning the nature of human creation and preservation, so it is not immediately clear that it might offer the grounds for understanding how a work might be said to bear a signature (or title) as captivating as "Nietzsche," for example. (Heidegger, we will recall, designates "Nietzsche" as the title for the irreducibly singular "matter" of Nietzsche's thought.) Heidegger remains faithful to the assertion of *Being and Time* that the address that has its source in another Dasein's relation to an alterity is essentially the address of history and is therefore anonymous. He thus elides in his discussion the place of the artist in the artistic process as a "living personality" (Heidegger's term in the *Habilitationsschrift*).[3] But the place of Dasein in the history of Being is still irreducible for Heidegger: as he says in his "Addendum," "Being needs man and is not without man" (*H,* 74/86). And so the work of art, inasmuch as it opens a history, as Heidegger asserts in this essay, must necessarily also pose the question of man. I will pursue this implication by introducing Heidegger's own description of human finitude into his description of the finitude of truth as it is traced out originally in art.

I begin by defining the sense in which the work of art might be understood as an address and by defining how this address is constituted in formal terms. As I proceed, it will become increasingly apparent why the address in question cannot be understood in terms of a traditional model of communication whereby an artist might communicate with a public by expressing himself to that public. The work is not even addressed by one Dasein to another Dasein. Rather, as Heidegger suggests, it is offered to truth, or it offers itself as a site for the event of truth (to which belongs also the holy), in such a way as to become its address. There is a communication (*Mitteilung*), but it passes by way of a separation (*Teilung*) that is finally, as I want to show, of an abyssal nature. The creator and the receiver are communicants in Heidegger's definition of art, but their shared identity and thus their community are founded upon an irreducible alterity that appears in the form of a certain strangeness in the work.

I use the term "address" initially on the basis of Heidegger's

[3]See Chapter 1, note 16 above.

134

description of the work's reception. Heidegger names reception "preservation" and describes this act by drawing explicitly upon the concept of Entschlossenheit from *Being and Time*. Preserving, Heidegger says, is "standing within the openness of beings that happens in the work," and standing within, he writes, is made possible in resolute Existenz: "outstanding standing-within the essential sunderance of the clearing of beings" (*H,* 55/67). The work of art itself is a projection of truth, the projection of the clearing or opening of Being. It is a projection (*Entwurf*) in the sense of a design or sketch, as we will see, but it is also "the re-lease of a throw," Heidegger says, and is cast toward a defined group of preservers: "The poetic projection of truth that sets itself into work as figure is also never carried out in the direction of an indeterminate void. Rather, in the work, truth is thrown toward the coming preservers, that is, toward a historical group of men" (*H,* 63/75). As a projection of truth, the work is an articulation of a still undisclosed history of Being into which the preservers have been cast. It is addressed, then, to the defined group for whom the work can become a destiny: "What is projected by it is only the withheld vocation of the historical being of man itself" (*H,* 64/76).

The work's address comes upon its preservers as a thrust (*Stoss*) of what is termed *ungeheuer:* extraordinary, awesome, sublime. It is not a simple address, so to speak; as we shall see shortly, it is founded in a paradoxical dynamic of approach and withdrawal. The work thrusts forth not the truth "itself" but rather the fact that truth has happened and happens in the work as having happened. Heidegger terms this appearance of the fact that truth has taken place in the work the createdness of the work of art. Art is distinguished from other modes of production, Heidegger argues, in that art bears and casts forth its createdness, not the fact that the work has been created by an individual artist, but rather "that unconcealedness of what is has happened here, and that, as this having happened, it happens here for the first time; or, that such a work *is* at all rather than is not" (*H,* 53/65). The work's very "reality"—its indepen-dent, thingly nature—is a function of the degree to which it manifests in itself and casts forth the unconcealment of beings. Following a kind of Hölderlinian syntax ("the more . . . the more"), Heidegger writes:

The event of its being created does not simply reverberate through the work; rather, the work casts before itself the eventful fact that the work is as this work, and it has constantly this fact about itself. The more essentially the work opens itself, the more luminous becomes the uniqueness of the fact that it is rather than is not. The more essentially this thrust comes into the Open, the stranger and more solitary the work becomes. [*H*, 53/65–66]

The projection of truth, then, comes as the work withdraws into what Heidegger terms "the constancy of its resting within itself" (*H*, 53/65). The work stands back and thus thrusts forward the fact "that it is," manifesting thereby the occurrence of truth.

The description of the work's createdness recalls forcefully, of course, the discussion in "What Is Metaphysics?" in which Heidegger describes the encounter with the nothing in anxiety. Heidegger argues there that, as Dasein enters the movement of Nichtung—the essence of Being's "throw," the repulsion (Abweisung) of the nothing that expels (Verweisen) being in its totality—Dasein experiences the whole of what is receding from it. The experience of the nothing that is the condition of Dasein's transcendence of being in its totality and of the revelation of beings in general is nothing more than the uncanny experience whereby things slip away and stand apart as strange or other. The nothing appears, then, in the strangeness of things when they stand apart from us *as things*, and thus it appears in a kind of originary contrast wherein beings stand out against that which makes it possible for them to be. But this (non) emergence of the nothing, Heidegger states, appears only in the phrase by which we attempt to articulate this experience: "that they are beings—and not nothing."

Heidegger's description of this speech act might bear some emphasis here, since it directs our attention to the fact that a similar "performance" is said to characterize the work of creation in art and to be part of what appears in the work's createdness, thus part of the work's "address." Heidegger writes that the spoken phrase "and not nothing" is not an appended clarification to the recognition of beings as such. Rather, he says, "It makes possible the openness of beings in general" (*W*, 114/105). The very words "and not nothing" are said to make possible the emergence of what is as such. This may seem a curiously literal interpretation of Heidegger's argument, but it is supported by the fact that, in "The Origin of the Work of Art," Heidegger attributes to the work itself a similar enunciation. Attending to the insistence of quotation marks in the German edition of "The Origin of the Work of Art," we recognize that Heidegger is arguing that the "that" of the phrase "that it is" itself stands forth or, as at the conclusion of the passage in question (*H*, 53/66), that the phrase "Dass es sei" ("that it be," more clearly a performative) is offered as the work withdraws in its solitude.

I will not try to define at this point how we are to understand in formal terms Heidegger's startling assertion that the work sets forth in its withdrawal the words "Dass," "Dass es sei," and (a third statement adduced by Heidegger) "factum est." We are not dealing here with a form of enunciation that would be audible or visible in any traditional sense (though a poet like Hölderlin, as I will note in my next chapter, does in fact make manifest a performance such as "Dass es sei" in his writings). But two observations should be made here. First, the "address" in which the work casts forward the fact of its being is ultimately of the nature of a speaking—a point that, while somewhat obscure in "The Origin of the Work of Art," is hardly surprising when we consider Heidegger's assertion late in his essay that the human project of Being is first a linguistic event. Art, Heidegger says, is essentially poetry (*Dichtung*); as such, it has its source in language, which "alone brings what is, as something that is, into the Open for the first time" (*H*, 61/73). A second observation follows from the originary nature of the speaking that occurs in the work of art: the creative "performance" that happens in art and that is cast forward in the work's createdness happens originally in the work itself. The work of art does not exist without the artist's creative act, but it bears in itself the origin of this act.

The performance in question (taking first the work's "Dass es sei") is in itself quite paradoxical, since it opens upon (and opens) the conditions of its own enunciation. Creation, says Heidegger, is a "bringing forth" of unconcealment which, while initial or inaugural, is still always the drawing out and reception of a relation to unconcealment. It is initial in that it consists in a project, an anticipatory "sketching out" (*Entwurf*), but such a project is already a response. We are turning here, once again, in a version of the hermeneutic circle that will become more clear in the course of this chapter. But Heidegger insists further upon the repetitive structure of the event in question by arguing that such a performance, as a creative act, is to be thought from out of the work itself. Any creative intention on the artist's part must be understood as proceeding from what first happens in the work, the event that "first gives to things their look and to men their outlook on themselves" (*H*, 29/43). The measure to which the artist answers in shaping his creation first opens in the work. Hence Heidegger reiterates the paradox that the work demands (*fordern*, *H*, 30/44) and requires (*H*, 31/45) its "setting up" (*aufstellen*) because in its own work-being it is something that sets up (*H*, 30/44). Creation belongs originally to the work. The artist's "that it be" (to the extent that we may finally attribute this enunciation to the artist at all) answers to, and is a repetition of, a more original saying that happens in the work, and it is as such a repetition that the enunciation is drawn forth or drawn out in the work itself: "Im Hervorbringen des Werkes liegt dieses Darbringen 'Dass es sei' " ("In the bringing forth of the work [the genitive both subjective and objective] there lies this offering 'that it be' ").[4] In a similar fashion, the preserver's "that it is"—if I am assigning it correctly, and it is no less a performative for this reason, inasmuch as the act of preservation is creative (*H*, 74/62)—is *already spoken* and advanced by the work in its address. In the work itself there opens originally the very possibility of the linguistic act of reception that is the basis of any community, inasmuch as preserving the work "grounds being for and with one another" (*H*, 68/55). "Dass es sei" (re-marking, as the artist's enunciation, the speaking that makes this creative act possible), "Dass" (re-marking in advance and making possible the preserver's response), and "factum est" (re-marking the work's reality) are what the work *says*, to the extent that a painting like the one by Van Gogh analyzed by Heidegger is said to "speak" to us (*H*, 21/35). These

---

[4]"Dass es sei" is the only apparent trace of the artist's intention, though the artist is merely answering to a more original speaking that occurs in the work. Nothing else of the artist appears in the work's working. As Heidegger writes, "Precisely where the artist and the process and the circumstances of the genesis of the work remain unknown, this thrust, this 'that it is' of createdness, emerges into view most clearly from the work" (*H*, 53/65). "Dass es sei," necessarily depending upon the artist's intervention and thus *of* the artist, is nevertheless the *work's* saying. We see here to what extent Heidegger has virtually effaced the "signature" of the artist.

words articulate the work's address as it withdraws in its solitude and remark the opening of the human acts of creative speaking in which a community is founded.[5]

Drawing a final point now from the reference to the argument of "What Is Metaphysics?" and concluding this initial consideration of the work's address, we might surmise that the preserver's experience of the happening of truth in the work—that it is at all rather than is not—is initially a "fascinated repose." For Heidegger, the arresting or fascinating quality of art would be grounded in the occurrence of truth. The throw of the work's projection of truth, in any case, transports the receiver into the breach of the openness of beings as it withdraws into this same space:

> The more solitarily the work, fixed in the figure, stands on its own and the more cleanly it seems to cut all ties to human beings, the more simply does the thrust come into the Open that such a work *is*, and the more essentially is the extraordinary [*das Ungeheure*] thrust to the surface and the long-familiar thrust down. But this multiple thrusting is nothing violent, for the more purely the work is itself transported into [*entrückt*] the openness of beings—an openness opened by itself—

[5]The precise status of these words born by the work remains to be defined in a more lengthy examination of the nature of the "speaking" that occurs in the work of art—that is to say, in a reading of *On the Way to Language*. Here I will note simply that the original saying that is repeated and brought forth in a phrase such as "Dass es sei" must be thought as issuing from the difference originally traced out in the work. This point is made clear in the first essay of the German edition of *On the Way to Language*, translated in *Poetry, Language, Thought* under the title "Language" (see, in particular, *US*, 29–30/207), where what is termed a "demand" in "The Origin of the Work of Art," as I noted above, is named a "bidding" (*Heissen*) and a command (*Geheiss*). I add also that the three "statements" appear almost as inscriptions on a monument that take their relief against (and thus bring forth) the unpresentable tracing of the "rift-design" (a notion to which I shall return shortly). The monumental aspect of the work's address may be heard in Heidegger's explication of the words "factum est" that, as held forth, mark the work's createdness: "that unconcealedness of what is has happened here, and as this having happened happens here for the first time" (*H*, 53/65). I stress the monumental aspect of these words inscribed in the work in order to signal in advance the paradox of a "speaking" that remarks a "tracing" (the "rift-design") and that Heidegger has apparently no difficulty relating to the kind of tracing that occurs in graphic or plastic art. In my development of the formal constitution of the work's address, I will follow Heidegger in describing a notion of form that is most easily conceived in relation to the plastic arts. But it should not be forgotten that Heidegger's propositions concerning the work's form hold for all works of art, including those conceived in language.

the more simply does it transport us out [*herausrückt*] of the realm of the ordinary. [*H,* 54/66]

The work's thrust comes as a pull. But while we speak of the *space* that opens in this "multiple throw," we must think also in terms of the very movement of history: "Whenever art happens—that is, whenever there is a beginning—a thrust enters history, history either begins or starts over again. History means here not a sequence in time of events of whatever sort, however important. History is the transporting [*Entrückung*] of a people into its appointed task as entrance into [*Einrückung*] that people's endowment" (*H,* 65/77). The work's address, then, comes in an event that transports its preservers into the double movement that we find in each description of the hermeneutic circle. The work addresses Dasein as Dasein's *witness.*[6]

To describe now the formal constitution of this uncanny address, it is necessary to define how the work's particular composure—what Heidegger terms its self-subsistence (*Insichselbststehen*) and its quality of resting in itself (*in sich beruhenden*)—represents a configuration of truth. We must describe how the work of art casts the measure of being—the rule or the schemata for the emergence of things—on the ground of the earth and thus how the work comes to stand forth in the strangeness of a self-subsistent thing.

Heidegger argues that the work achieves its peculiar identity, its "standing within itself," when it stands outside all practical relations (something that is not the case, despite appearances, in the museum, where the work is an object of the art industry and already caught up in a process of exchange). This is not to say that the work is located somewhere outside history and undetermined by social relations; rather, the work achieves its solitude or self-subsistence as it stands within those essential historical relations that define a world and that are first cast by the work itself. The work is fundamentally historical in nature.

The work founds the determining relations of the world in which it emerges as it brings about the differentiation and articulation of what Heidegger designates as world and earth. The world of a

[6]I refer to my argument in Chapter 1, of course, but also to Heidegger's essay "Hölderlin and the Essence of Poetry," in which Heidegger speaks of the poet as a "witness."

people is described here as the "governing expanse" of the context of relations in which human actions acquire meaning: "World is the ever-nonobjective to which we are subject as long as the paths of birth and death, blessing and curse keep us transported into Being. Whenever those decisions of our history that relate to our very being are made . . . there the world worlds" (*H*, 30–31/44–45). Projecting upon birth and death, blessing and curse, victory and defeat (a series of terms that Heidegger couples in the manner of Heraclitus), the human Dasein, as a people, is exposed to Being and opens to a decision concerning its historical destiny. In its decisions upon the historical possibilities that open to it (following here the schema described in paragraph 74 of *Being and Time* [*SZ*, 384–85/436–37]), it engages in a struggle of differentiation and definition in which human actions acquire meaning and in which a relation to what is is defined. Thus the opening of a world also measures the relations between existent things, giving them proximity or distance, their particular temporal status (their "lingering or hastening," Heidegger says), and their "scope and limits" (*H*, 31/45). The world, though itself invisible, is the condition of visibility for things and gives its rule or law to things as that which directs the way they come to stand.

But the world opens only on the ground of the earth, whose very nature is to resist the world's "self-opening." Earth is not to be understood merely in terms of materiality; it is that which "shelters" in the emergence of physis. The earth is brought forth in the work of art in its distinctive nature as part of a world ("The rock comes to bear and rest and so first becomes rock; metals come to glitter and shimmer, colors to glow, tones to sing, the word to speak" [*H*, 32/46]), but the earth emerges always as that which conceals itself and shrinks from disclosure. It shows itself in a kind of reserve, resisting any technical-scientific description. (We may describe precisely the physical characteristics of rock, metals, colors, sounds, or words, but this description fails to capture their essential nature that partakes of both the muteness of material things, a certain inaccessibility, and their presence in the world of man; we may measure the stone's weight, but this calculation cannot give us this weight's burden.) At the same time, however, the earth's reserve does not entail undifferentiation. Heidegger expresses this in a striking passage:

The earth appears openly cleared as itself only when it is perceived and preserved as that which is by nature undisclosable, that which shrinks from every disclosure and constantly keeps itself closed up. All things of earth, and the earth itself as a whole, flow together into a reciprocal accord. But this confluence is not a blurring of their outlines. Here there flows the stream, restful within itself, of the setting of bounds, which delimits everything present within its presence. Thus in each of the self-secluding things there is the same not-knowing-of-one-another. The earth is essentially self-secluding. [*H*, 33/47]

This passage is essential to our understanding of Heidegger's assertion that the work of art brings the conflictual pair earth and world into the unity of a single differential configuration. Heidegger argues that earth and world come to be themselves and assert their respective natures as the work draws out the essential traits of their conflict. The work traces out the intimacy of their mutual, though conflictual, belonging in what Heidegger terms a "basic design," an "outline sketch" (*H*, 51/63). He terms this sketch a "rift" (Riss) or "rift-design" and says that "it brings the opposition of measure and boundary into their common outline" (*H*, 51/63). We understand "measure" immediately as a reference to world, and in the light of the passage I have just quoted, we may see that "boundary" refers to the setting of bounds that occurs in the self-seclusion of the things of the earth. In the earth's setting of bounds, there is a "self-seclusion," a "separation," but these bounds do not define relations among things—there is in the things of the earth a "not knowing of one another." Only when the world opens and marks these bounds *as bounds* does the "reciprocal accord" of things become a mutual relatedness. Their limits then serve to mark them off against one another and thus to define a relational context.

The opening of a world may thus be understood as a kind of differential articulation of what is. Heidegger defines this differentiation (taking this last term as a verb) by thinking with his language in a way that defies any traditional conceptual analysis. He invites us to think the Riss as a scission and as the tracing of an outline (the first stroke, so to speak, of a project, Entwurf) that draws out, and gathers into a unity through a kind of differential traction, the fundamental traits (*Grundzüge*) of the happening of truth in the conflict of world and earth. The verbal "work" to which I have referred, and by which Heidegger draws together the notions of tearing or opening, tracing, pulling, and gathering, entails an activation of the semantic network formed by the verbs *reissen* (which can mean to pull or to draw as well as to tear and whose etymology crosses that of the English "writing"), *ziehen* (to draw or pull and, as an intransitive verb, to move; from "ziehen" also comes "Zug," a drawing or traction, progress or passage, but also a trait, stroke, or feature: hence Grundzug), *zeichnen* (to draw, delineate, or mark, as with a sign, *Zeichen*) and, later, in the essays on language, *zeigen* (to show, point, or indicate).[7] With the term "Riss," Heidegger names the initial opening and gathering tracing of the difference or conflict between world and earth that first brings them into their essential natures. (And as always, Heidegger is attempting to think the terms of a relation from out of the relation itself—the terms are not first given and then enter into relation; they first assert themselves in their identity in the play of their mutual belonging.)[8] The tracing of their difference is the source of the unity of the conflicting elements. As it draws earth and world into their intimacy, it becomes itself a "self-overreaching gathering" (and we have here a first sign of Heidegger's reading of Nietzsche in this essay). The conflict is not a discord, Heidegger says:

> In essential striving, rather, the opponents raise each other into the self-assertion [*Selbstbehauptung*] of their natures. Self-assertion of nature, however, is never a rigid insistence upon some contingent state, but surrender to the concealed originality of the source of one's own being. In the struggle, each opponent carries the other beyond itself.

[7]From this brief evocation of the semantic network that Heidegger sketches out with his notion of the Riss, it should be apparent that Jacques Derrida's notion of writing offers a most powerful interpretation of the originary tracing that Heidegger will later name "the unity of the essence of language" (*US*, 251/121). For Derrida's own discussion of the Riss and his important emphasis on the contracting or tractive nature of the trait, see "Le retrait de la métaphore" *Poesie* 7 (1978); 103–26. See also Rodolphe Gasché's discussion of this essay in an excellent article entitled "Joining the Text: From Heidegger to Derrida," in *The Yale Critics: Deconstruction in America*, ed. Jonathan Arac, Wlad Godzich, and Wallace Martin (Minneapolis: University of Minnesota Press, 1983), pp. 156–75.

[8]One of the clearest statements of this notion comes in "Identity and Difference," in the commentary of Parmenides' maxim that thought and Being are the same. There, Heidegger asserts that we must think the identity of the terms on the basis of the "cobelonging" that is named in "the Same."

Thus the striving becomes ever more intense as striving, and more authentically what it is. The more the struggle overdoes itself on its own part, the more inflexibly do the opponents let themselves to into the intimacy of simple belonging to one another. [*H,* 35/49; my emphasis]

The conflictual relation of world and earth, then, is traced out in the Riss, which, in turn, is fixed in place and set up in the work in figure or shape (*Gestalt*). Here again, we see Heidegger working through his language, and in such a way as to rejoin his interpretation of the Greek notion of thesis (*H,* 72–84). The Riss, Heidegger says, is set back into the earth (*zurückgestellt*) in wood, stone, word, color, or tone, and in such a way that the earth, through its emergence in relation to the world set up in the work (*aufgestellt*), sets the Riss forth (*herstellt*) into the Open of their conflict (opened by the Riss itself). The Riss is thus fixed in place (*festgestellt*) and composed (*gefügt*) in such a way that it is brought into the limit traced in the work's form. The *Stellen* that is to be heard in Gestalt (like the *Setzen* that Heidegger uses in the phrase by which he defines art—*das Ins-Werk-Setzen der Wahrheit,* the setting-into-work of truth [*H,* 73–86]) is not to be heard as a positing in the sense defined in the metaphysics of subjectivity, that is, as the positing of an object for the subject that represents. It is to be understood rather as a setting forth into unconcealment that draws out and draws forth the relation to unconcealment. When the statue of the god is set up in the temple, for example, it is not set up as an object of aesthetic contemplation but rather offered to the god in praise and as an invocation and reception of its presence (*H,* 30/44). This example underscores Heidegger's implicit argument that a work of art opens a relation to the holy (even when this relation must be thought in terms of an absence; Heidegger will treat more explicitly the relation between art and the holy in his readings of Hölderlin). But the example also holds more generally for the relation between art and truth. As I said at the outset of this chapter, the work is addressed to some alterity and not posed by man for man.

The Riss, then, is not posited or presented by the work. It is, properly speaking, unpresentable, for it is no thing that is. It appears only, and can only be, as we will see, in the movement of repetition by which it is drawn out in the work's setting forth of

144

the earth (a setting forth, again, that occurs only from out of the Riss itself as the opening and gathering of the conflict of world and earth). The work's form essentially retraces this opening tracing that makes possible any delimiting form. Any limit in the essential sense defined by Heidegger, namely, that limit in which something that is comes to stand, remarks the Riss, or is traced from out of the Riss.[9] But the Gestalt of the work of art remarks in an evident fashion this originary differentiation (this again, is the work's createdness and, as we will see shortly, the source of the work's strangeness). Setting forth and composing in this fashion the conflict of world and earth, the work comes to bear and manifest in its very composition their intimate belonging. Setting the Riss into figure (and this is the work's "working"), the work thus achieves its own peculiar, gathered unity, that self-sufficiency that strikes our attention in the work of art.

The composure of the work of art is indeed, according to Heidegger, *ce qui frappe d'abord.*[10] But in order to account for the strangeness or uncanny quality that makes this composure so

---

[9]This understanding of the notion of limit is developed in the "Addendum" to "The Origin of the Work of Art" (*H,* 71/83) and also, at some length, in *An Introduction to Metaphysics.* In the following passage, Heidegger suggests how form is to be defined in relation to this notion: "The words *ptōsis* and *enklisis* mean falling, tipping, inclining. This implies a deviation from standing upright and straight. But this erect standing-there, coming up [*zum Stande kommen,* coming to stand] and enduring [*im Stand bleiben,* remaining in standing] is what the Greeks understood by Being. Yet what thus comes up and becomes intrinsically stable [*ständig*] encounters, freely and spontaneously, the necessity of its limit, *peras.* This limit is not something that comes to being from outside. Still less is it a deficiency in the sense of a harmful restriction. No, the hold that governs itself from out of the limit, the having-itself, wherein the enduring holds itself, is the Being of what is; it is what first makes being into a being as differentiated from nonbeing. Coming to stand accordingly means: to achieve a limit for itself, to limit itself. Consequently a fundamental characteristic of what is is *to telos,* which means not aim or purpose but end.... Limit and end are that wherewith being begins to *be.* It is on this basis that we must understand the supreme term that Aristotle used for Being, *entelecheia*—the holding (preserving)-itself-in-the-ending (limit).... That which places itself [*sich Stellende*] in its limit, completing it, and so stands, has form, *morphē.* Form as the Greeks understood it derives its essence from an emerging placing-itself-in-the-limit" (*EM,* 46/60)

[10]"What first strikes the attention"—a phrase referring again to Mallarmés "Préface" to "Un coup de dés..." (*Oeuvres complètes,* p. 455) and to his remark concerning a "spacing" in his poem that Heidegger's meditation on the Riss may help us to think.

arresting, it is necessary to recognize how the composing of the rift-design gives a configuration of truth, whose appearance, for Heidegger, is always marked by a certain strangeness. Heidegger, in fact, accounts for the work's self-subsistent quality both in formal terms (in terms of the work's composition—its tracing of the Riss in figure in its use of the earth) and with reference to his understanding of the event of truth (shown by the work's standing back in its "createdness"). The happening of truth is at work *in* the work (*H,* 45/58) as the gathering of the conflict between world and earth: "The independence or self-composure of the work is grounded here," Heidegger says (*H,* 45/58). But at the same time, the "steadfastness of the work's self-subsistence" is constituted by the work's "thrust" as it withdraws and casts forth the fact of its createdness, the fact that truth has happened. Both of these explanations of the work of art's distinctive independence must of course be thought together, though the second explanation of the work's self-subsistent nature derives from a more profound conception of the work's composing of the conflict of world and earth. The organization of "The Origin of the Work of Art" itself manifests the fact that Heidegger is moving to another level of reflection when he defines how truth happens in the battle between world and earth; Heidegger moves to think the essence of the "intimacy" of world and earth when, midway through the essay, he turns to ask "What is truth?" (*H,* 36/50). But the linear movement of the essay can betray the nature of the transition that is effected, or it can lead us to overlook the nature of what Heidegger is exploring. Again, Heidegger is asserting that the work fashions and bears *in itself* the event out of which it comes to stand. "Composure" describes both the work's formal aspect and the uncanny effect of the event of truth. In order to sharpen the sense of this paradox, let us consider more closely how the founding differentiation effected by the Riss constitutes the event of truth.

Heidegger defines truth, we have seen, as the unconcealedness of beings: alētheia (in a sense of this term left unthought by the Greeks themselves, Heidegger insists). Unconcealedness is what first makes a thing available to a propositional statement which is true by virtue of its correspondence with the thing. Heidegger's argument is simple and powerful: a thing must offer itself to our representation if our representation is to conform to it. Not only the particular thing must lie open, Heidegger says, but beings as a whole must in some way be unconcealed; the realm in which things offer themselves to representation must itself be disclosed. Heidegger describes this event as follows:

> Beyond what is, not away from it, but before it, there is still something else that happens. In the midst of beings as a whole an open place occurs. There is a clearing, a lighting. Thought of in reference to what is, to beings, this clearing is in a greater degree than are beings. The open center is therefore not surrounded by what is; rather, the lighting center itself encircles all that is, like the nothing which we scarcely know.
>
> That which is can only be, as a being, if it stands within and stands out within what is lighted in this clearing. [*H*, 39–40/53]

Yet the clearing from which beings stand forth unconcealed is at the same time, Heidegger says, a concealment. Concealment occurs as beings obstruct one another—hiding and obscuring—and, second, as beings "refuse themselves." This second form of concealment may be understood in relation to Heidegger's description of nihilation in "What Is Metaphysics?" Nichtung, composing the very Being of what is, refuses or repels (*abweist*) being in its totality; it "makes possible in advance the revelation of beings in general" (*W*, 114/105). Similarly, concealment as refusal is "the beginning of the clearing of what is lighted" (*H*, 40/53). It appears in the conflict of truth as the self-closing of the earth, and it is the source of the work of art's own withdrawal.

Truth, then, is the conflict of clearing and concealment by which an "open center" (*Mitte*) is won. The relation of world and earth, Heidegger says, is to be thought on the basis of the opening of the Open: "To the Open there belong a world and the earth" (*H*, 42/55). With the notion of the Riss, Heidegger draws together the conflictual pairs world/earth and clearing/concealing (the latter pair, again, the source of the relation named in the former). The Riss draws out the basic features of the event of truth ("the rise of the lighting of beings") by tracing the "common outline" of world and earth (*H*, 51/63)—their original differentiation and articulation. Tracing out the intimacy of conflict, the Riss sets forth the openness of the Open, holding open (as the *Austrag*, the settlement of the conflict) the clearing "within which what is stands, and from which it sets itself back into itself" (*H*, 42/55). Within this Open the work comes to stand in its essential limits, standing out, so to speak, against the outline or horizon that it draws with the Riss. Standing out or back in this way, the work manifests the fact that unconcealedness has occurred. But at the same time, this unconcealedness is happening *in* the work or through the work—it is opened by the work and born in it in the composed Riss. Thus the work traces out and makes manifest the conditions of its own emergence.

We can put this assertion another way by saying that the work brings about a setting of limits in the differentiation of world and earth. The work sets forth those limits within which a thing may stand as a thing. And the work itself comes to stand within the limits that it brings forth and makes manifest. Standing in these limits, it makes these limits appear *as limits*. The work thus stands forth through a play of contrast instigated by the work itself. The work carries with it its own backdrop. Or we might say simply that the work contrasts with itself. Heidegger is thus offering in his description of the work of art an instance of identity founded in difference.

The term "backdrop" might suggest a kind of stage—a metaphor that I would be hesitant to use, except that Heidegger himself employs it (though only in passing, and in asserting that the work of art is not a *rigid* stage) when he argues that the event of unconcealment entails essentially a contrasting that derives from what he calls a double concealment. To this point I have stressed the form of concealment that Heidegger calls "refusal"—the concealment that has its source in Nichtung. But the second concealment is perhaps no less fundamental, if only for the fact that one can never tell, according to Heidegger, which form of concealment one is dealing with (and particularly, one might suspect, in the work of art). Concealment, Heidegger says, conceals (*verbirgt*, and elsewhere *versagt*—these express the refusal of Nichtung) and dissembles itself (*sich verstellt*). Heidegger introduces the second form of concealment as follows: "But concealment, though of another sort, to be sure, at the same time also occurs within what is lighted. One being places itself in front of another being, the one helps to hide the other, the former obscures the latter, a few obstruct many, one denies all" (*H*, 40/54).

The first sense of *verstellen* is one thing blocking or obstructing another—if only because what is thus hidden has been put in the wrong place. But Heidegger continues to develop a second meaning of verstellen:

> Here concealment is not simple refusal. Rather, a being appears, but it presents itself as other than it is. This concealment is dissembling. If one being did not simulate another, we would not make mistakes or act mistakenly in regard to beings; we could not go astray and transgress, and especially could never overreach ourselves. That a being should be able to deceive as semblance is the condition for our being able to be deceived, not conversely.
>
> Concealment can be a refusal or merely a dissembling. We are never fully certain whether it is the one or the other. Concealment conceals and dissembles itself. This means: the open place in the midst of being, the clearing, is never a rigid stage with a permanently raised curtain on which the play of beings runs its course. Rather, the clearing happens only as this double concealment. [*H,* 40–41/54]

"Verstellen" is thus also to be understood as disguise or dissembling. It is only a possibility, Heidegger says ("Die Verbergung kann ein Versagen sein oder nur ein Verstellen"). Though we are never sure, he adds, with which we are dealing. And though merely a possibility, *Verstellung* belongs essentially to *Verbergung.* Concealment (Verbergung) both conceals itself (*sich verbirgt*) and dissembles itself. A posing as something other than itself belongs to the concealing denial—the Nichtung—that provides the source of all clearing. Physis loves to hide, Heraclitus said—it withdraws or reserves itself, with pleasure or joy; Heidegger adds (perhaps explicating the "pleasure" for us) that this hiding is also a disguising or a playing at. The hiding disguises itself.

But what would hiding, which surely cannot appear insofar as it hides itself (and it must appear in art), disguise itself as, except disguise, when disguise appears as disguise, when disguise appears? In art, concealment appears (*erscheint*) inasmuch as the event of truth—a play of concealment and unconcealment—somehow comes to show there. But it appears in disguise or as disguise. What else is art but Schein (semblance, mere appearance), even if this Schein must be thought as grounded within the horizon of truth? So in art, we think we see disguise—that is what Nietzsche thought in any case; Nietzsche asserted that art would be disguise appearing *as* disguise, as a disguise for which no true unveiling is possible. But according to Heidegger, we see in fact reserve, withdrawal. He adds, though, that we can never be sure—at which proposition, we would probably see Nietzsche's smile.

So we might add now that the work's self-contrasting must be understood also, or is perhaps inseparable from, a kind of posing in a theatrical sense—or rather a certain figuring (in the sense of "figuring as"). The differential outline of world and earth, as it sets itself back into earth in figure or Gestalt, is concealed and dissembled even as it is brought forth, and a certain figurality thus comes to belong to the work's distinctive composure. The work somehow brings forth the fact that it is a *figure of* . . . something—the event of truth. But truth is no thing that is, and is nowhere other than in the work; so we might say no more than that it is the figure of . . . nothing, other than itself. This is to say, if we follow out the logic of this argument, that the work shows figurality itself. I will return to this point in Chapter 5 when I take up Heidegger's reading of Hölderlin's "Andenken."

The paradoxical elements of the definition that I have pursued thus far—that the work of art works as an uncanny address whose formal structure constitutes an identity founded in difference— belong essentially to the logic of the finitude of truth. I have examined this logic from its objective or formal end, so to speak, considering how truth occurs *in* the work. But the proposition "art is the setting into work of truth" might be explored also by taking truth as its subject. Heidegger cautions that the phrase is ambiguous (*H*, 73/86) and that truth is neither subject nor object. Nevertheless, the two directions in which the phrase points reflect distinct movements in Heidegger's essay. (These movements are indicated expressly in the series of questions posed immediately before the section entitled "Truth and Art" and from which I draw two: What is the nature of the work that it might bring about, through the creation belonging to it, the happening of truth? What is the nature of truth that it can be set into work or, even under certain conditions, must be set into work, in order to be *as* truth?) To demonstrate the ambiguity of the phrase in question, Heidegger pursues both "slopes" of the ambiguity and forces his reader to entertain both movements without canceling them in a dialectical fashion. Considering truth as the subject of the phrase in question, we note that Heidegger attributes to the nature of truth an "impulse [*Zug*] toward the work" (*H*, 48/60). Truth can only be insofar as it establishes itself in some being—it does not exist outside or before its determination (by the work as thing). Truth can only become itself as a singular event and attain constancy by setting itself up within the sphere opened by truth itself:

> The openness of this Open, that is, truth, can be what it is, namely *this* openness, only if and as long as it establishes itself within its Open. Hence there must always be some being in this Open, something that is, in which the openness takes its stand and attains its constancy. In taking possession thus of the Open, the openness holds open the Open and sustains it. Setting and taking possession are here everywhere drawn from the Greek sense of thesis, which means a setting up in the unconcealed. [*H*, 48/61]

Truth, then, must pose itself or, in the context of art (there are other contexts),[11] must figure itself in order to occur. Setting itself up in this way, as we see, truth "takes possession" of its Open and affirms itself (becoming *this* openness); we might say that it assumes power over itself or comes to power in this act of figuration. And since Heidegger names truth's impulse toward the work a will (*H*, 50/62), we see that he is thinking the event of truth in the work in terms of a will to power (as Heidegger describes it in his *Nietzsche*).[12]

---

[11]Heidegger writes in "The Origin of the Work of Art": "One essential way in which truth establishes itself in the beings it has opened up is truth setting itself into work. Another way in which truth occurs is the act that founds a political state. Still another way in which truth comes to shine forth is the nearness of that which is not simply a being, but the being that is most of all. Still another way in which truth grounds itself is the essential sacrifice. Still another way in which truth becomes is the thinker's questioning, which, as the thinking of Being, names Being in its question-worthiness" (*H*, 49/61–62).

[12]The interpretation of Nietzsche's concept of art as developed in *Nietzsche* would seem to confirm this observation. Truth for Nietzsche, we will recall, is a fixed semblance necessary to the living being; art, however, is the affirmation of semblance wherein life appears in its perspectival character and in its essence as becoming. Heidegger expresses this in a way that parallels the formulations of the event of truth in art in "The Origin of the Work of Art." Art, he says, "is not an immobilizing, but a liberating for expansion, a clarifying to the point of transfiguration, and this in two senses; first, stationing a thing in the clarity of Being; second,

But in taking truth as the subject of the phrase "the setting into work of truth," we risk obscuring the determined character of its "self-establishing" (just as a subjectivist interpretation of the Will to Power—such as that posited in one moment of Heidegger's interpretation of Nietzsche—obscures its determined character and the nature of the difference at work in eternal recurrence). Truth's "Zug zum Werk" must be thought in relation to the draw of the rift-design as it is initially traced out in the work's form (and thus in the work's "thingly" character). To reiterate the point made immediately above: the setting up of the conflict of truth in the work is a repetition of the conflict that *first lets this conflict be*. The conflict must be figured. Heidegger expresses this paradox succinctly when he states, "Truth happens only by establishing itself in the conflict and sphere opened up by truth itself" (*H*, 49/61). Truth opens in a sphere opened by the work of art—but this sphere itself only opens with the event of truth; there is a repetition by which truth comes to be. The work "instigates" (*H*, 36/49) the striving in which the Open is won, and thus we may say that the pose or figure comes first: the origin (the event of truth) is determined.

Yet, while Heidegger develops this problem at some length, he nevertheless elides an essential dimension of it. He remarks in the "Addendum" to "The Origin of the Work of Art" (written twenty years after the essay, in 1956), that if truth is taken as the subject of the phrase "the setting into work of truth," then "Art is conceived in terms of disclosive appropriation." He adds: "Being, however, is a call to man and is not without man. Accordingly, art is at the same time defined as the setting-into-work of truth, where truth *now* is 'object,' and art is human creating and preserving" (*H*, 74/86). But the *human* (*menschlichen*) relation to art, he says, remains ambiguous in his essay: "In the heading 'the setting-into-work of

---

establishing such clarity as the heightening of life itself" (*N*1, 249/1, 216). The latter definition of the essence of the Will to Power as an Eternal Return is also echoed in "The Origin of the Work of Art" in Heidegger's statement that the conflict of truth "overdoes itself on its own part" in the work of art (*H*, 35/49) and is a "continually self-overreaching gathering" (*H*, 36/50). Truth appears in art, then, in a distinctly Nietzschean configuration. We might note in this respect that Heidegger was reworking "The Origin of the Work of Art" during the winter semester of 1936–37, the period of the lectures that were published in the first volume of *Nietzsche* under the title "The Will to Power as Art." See Krell's translation of *The Will to Power as Art*, vol. 1 of *Nietzsche*, p. 118.

truth,' in which it remains undecided but decid*able* who does the setting or in what way it occurs, there is concealed the *relation of Being and human being* [*der Bezug von Sein und Menschenswesen*], a relation that is unsuitably conceived even in this version—a distressing difficulty, which has been clear to me since *Being and Time* and has since been expressed in a variety of versions" (*H*, 74/87). A distressing difficulty—what is said to refuse itself to articulation here is one of the central questions, if not *the* central question, of Heidegger's early philosophy. The context of the remark should not mislead us as to its scope; while it appears in an addendum to Heidegger's essay on art, it refers, as Heidegger points out, to a problem that first emerged in *Being and Time* and was addressed repeatedly thereafter.

The problem of the relation between Being and human being, I would argue, is a kind of obstacle that "maltreats" Heidegger throughout his project much in the way that the problem of the foundation maltreated Kant, as Heidegger asserts, and the problem of the center maltreated (*maltrātierte*, N1, 24/1,6, as cited above in Chapter 2) Nietzsche. Here, in "The Origin of the Work of Art," Heidegger fails, he says, to bring forth the relation of Being and human being, and even fails to conceive it properly. How can we understand this failure?

We begin to approach it, I believe, by asking what Heidegger has omitted in his account of the setting into work of truth. First, we know from texts such as *Being and Time*, "What Is Metaphysics?," and *An Introduction to Metaphysics* that the relation of Being and human being only exists or only comes to be inasmuch as Dasein casts this relation in a creative project. Dasein's project is essentially a *response* and is thus passive or receptive in nature—this, too, Heidegger stresses in "The Origin of the Work of Art." But it is passively *active*—in a sense now that pushes both of these terms beyond their accepted meaning—in that the response first allows the call to occur. To use the language of "The Origin of the Work of Art," the project "traces out" the conditions of its own possibility, or initially poses them, since they do not exist before the act of projecting.[13] The project first opens the relation of Being and

---

[13]For this discussion, I refer once again to my first chapter. See also Jean-Luc Nancy's recent presentation of the hermeneutic circle in *Le partage des voix* (Paris: Galilée, 1982).

human being, and Heidegger adds that Being *is* only in this relation. This is what Heidegger terms the finitude of Being. As he says in his "Addendum" to "The Origin of the Work of Art," "Being is a call to man and is not without man."

In this same event, however, human finitude is defined or determined. That to which the project responds—but which, again, *is* not before the response or does not exist except in relation to the response—is the throw of Being that Heidegger defines in "What Is Metaphysics?" as the event of Nichtung. The opening of Being in Nichtung throws or drives Dasein, as Heidegger says, into the freedom of undertaking technē, or a creative project of Being. As we have seen, Heidegger writes of this originary opening, "So abyssally does the finitizing [*Verendlichung*] dig into Dasein, that the most authentic and deep finitude [*Endlichkeit*] refuses itself [*sich versagt*] to our freedom" (W, 118/108). The opening of Being that Dasein is called upon to hold open—the there or *Da* of Dasein itself—exceeds Dasein's hold. It is a kind of abyss. Finitude, understood in this way, is the limit beyond all limits—even more fundamental to human being than the experience of mortality insofar as the relation to death becomes a resource for speculative mastery. And insofar as Dasein first draws out or traces this limit in the creative project, first *discovers* it in the project, the creative project, *as a work of art*, must manifest this limit. Or when the work manifests its limits *as limits* (to adopt the formulation I offered a moment ago), it must in some way mark the fact that *for Dasein* the opening of Being that is established in the work is abyssal in nature.

Now, a limit *as* a limit marks a relation and thus, in some sense, an opening to some other, some alterity that stands in relation with what is marked as being the same. Here the limit, as limit, is an opening to man's finitude. This finitude is characterized, as we have seen, by the fact that it reserves itself or refuses itself (*sich versagt*). The most intimate proximity of Being and human being, in other words, withholds itself (as always, the closest is what is most distant). But again—and I reiterate this because I think we can glimpse here an instance of the furtive logic of the trace—it withholds itself only inasmuch as it is somehow marked in the work. The yawning of the abyss that is finitude only opens in the creative project. Thus the work must mark the reserve of Dasein's most intimate, most reserved being, if only as a veil. It must bear a trace of Dasein's self-reserving finitude—it must somehow open to this abyssal opening. The address of the work in which the work casts forward the fact of its createdness must also be a designation or manifestation of this withheld origin, or of the origin *as* withheld.

Thus, paradoxically, the work's reserve—the effect of withdrawal or self-subsistence that belongs to the work's self-delimitation as a tracing of the rift-design—marks a kind of excess. The reserve of the work is the appearance of a more profound reserve that belongs to the finitude of Dasein. The work's reserve—if we pry at this logic somewhat—is thus strangely or uncannily excessive. It thus fascinates (inasmuch as fascination belongs to Dasein's original experience of the openness of beings); it promises a glimpse of Dasein's naked exposure to the openness of Being, its finitude, but it gives only a glimpse of the self-refusal of Dasein's intimate being. The work's address, if it works as a promise or offer, is also in fact an interdiction, or it repeats an interdiction that is constituted in an abyssal structure of reserve (for Dasein's reserve answers to a reserved offer of Being). The work shows the interdiction of the origin; it poses the origin as interdicted. This is the strange law of the work that appears in the work's equilibrium.[14]

Reading the problematic of Dasein back into "The Origin of the Work of Art," as I have done here, essentially brings forth an "abyssal" quality of the work of art that Heidegger has perhaps already identified when he declares "truth is untruth" at the beginning of the paragraph in which he sets out the necessity of truth's posing itself in its Open. But staying only in the terms developed here, we recognize that the work's rift-design must in some way mark the opening to something that exceeds the "hold" of the work's formal boundaries. Thus, if the work opens beyond

[14]In the final section of *Der Satz vom Grund,* Heidegger contrasts the *ratio* or calculus that Hölderlin finds in the measure of the work of art with the *mathesis* of the subject of representation (that is, the capacity of the subject to assure itself of what is by posing the object before itself in representation as calculable and hence mathematically accessible). Hölderlin, he says, gives to the word "calculus" a more profound sense in his meditation on the equilibrium or balance of the tragic work in his "Notes to Oedipus." The law or calculus of the work appears, as I will note in Chapter 5, in the work's equilibrium. The law in question, according to Hölderlin, is a ground for poetic representation and is derived from the very means by which a thing may appear as a thing—the conditions of its phenomenal manifestation.

itself in this way, we may have cause to question Heidegger's assertions concerning the gathered, unified nature of the work. The work's unity and self-repose, in any case, must be fragile or somehow "exposed"—exposing something other than itself.

Heidegger, reminding us of the traditional definitions of artistic figuration, asserted at the outset of his argument that the work of art "says something other than the mere thing itself is, *allo agoreuei*. The work makes public something other than itself; it manifests something other; it is an allegory." He added, "In the work of art something other is brought together with the thing that is made. To bring together is, in Greek, *sumballein*. The work is a symbol" (*H*, 4/19–20). We understand by the end of "The Origin of the Work of Art" that the thingly quality of the work to which something else may be added can only be understood in relation to the event of truth by which the *real* thing comes to be. The work's reality—its *factum est*—can only be thought in terms of the setting into work of truth. But truth, which has an impulse to be joined in the work, or joined *with* the work (sumballein), is not reducible to the work in the sense that the work would contain it wholly, as the symbol might be said, in a certain Romantic formulation, to contain its signified within it. Truth as the event of unconcealment occurs nowhere but in the work, but it is also more than the work or other than the work (which we know if only because truth appears only in *contrast*, in the "that it *is*" of the work, and through a kind of ongoing deferral—the appearance of the fact *that* the work is is an appearance of the fact that truth happens as having happened).

Being needs the work, to put it simply, but is not reducible to the work; the work preserves, we might say, the ontological difference. But the tracing of this difference in the work is also the tracing of the self-refusal of human finitude, which, of course, belongs to the refusal of truth itself, but also seems uncannily excessive. Again, Heidegger could not fully incorporate this notion of human finitude into his description of the event of truth. Heidegger was repelled, in any case, by Nietzsche's own effort to bring it forth in texts such as *Ecce Homo*—an effort that included foregrounding the *verstellen*, the disguise that belongs to truth's own self-refusal. However we understand finally the excessive nature of human finitude—its refusal to any formal definition, to any structure (*Gefüge*)—we may say at least that the work of art is also, necessarily, an allegory of human finitude. For this, it possesses a strange beauty.[15]

II

The testimony of Hölderlin and Nietzsche, as I have suggested, indicates that the "strange beauty" of art is indeed not a manifestation of the self-gathering of Dasein in the nearness of Being but rather (or also) the sign of an instability, an ambiguity, or a disruption in that relation. The very decisiveness of Heidegger's interpretations of these texts points to his own obscure recognition of this fact. We see this most clearly in Heidegger's interpretation of Nietzsche in his commentary on the question of art. Many assertions from Heidegger's argument in "The Origin of the Work of Art" recur here, so this commentary is of particular interest in the context of the preceding discussion. But most noteworthy is the fact that these assertions appear to fend off a danger perceived in Nietzsche's testimony concerning the relation of Being and human being. Nietzsche, as I have said, foregrounds this relation in his own project, and thus Heidegger's treatment of this problem in Nietzsche's text is of particular interest for us here.

In Chapter 2 I sought to demonstrate that Heidegger, precisely in relation to the question of the situation of Dasein in a project of Being, recognizes something like a notion of "disaster" in Nietzsche's understanding of tragic experience. Heidegger invites us to think eternal recurrence as a project of being in its totality and within the configuration of the paradoxical movement of the hermeneutic circle. To think the Eternal Return, as we have seen, is to reach back to the open foundation of thought; the movement, and that which it thinks, is the *circulus vitiosus deus*. This "open foundation" figures briefly in Heidegger's argument as an equivalent of the groundless foundation of Dasein—an abyss (Abgrund). Thus,

[15]Gérard Granel's remarkable statement ("Et Tu, quis es?") in the issue of *Critique* entitled *La philosophie malgré tout* (no. 369, February 1978) suggests this term (though in a larger context). He writes: "Every human occupation conjures too soon its nothingness, and this in effect produces in it 'holes'—an ataxy, an amnesia, a strange beauty, a clumsiness, a dwarfism, a giantism, finally whatever form of the unexpected and the unheard that *happens* to this practice, and upon which it cannot turn back (which is therefore its history and its destiny at the same time)" (p. 179).

the reference to Nietzsche's understanding of the Dionysian in *Nietzsche* as an interpretation of what the Greeks of the Golden Age called deinon and deinotaton (N1, 151/1, 128) points immediately to the presentation in *An Introduction to Metaphysics* and to the disappropriating elements of tragic experience. But in the general movement of Heidegger's essay, the Dionysian is described by Heidegger as always bound, always mastered in the artist's "free disposition" over its conflict. Difference, returning constantly as the source of creative activity, is subsumed in the creative self-affirmation of a *unified* will to power. Heidegger's discussion of art at the beginning of his *Nietzsche*, though merely "preliminary," sets this argument in place.[16]

I begin by resituating the question of art in relation to my discussion in Chapter 2. We will recall that amor fati, as an artistic mode of being, names the creative mode of encounter with the Being of what is—its transfiguration or trans-formation in which a historical destiny takes form. This transfiguration is both the fundamental event of being in its totality, its process of self-creation, and a movement of transition between epochs, the transvaluation in which Nietzsche thinks the overcoming of nihilism. Amor fati, as a relation to destiny or to the *fatum*, is a *revolt* in that it occurs as a "counterthought" to the destiny of nihilism. Heidegger reads the countermovement of this thought as an inversion of Plato, but again, the circle described by this movement of inversion is not a closed one. The turn (*Wende*) that is required by the experience of distress (*Not*) in the encounter with the essence of nihilism consists in a constant turning back into this necessity (*Notwendigkeit*), which is the destiny of Being that opens with the death of God. The thought of the Eternal Return (in which the essence of nihilism attains form) brings the thinker into an ever more profound confrontation with the terrifying character of what is thought in

---

[16]Heidegger's discussion of the question of art is meant to serve as a preliminary approach to the "metaphysical horizon" in which the question of the situation of man in a project of Being arises—that is, the horizon that opens with the thought of eternal recurrence and with the attendant fusing of Being and becoming, action and reaction (N1, 160–61/1, 136). But Heidegger never comes "full circle" to pose the question of art on the basis of his most far-reaching analyses. Furthermore, his description of eternal recurrence as a *repetition of difference* is so allusive, or so muted, that a more critical development of this notion in the context of art becomes extremely difficult.

the thought—the overcoming of nihilism is an entry into relation with that which constitutes its essence. The passage involved in this downgoing is thus in two directions at once, and the revolt or counterthought describes a figure of repetition.

As we have seen, Heidegger isolates the conflictual element of this creative act of figuration in the discord that exists between art and truth. Art's transfiguration is a countermovement in which the essence of being (the perspectival Scheinen) opens and appears and in which art turns against truth. In art the event of truth (here in a nonmetaphysical sense) occurs as the Eternal Return. Art, again, is the fundamental event of being in its totality, whose "fundamental law" is conflict as such.

From Heidegger's description of this discord that defines the tragic character of being, it is difficult to determine either the nature of this discord or the nature of the appearance (*Aufschein*) of transfiguration—the revelation of the Eternal Return. This obscurity in Heidegger's argument is related to a fact to which Heidegger points with some insistence—the fact that Nietzsche defines the essence of art not on the basis of the work of art but rather from the perspective of the artist's activity. But the obscurity derives also from the ambiguity in Heidegger's interpretation of Nietzsche's understanding of the nature of truth. The nature of the tragic discord and the nature of (its) appearance in art remain essentially undefined because of the conflict that structures Heidegger's own interpretation.

In one direction of the argument, art's turn against truth is defined as a dialectical movement of *Aufhebung* (since both art and truth are subsumed into a "higher" unity in Will to Power); but in another direction of argumentation, the event of art's turn figures as the conflict that presides in the event of truth as alētheia. If we pursue this last perspective, then we find the relevant context for Heidegger's description of the conflict of art and truth in "The Origin of the Work of Art." "Conflict" might then be understood in terms of the work's thrusting forth its sketch of the unconcealedness of what is: "By virtue of the projected sketch set into the work of the unconcealedness of what is, which casts itself toward us, everything ordinary and hitherto existing becomes an unbeing. This unbeing has lost the capacity to give and keep being as measure" (*H*, 59–60/72). This phrase describes nicely what Nietzsche understands by the critical and "untimely" nature of thought as it becomes an affirmative and artistic power. The thrust of art is monstrous: "The more solitarily the work, fixed in the figure, stands on its own and the more cleanly it seems to cut all ties to human beings, the more simply does the thrust come into the Open that such a work *is* and the more essentially is the extraordinary [*das Ungeheure*—Hölderlin's word for the tragic] thrust to the surface and the long familiar thrust down" (*H,* 54/66). Truth is the fixed, commonly shared appearance that a species must pose for its survival. But art turns against this fixed appearance and allows for the surge of the creative source that in "The Origin of the Work of Art," is the play of concealment and unconcealment (what Heidegger terms in his reading of Hölderlin, and in reference to Nietzsche, the "Dionysian"—a play of presence and absence whose symbol is the mask).[17]

"The Origin of the Work of Art" reveals itself all the more clearly as the decisive context for Heidegger's remarks on art in *Nietzsche* when we recognize that the Will to Power is described in the latter volume as a *differential articulation* very much like the difference of world and earth. The Will to Power appears as difference first in the conflictual articulation of art and truth—it is that *same,* out of which art and truth diverge. But thought more profoundly as the unity of art and truth, it is the perspectival Scheinen, a bringing-to-appear that occurs as a process of life's becoming-form. Heidegger describes this process as a version of the relation between *physis* and *nomos,* as we will see shortly, and thus Will to Power comes to appear in Heidegger's description of the artistic process under the guise of truth, as the event of unconcealment whereby things are brought to stand within their essential limits.

In short, Heidegger finds in Nietzsche another version of the conflict described in *An Introduction to Metaphysics* and in "The Origin of the Work of Art"—a conflict, Heidegger says, that was first thought profoundly by Hölderlin. All of these interpretations are part of Heidegger's effort to articulate with his notion of art or Dichtung the "hidden stylistic law" of the German destiny:

> It is enough if we gather from the reference [to Hölderlin's contrasting of "the holy pathos" and "the Occidental *Junonian* sobriety of

[17]See Chapter 5, note 11 below.

representational skill"] that the variously named conflict of the Dionysian and the Apollonian, of holy passion and sober representation, is a hidden stylistic law of the historical determination of the German people and that one day we must find ourselves ready and able to give it shape. The opposition is not a formula with the help of which we should be content to describe "culture." By recognizing this antagonism, Hölderlin and Nietzsche early on placed a question mark after the task of the German people to find their essence historically. Will we understand this cipher? One thing is certain: history will wreak vengeance on us if we do not. [N1, 124/1, 104]

These words of 1936 underscore powerfully the fact that Heidegger's turn to the problem of art and Dichtung is part of his confrontation (however indirect) with the fact of National Socialism.

Heidegger's description of the artistic process as it is thought by Nietzsche may be described briefly as the production of the beautiful. Heidegger interprets Nietzsche's concept of the beautiful in the context of Kant's understanding of the term ("Kant alone grasped the essence of what Nietzsche in his own way wanted to comprehend concerning the decisive aspects of the beautiful" [N1, 130/1, 111]); "beautiful" is an object's radiant appearance as it comes forward *as* pure object. The beautiful is what pleases, what prompts in us an unconstrained favoring *(freie Gunst)* in which we "freely grant to what encounters us as such its way to be" (N1, 129/1, 109). This is not a "disinterested" relation to what is, if disinterest is taken to mean indifference or lack of engagement, as in the reigning misinterpretation of Kant's aesthetic thinking. Rather, aesthetic comportment is an engagement with the object of the highest sort, in which man first comes into the fullness of his essence (N1, 133/1, 113). For Nietzsche, such engagement is thought in terms of an object's corresponding to what we take ourselves to be and demand of ourselves, to that of which we are capable in a particular state of attunement; "beautiful" is that which *determines* us to ascend beyond ourselves to the full of our essential capability. This rapture, the essential aesthetic state, is the mode of attunement "in the sense of the supreme and most measured determinateness" (N1, 134/1, 113).

Creation, then, is a "rapturous bringing forth of the beautiful in the work" (N1, 135/1, 115). Heidegger regrets Nietzsche's failure to think creation on the basis of the essence of the work, but he finds a notion of determination and definition (what has to do with standards and with hierarchy [N1, 136/1, 116]) in the idealizing process that belongs to rapture. Rapture is an "extraordinary emphasis [*ungeheuren Heraustreiben*]" (N1, 137/1, 116) of the main features of the object. Rapture is drawn (*beziehen*) in anticipation to an ensemble of traits (*Gezüge*) or an articulation (*Gefüge*)—an attraction that can only have its source in a kind of overwhelming "throw." Heidegger accordingly cites Rilke's line from the "First Elegy," which is in his view wholly Nietzschean: "For the beautiful is nothing but the beginning of the terrible, a beginning we but barely endure" (N1, 137/1, 116). Creation is thus initially an encounter with the fatum (though here in terms of its inscription in an articulation of distinguishing traits), and thus creation appears as a configuration of amor fati.

Creation draws out the "major features" of the object as form. As in "The Origin of the Work of Art," Heidegger defines this concept in relation to the Greek concept of *morphē*: it is the limit and delimitation that brings a being into what it is and that brings it to stand in itself, the Gestalt. Heidegger's discussion is guided throughout by the terms of "The Origin of the Work of Art," though here the terrible or sublime is defined not as the emergence of truth but as Will to Power in its essence as Eternal Return (the apprehension of which in art inspires in Nietzsche a "sacred horror"). But as in "The Origin of the Work of Art," the gathering, composing element is form, and the same temporal paradoxes appear with respect to this element that determines the process in which it is realized. Rapture is form-engendering, but it becomes possible in the realm of form: "Form defines and demarcates for the first time the realm in which the state of waxing force and plenitude of being comes to fulfillment. Form founds the realm in which rapture as such becomes possible. Wherever form holds sway, as the supreme simplicity of the most resourceful lawfulness, there is rapture" (N1, 140/1, 119).

The creative event is thus the becoming of form—a relation of reciprocal determination, or a kind of interplay between a "physiological state of creative response" and the governing traits of form. Heidegger remarks that this opposition traverses Nietzsche's thought on art; it is said to produce a "constant scission" in his text between his conception of art as creative of values and hierarchies (art in its *decisive* function) and as an "explosion" of life's creative forces. But the two contradictory conceptions, Heidegger argues, are united in Nietzsche's conception of the essence of art in its supreme form as the "grand style": "Art in the grand style is the simple tranquillity resulting from the protective mastery of the supreme plenitude of life. To it belongs the original liberation [*Entfesselung*] of life, but one which is restrained; to it belongs the most terrific opposition, but in the unity of the simple" (N1, 148–49/1, 126).

"Style" in this perspective would refer to the manner of the project as it opens and holds open in its "free bearing" the original conflict. Heidegger calls this gathering of the conflict the "self-forming law" of the event:

An equally original freedom with regard to the extreme opposites, chaos and law; not the mere subjection of chaos to a form, but that mastery which enables the primal wilderness of chaos and the primordiality of law to advance under the same yoke, invariably bound to one another with equal necessity. Such mastery is unconstrained disposition over that yoke, which is as equally removed from the paralysis of form in what is dogmatic and formalistic as from sheer rapturous tumult. Wherever unconstrained disposition over that yoke is an event's self-forming law, there is the grand style; where the grand style prevails, there art in the purity of its essential plenitude is actual. [N1, 151/1, 128]

Let us recall that the event in question here is, in Heideggerian terms, the becoming of truth, its essencing. Here it is the becoming of a self-forming law: "What is inexhaustible, what is to be created, is the law. What art that dissolves style misinterprets as a sheer effervescence of feelings is in its essence the agitation of the discovery of law; such discovery can become actual in art only when the law drapes itself in freedom of form, in order in that way to come openly into play" (N1, 154/1, 130–31).

The law in question here, of course, is Eternal Return; the grand style, the self-shaping of this event of being in its totality. The Will to Power composes itself (transfigures itself) in form as eternal recurrence. But art remains the event of truth, Heidegger argues, since the self-gathering of will (which, as a differential element, an "open foundation," gathers itself and the terms of its conflict into "the unity of the simple") is a self-assimilation and self-presentation: the accomplishment of truth as homoiōsis. The Dionysian is fully appropriated within this "metaphysical horizon."

It would be appropriate to enumerate what Heidegger has had to exclude from Nietzsche's text in order to delimit this metaphysical dimension of his thought. We would begin by noting that Heidegger himself is quite clear about his hermeneutic decisions. He has effectively bracketed the totality of Nietzsche's productions with the judgment that none of the writings constitute a work in the essential sense of this term defined in "The Origin of the Work of Art." The works published by Nietzsche constitute only "foreground" to "Nietzsche's philosophy proper" (N1, 17/1, 8) (*Thus Spake Zarathoustra* is a "vestibule"), and the posthumous *The Will to Power* fails to answer to an essential form that refused itself (*sich versagte*, N1, 485) to even the thinker. Still, Heidegger pretends to recognize Nietzsche's fundamental thought in fragments from *The Will to Power* that in his view *distinguish* themselves in relation to one another not only by their content but also by their inner structural form and the rigor of their saying (N1, 487). We might conclude from Heidegger's suggestions that the essential form of Nietzsche's philosophy is to be described with a newly founded thought of the fragment; but Heidegger quickly asserts that he seeks not to read *The Will to Power* but rather to follow Nietzsche's "hidden course of thought" toward the thought of Will to Power and to think the latter's most intimate law and structure.

But aside from Heidegger's general reservations concerning writing, as announced in *What Is Called Thinking?*,[18] one of the most noteworthy arguments for bracketing Nietzsche's written testimony bears upon those works that are an expression of the man Nietzsche. Heidegger refuses to consider the work in relation to the man, as he argues at the beginning of "The Will to Power

---

[18]"For anyone who begins to write out of thoughtfulness must inevitably be like those people who run to seek refuge from any draft too strong for them. An as yet hidden history still keeps the secret why all great Western thinkers after Socrates, with all their greatness, had to be such fugitives. Thinking has entered into literature, and literature has decided the fate of Western science" (WHD, 52/17–18).

as Knowledge," since such a perspective would involve a historiographical or psychological approach and would fail to grasp the Being and the world that ground the work (*N*1, 474). But he also discounts the works in which Nietzsche himself speaks, preemptively, rather than allowing them to speak for themselves. *Ecce Homo* (but also *The Wagner Case, Nietzsche contra Wagner, Twilight of the Idols,* and *The Antichrist*) would be an example of a "peculiar restlessness" that possessed Nietzsche in the last year of his lucidity (the time of his *greatest lucidity,* Heidegger argues elsewhere [*N*1, 487]): "He could no longer wait for the long gestation of a broadly conceived work that would be able to speak for itself, on its own, as a work. Nietzsche himself had to speak, he himself had to come forth and announce his basic position vis-à-vis the world, drawing the boundaries which were to prevent anyone's confusing that basic position with any other" (*N*1, 17/1, 8).

Ecce Homo would be an instance of Nietzsche's speaking *for* his position, representing his philosophy (and thereby necessarily misrepresenting it). A distance would open between Nietzsche and his philosophy proper; or more accurately, "Nietzsche" would be there as a screening, supplemental voice. Clearly, Heidegger is refusing to accept Nietzsche's assertion that he is exhibiting his philosophy *in himself*—that the Nietzsche of *Ecce Homo* is an exemplary subject of the Will to Power. Heidegger is anxious to distinguish the subject that speaks in *Ecce Homo* from the subject that he wants to claim is the subject of metaphysics, even though he cautiously recognizes in "The Will to Power as Knowledge" the voice of *Ecce Homo* as that of a fatality. But this recognition is indirect and marked by a reservation. Heidegger refers to the subject of *Ecce Homo* as a fatality only in order to dismiss the psychologistic readings of the text that interpret it as a sign of Nietzsche's imminent collapse (and on this basis we might wonder how we are to understand Heidegger's reference to Nietzsche's "restlessness"—a question that is all the more interesting if restlessness is not a psychological phenomenon). But in the very gesture by which he suspends the question of madness, he alludes to a danger in Nietzsche's various acts of self-exhibition (for the problem, indeed, extends well beyond *Ecce Homo*). Despite his most intimate will, Heidegger asserts, Nietzsche became the instigator and promoter of an intensified spiritual, corporal and intellectual auto-dissection and a setting on stage of man that ultimately and indirectly had as a consequence an abandoned exhibiting of all human activity in "sound and image" through photomontage and reportage...

Nietzsche composed for himself an ambiguous figure [*Gestalt*], and had to do so within his own sphere and that of the present time. It is up to us to grasp behind this ambiguity the unique and the forward pointing, the decisive and the definitive. [*N*1, 474]

Nietzsche's self-exhibition thus requires severe interpretive decision, not only because it is "ambiguous" in nature, but also because it prompts (perhaps because of its very ambiguity) a kind of mimetic contagion during this end period of the metaphysics of subjectivity that lies under the domination of the "dictatorship of publicity" (*W*, 317/197). What is most remarkable about Heidegger's words concerning *Ecce Homo* and the indirection of his treatment of the text is that it would seem entirely possible for Heidegger to follow Nietzsche's lead in identifying the subject of *Ecce Homo* with the subject of the Will to Power. ("*Revaluation of all values*: that is my formula for an act of supreme self-examination [*Selbstbesinnung*] on the part of humanity, becomes flesh and genius in me.")[19] Even if Nietzsche's "gratuitous" act of telling his life to himself in *Ecce Homo* (giving himself this gift in return for the "presents" of the year: *Twilight of the Idols*, etc.)[20] is not itself an act of self-examination, could Heidegger not contain the secondary effects of this *Darstellung* with his description of the dominance of the image in the modern metaphysics of subjectivity? If Heidegger merely alludes to this argument indirectly, it is perhaps because the paradoxical freedom of which Nietzsche bears witness in *Ecce Homo* ("that neutrality, that freedom from all partiality in relation to the total problem of life")[21] escapes not only Heidegger's description of the Will to Power's *self-contained* or self-assimilating nature as a process of homoiōsis but also the horizon of truth thought as alētheia. Nietzsche may well be exhibiting aspects of the relation

[19]*Ecce Homo*, trans. Walter Kaufmann (New York: Random House, 1967), p. 326.
[20]Ibid., p. 221.
[21]Ibid., p. 222. For an excellent discussion of the nature of this freedom, see Rodolphe Gasché, "Autobiography as *Gestalt*: Nietzsche's *Ecce Homo*," in *Boundary 2*, vol. 9, no. 3, and 10, no. 1 (Spring/Fall 1981): 271–90.

of Being and human being that not only are perhaps offensive to Heidegger's reserve but also pose a threat to the possibility of holding Nietzsche at a distance within the boundaries of the question of the truth of Being.

Indeed, as regards Heidegger's sense of propriety, he is excluding from the essential form of Nietzsche's thought the self-exposition that characterizes *Ecce Homo* in a way that parallels his approving citation of Nietzsche's statements concerning the artist's lack of shame:

> Nietzsche says (*WM*, 814), "Artists are *not* men of *great* passion, whatever they like to tell us—and themselves as well." Nietzsche adduces two reasons why artists cannot be men of great passion. First, simply because they are artists, i.e., creators, artists must examine themselves; they lack shame [*Scham*] before themselves, and above all they lack shame before great passion; as artists they have to exploit passion, hiding in ambush and pouncing on it, transforming it in the artistic process. Artists are too curious merely to *be* magnificent in great passion; for what passion would have confronting it is not curiosity but a sense of shame. Second, artists are also always the victims of the talent they possess, and that denies them the sheer extravagance of great passion. "One does not *get over* a passion by portraying it; rather, the passion *is over when* one portrays it" (*WM*, 814). [N1, 121–22/1, 101][22]

These citations from Nietzsche pose a difficulty in the context of Heidegger's argument, since Heidegger is demonstrating that the artist manifests the Will to Power in its most perspicuous form. Heidegger will not define in the course of his argument how the self-grasping and self-fashioning in form of the artistic Will to Power is to be distinguished from artistic curiosity and its productions. But "curiosity" as it substitutes for shame in this passage appears in *Ecce Homo* as a kind of pleasure in self-exhibition that is

---

[22]A related theme surfaces again in "Alētheia (Heraklit, Fragment 16)": "Being present is the uncovering concealing of the self. Appropriate to this way of being is modesty [*die Scheu*]. This latter is the reserved remaining concealed before the approach of what presents itself. It is the sheltering of what becomes present in the inviolable nearness of what constantly remains in coming, a coming that remains an increasing veiling of itself. This modesty and everything high related to it must be thought in the light of remaining-hidden" (*VA*, 263).

no less "shameless" and that in its excess veers into the self-parody of histrionism. Pierre Klossowski very deftly adopts Nietzsche's words concerning Dostoevsky to describe *Ecce Homo* in this respect: "a frightening and ferocious mockery of the Delphic 'know thyself,' but tossed off with such an effortless audacity and joy in his superior powers that I was thoroughly drunk with delight."[23] Such self-parody is hardly compatible with Heidegger's description of an artistic "free disposition" over the articulation of artistic passion (*Rausch*) and form in the "grand style." If anything, it is a sovereign exhibition of the impossibility of such mastery, of such a founded becoming-form.[24]

The instability of the self that speaks in *Ecce Homo* is marked by a voice that seems capable of saying almost anything ("Perhaps I am a buffoon"). In this sense, it is the voice of no one. Or we might say that its extravagance marks the figural character of the persona(e) that speaks with it (and again, it is the voice of no one). Nietzsche speaks *as* a fatality in *Ecce Homo*; in so doing he brings forth the irreducibly figural or fictive character of the self's act of self-positing—remarking the fact that any "posing" of the self is also and always a Darstellung, a mimesis, and that such posing is inherently unstable, even volatile in nature.[25] Indeed, the voice of

[23]*Nietzsche et le cercle vicieux* (Paris: Mercure de France, 1969), p. 323. The full letter of March 7, 1887, to Peter Gast is presented and translated by Peter Fuss and Henry Shapiro in *Nietzsche, A Self-Portrait from His Letters* (Cambridge: Harvard University Press, 1971), pp. 97–98.

[24]Jean-Luc Nancy's description of *Ecce Homo* would support this interpretation. In the context of his analysis of Nietzsche's concept of "probity," he writes the following: "But it happens that *Redlichkeit* [honesty or probity] is also a gazing without feigning and without concessions upon the universality 'of delirium and of error.' . . .

"It is this madness that *Ecce Homo* (which might well be the book of *Redlichkeit* par excellence) confronts by playing it out, but plays with also in confronting it. For what this book confronts—brutally—is at bottom the impossibility of designating to humanity, to human thought, the act of its self-examination [*Selbstbesinnung*] (as the *Umwertung* is found defined there; cf. 'Why I am a Destiny, I') without pulling away from it any seat, any support, any foundation, any *selbst* for this *Selbstbesinnung*—proposing to it, at this moment, only the *selbst* of Nietzsche himself, which is as much as to say (for this exhibition has nothing subjectivist about it, we are not coming back to 'Monsieur Nietzsche'), nothing, a *guignol*, and nevertheless for this, precisely for this, the first 'honest man' the first *anständig* man, which must imply some *Redlichkeit*. . . . Probity is probity before the *unbearable* nature of the thought of truth" ("Notre probité!" *L'impératif catégorique* [Paris: Flammarion, 1983], pp. 71–72).

[25]In his "Typographie" (in *Mimesis: Des articulations* [Paris: Flammarion, 1975], pp.

Ecce Homo reflects the createdness of its persona in a way that paradoxically inverts the distinctive character of the work of art as Heidegger describes it in "The Origin of the Work of Art." If the work of art, as a work of Dasein, marks the reserve of truth with its own reserve or withdrawal, Nietzsche's voice in *Ecce Homo* seems to mark its finitude (its self-positing as the opening to an unpresentable alterity) in its very lack of reserve. The voice of *Ecce Homo* is too bright (in an acoustical sense), just as in his last year—the year of greatest lucidity—"everything about him radiates an excessive brilliance" (*N1*, 23/1, 15), a phrase that points to Hölderlin. It is as though the I of *Ecce Homo* itself marks a limit like that of the work of art insofar as the work marks "the possibility of disaster." But whereas this limit, defining the ontological difference, is said to "gather" in the work of art, the freedom of the I in *Ecce Homo* (and the instability or volatility of the self that moves through identities in Nietzsche's last weeks of lucidity) points to an experience of difference that is not unifying or gathering. When Nietzsche *mimes* the reserve of truth with his excessive act of self-exhibition, he exposes the abyss of truth—or the abyss that opens in the relation of Being and human being.

Would mimesis name what troubles Heidegger in the relation of Being and human being as it manifests itself in art? What I have called the anonymity of Nietzsche's voice in *Ecce Homo* and the freedom of the I that speaks in that text might also be described as a "plasticity" or an "open" capacity for shifting roles or characters that is to be understood not as a constitutive lack of identity (the concept of lack consistently brings us back to the metaphysical subject, as has been demonstrated in readings of psychoanalytic theory) but rather, as Lacoue-Labarthe has suggested,[26] as what

---

166–270), Lacoue-Labarthe analyzes Heidegger's effort to think all of the derivatives of *Ge-stell* (*Stellung, Vorstellung, Herstellung, Aufstellung, Darstellung,* etc.) within the horizon of *alētheia* and, as part of this effort, Heidegger's gesture of thinking *Darstellung* in terms of *Herstellung* (with which he translates *poiēsis*). Reducing all fictioning to a notion of production, Heidegger sidesteps the problem of mimesis in some of its more unsettling dimensions. With this discussion of *Ecce Homo*, I am working very much in reference to Lacoue-Labarthe's extraordinarily rich discussion of the problem of mimesis. Translations of "Typographie," "La transcendance finit dans la politique," and the essays on Hölderlin that I will cite in the next chapter are part of *Typography,* a volume of essays by Lacoue-Labarthe, to be published by Harvard University Press.

[26]"Typographie," p. 246.

ek-sists or de-sists in any self-identification or self-affirmation. The extravagance of the voice in *Ecce Homo* manifests that the self there affirmed is a mask—but no stable identity, no true subject, lies behind this play. There is, so to speak, only an echo of anonymity that signals to us that "Nietzsche" is giving himself "for" Nietzsche or "as" Nietzsche, the veiling or representation (Darstellung) being irreducible or originary.

If "Nietzsche" names both the "matter" of Nietzsche's thought and the unstable play of identity in which it takes form and gives itself, then any possibilty of a definitive Auseinandersetzung with Nietzsche is suspended. Not only does this voice have a possibly contagious character (with all the powers of fascination or capture that Plato accorded to mimesis in the third book of his *Republic*), but in its anonymity, it is perhaps impossible to lose. The very form of Heidegger's reading of Nietzsche, spreading as it does through a long series of texts, is a sign that Heidegger suffered such a capture.

"Mimesis" is hardly an *answer* to the question of the nature of the instability in the relation of Being and human being that Nietzsche foregrounds in his writing. The term, in effect, simply reposes the question. If it names the particular "plastic" character of what Nietzsche terms the Will to Power (a "plasticity" defined nicely by Deleuze in *Nietzsche et la philosophie*),[27] we have still to define how we might understand the finite nature of this differential element. More specifically, Heidegger implicitly invites us to ask to what extent the instability in the self-affirmation of Dasein derives from the thetic character of this act. (Let us recall that the question of man emerges in the context of the problem of the "setting into work of truth" and thus, as Heidegger explains in his "Addendum," in relation to his interpretation of the Greek notion of thesis.) Here, of course, the question of language presents itself.

But the question of language, as it emerges here, is very much a limit question for Heidegger inasmuch as it involves what we might term, following Blanchot, the literary possibilities in language. To follow Heidegger as far as he might take us in this direction, it would be necessary to examine in much greater depth

---

[27]Gilles Deleuze, *Nietzsche et la philosophie* (Paris: Presses Universitaires de France, 1973). See, in particular, chaps. 1 and 2.

Heidegger's meditation on language. But it would be necessary also to leave Heidegger's text in order to define how this question indeed forms a limit for Heidegger's thought. We would need to turn, for example, to Blanchot's experiments (among others) in theory and fiction—and this, of course, must be another project.[28]

Here I have sought to work more modestly from within the terms of the problematic opened by Heidegger in his reading of Nietzsche and to demonstrate how Heidegger turns away from the unsettling dimensions of the problematic of Dasein. Heidegger cannot accommodate in his description of artistic being the accents of the histrion. He follows, rather, the strain in Nietzsche's text that reflects Nietzsche's effort to combat his experience of self-dissolution. But the strain of self-affirmation in Nietzsche's text is indissociable from Nietzsche's experience of dispersion or disappropriation, and the effort to escape this experience (traced admirably by Klossowski in his *Nietzsche et le cercle vicieux*) is conjoined with a drive for lucidity that leads Nietzsche back to the delirium upon which his thought turns, as upon its axis. Nietzsche's

[28]Such a project might begin with a reading of Maurice Blanchot's "Literature and the Right to Death" ("La littérature et le droit à la mort," in *La part du feu* [Paris: Gallimard, 1949]). In this text Blanchot analyzes the nature of the particular positing by which the work , in Heidegger's terms, first traces out the possibility of the event of truth. Blanchot finds in the language of literature a certain opacity or material quality that resists any subsumption in the production of meaning but yet cannot be defined as pure substance or a brute, silent being. Literary language brings Dasein back to the abyssal conditions of its existence (the "bottom"—and "open"—end of the hermeneutic circle, we might say), and "appears" in literature as an element between earth and world (Blanchot's terms "day" and "night" bear something of a Hegelian inflection) that does not gather the two terms into the unity and intimacy of a differential relation but, rather, suspends or neutralizes the relation (creating a "relation without relation") and remains as a kind of residue after the conflict of world and earth. It is that element out of which the two conflictual terms emerge but which is never fully subsumed. The work's "reserve" in this context would belong to the thingly or material quality of language. The question of mimesis emerges as Blanchot defines the nature of the image in terms of these qualities of language and, in a remarkable meditation on the cadaver in "Two Versions of the Imaginary," describes the image as the site where "resemblance itself" appears. To this series of references, we might add Blanchot's reflections in "The Narrative Voice," in which Blanchot locates the kind of anonymity that I hear in the voice of *Ecce Homo* in a literary experience in which the limits of language are brought forth. All of the essays to which I have referred are collected in *The Gaze of Orpheus*, trans. Lydia Davis (Barrytown: Station Hill, 1981), a volume that provides an excellent introduction to Blanchot's extensive theoretical production. I might note as well that Blanchot explores throughout his fiction the experience of the uncanny.

project of thought, Klossowski suggests, must be thought in a figure resembling the one I have sought to describe as the double movement of the hermeneutic circle:

> *That a thought should climb only in descending, progress only in regressing.* —Inconceivable spiral, whose "useless" description is distasteful, to the point that one carefully refrains from admitting that it is described by the very movement of successive generations—or fixes only upon the climb of a spirit as long as it seems to follow, in harmony with culture, the ascension of history. And as for the rest, one leaves the descending movement of this spiraling thought to those whose specialty is the failure, the refuse, the waste of the function of thinking and living, who according to this convenient division of labor will hardly have to worry about this tension between lucidity and obscurity; unless it is to note, the day on which these last would pronounce themselves, *the one through the other,* that they would take on the *accent of delirium.*[29]

"Delirium" is perhaps one of the few modes in which the limit experience that we designate as "the relation of Being and human being" presents itself to us in this epoch—if only because we are not prepared to hear less extreme or less "disastrous" testimony. But art offers other accents as it describes the figure evoked by Klossowski, and I would argue that Heidegger invites us to think art, or creation in general, precisely as such a process wherein Dasein brings itself (with an empassioned lucidity) before its own limits.

To describe the historical style that emerges in Heidegger's thinking in terms of an intimate relation between gathering and dispersion, appropriation and disappropriation, is to force Heidegger's text back to the richest intuitions of the thinking that emerged in *Being and Time;* but it is also to enter into the most intimate movement of his thought, not only in the trajectory that leads through Heidegger's *Nietzsche,* but throughout Heidegger's writings. The full bearing of this statement (its justice, but also its direction in further readings) must remain latent in a study of this scope, and its elaboration does not belong to a single reader alone—an assertion I make knowing that I am not the first along

[29]*Nietzsche et le cercle vicieux,* p. 14.

this path. But it implies that, by remarking in each case the gap or the shadow that figures in Heidegger's efforts to formulate the gathering event of appropriation (just as Heidegger marked the irrecoverable distance that held Nietzsche's thought from itself, even as he placed Nietzsche at a distance), we follow him most faithfully—with the piety of the traitor, as Hölderlin would say.

5 /

Hölderlin's Testimony:
An Eye Too Many Perhaps

Heidegger may well turn aside from the question of the relation between Being and human being in "The Origin of the Work of Art." But in the reading of Hölderlin that begins to take shape at approximately the same time (Heidegger lectured on Hölderlin's hymns "Germanien" and "Der Rhein" during the winter semester of 1934–35, and in 1936 he first presented "Hölderlin and the Essense of Poetry"), Heidegger addresses forcefully the question of the human Dasein in relation to the problem of art. Hölderlin's writings are chosen for a meditation on the essence of poetry, Heidegger explains, because Hölderlin's poetic destiny is to say this essence poetically. This means, Heidegger says, that Hölderlin is the poet *of the poet* (*EHD*, 34), and he goes on to assert that Hölderlin's grounding of the poetic self is an exemplary act for the German people that defines their historical destiny.

But the gesture by which Heidegger assigns this destiny to Hölderlin and at the same time defines the poetic relation of Being and human being is no less problematic, I want to argue, than Heidegger's elision of the question of man in "The Origin of the Work of Art." Its forced character, even its violence, demonstrates that Heidegger perceives a danger in Hölderlin's meditation on the possibility of a poetic founding of the human Dasein. Indeed, I would suggest that the theme of danger as it appears in "Hölderlin and the Essence of Poetry" works symptomatically (in a way that resembles what Freud calls *Verneinung*) by veiling and unveiling Heidegger's recognition of the unsettling nature of Hölderlin's understanding of human finitude. For this understanding challenges Heidegger's own assertions concerning the unity and simplicity of the clearing of Being and the "gathering" appropriation of the human essence—assertions for which Heidegger calls Hölderlin as his chief witness.

I would not be the first, of course, to decry the violence of Heidegger's interpretation of Hölderlin. In fact, within the limits of this study, I can hardly consider the range of criticisms that have been made, nor even, in a more fitting, positive mode, consider the large number of issues brought forth in the literature concerning the implications of Heidegger's thinking encounter with Hölderlin's poetic thought. This literature is of particular interest at this moment of the development of Heidegger scholarship, I believe, because it is informed by the intense theoretical reflection that has developed in recent years out of the discipline of literary theory. The contemporary concern with the problem of the relation between philosophy and literature has brought into relief Heidegger's claim concerning the fundamental nature of the dialogue between poetry and thought, while Heidegger's own methods of reading have posed a significant challenge to the most basic assumptions of philological research.[1]

My own approach to Heidegger's interpretations of Hölderlin is shaped primarily by the guiding concern of this volume: the question of finitude as it presents itself in relation to the self-definition (or self-affirmation) of the human Dasein in a project of Being. But I might note here what I hope was already visible in my reading of "The Origin of the Work of Art," namely,

---

[1] A partial bibliography for this literature includes Beda Allemann, *Hölderlin und Heidegger*, 2d ed. (Freiburg: Atlantis Verlag, 1954); Else Buddeberg, *Heidegger und die Dichtung* (Stuttgart: S. B. Metzlersche, 1953); David Halliburton, *Poetic Thinking: An Approach to Heidegger* (Chicago: University of Chicago Press, 1981); Karsten Harries, "Heidegger and Hölderlin: The Limits of Language," *Personalist* 44 (1963): 5–23; Paul de Man, "Heidegger's Exegeses of Hölderlin," in *Blindness and Insight*, 2d ed. (Minneapolis: University of Minnesota Press, 1983), pp. 246–66; Michael Murray, "Heidegger's Hermeneutic Reading of Hölderlin: The Signs of Time," *Eighteenth Century* 21, no. 1 (1980): 41–66; Otto Pöggeler, "Heidegger's Begegnung mit Hölderlin," *Man and World* 10, no. 1 (1977): 13–61; and David A. White, *Heidegger and the Language of Poetry* (Lincoln: University of Nebraska Press, 1978).

that I am trying to prepare the ground for a formal understanding of the "arresting" character of the matter of Heidegger's thought ("Heidegger") inasmuch as it comes to be only as it is *written* (to recall Derrida's term for the trace structure in his own interpretation of the finitude of Being), and thus inasmuch as its "arrest" is the work of a text. In this way, I am attempting to approach the question of language in Heidegger's text in a way that goes beyond a conceptual or thematic approach to this question (as Heidegger invites us to do) but that follows Heidegger in his performative reflection on how language works. Thus I hope in this reading to address some of the basic concerns in current theoretical and philosophical questioning concerning the nature of the text and the act of interpretation. With this reference in mind, I will undertake in this chapter, in a reading of Heidegger's essay "Andenken," a lengthy consideration of what Heidegger designates as the reflexive character of Hölderlin's poetry.

We may glimpse the nature of the divergence between Hölderlin's poetic experience of the relation between Being and human being, and Heidegger's appropriation of this experience, in Heidegger's use of the figure that I would like to take up as a leitmotif for this reading. From Hölderlin, as I have said, Heidegger draws the figure of the "eye too many" to designate the mark of Western man's tragic destiny. In Heidegger's view, Hölderlin expresses his own historical essence as a poet with this same phrase concerning Oedipus. In "Hölderlin and the Essence of Poetry," Heidegger writes: "This poet thinks poetically out of an excess of pressure from the ground and center of Being. The words said of Oedipus in the late poem 'In lovely blueness . . . ' apply to Hölderlin himself: 'King Oedipus has an eye too many perhaps'" (*EHD*, 47). This designation applies to Hölderlin, Heidegger says, because he is the poet of the poet—not by virtue of some specifically modern failing, an excessive self-consciousness experienced as a lack before the plenitude of Being, but rather by virtue of the excessive richness of his experience of belonging to the intimacy of Being. The "eye too many" marks Hölderlin as a witness to the modern German historical destiny.

Heidegger is quite justified in identifying Oedipus's destiny with Hölderlin's own on the basis of the line from "In lovely blueness. . . ." But what Heidegger describes (and, with much of the philosophical tradition, admires) as Oedipus's "wild and radical assertion of his fundamental passion" (*EM*, 81/107) receives, as we might also gather from "In lovely blueness . . . ," a far more ambivalent characterization from Hölderlin. In his "Notes to Oedipus," Hölderlin names Oedipus's tragic quest for his identity as a self-conscious subject "the desperate struggle to come to himself, the extravagant search for a consciousness," and further describes this struggle as "the insane questioning in search of a consciousness."[2]

For Hölderlin, Oedipus's "eye too many" is the sign of a particularly modern malady. Correspondingly, the tragedy of Oedipus is, in Hölderlin's view, a presentation of a catastrophic suspension of Oedipus's speculative overreaching and the catharsis of his interpretive passion. Oedipus suffers a kind of exile, an *irreversible passage* away from the Greek "oriental" nature that Hölderlin describes as an "excentric enthusiasm" or "sacred pathos"—a panic drive toward unification with the divine whose counterpart Hölderlin finds in modern art (in Schiller's sentimental mode) and modern thought (the speculative tendency of modern philosophy). When Heidegger, in his lectures of 1934–35, describes this same destiny (as I will demonstrate) in terms of an *accomplishment* of Oedipus's original drive for unity, he redresses—in a way that is very close to being dialectical, and perhaps inevitably so—some of the most radical elements in Hölderlin's thought on tragedy. In the same gesture, he fails to recognize the "monstrosity" of Hölderlin's image of Oedipus's eye too many and its meaning for Hölderlin as he reflects upon his own inability to know the measure of his experience as a poet.

In his book-length study of Heidegger's reading of Hölderlin, Beda Allemann recognized the importance of Hölderlin's "Notes to Oedipus" and "Notes to Antigone" for understanding the distance Hölderlin takes from the metaphysics of subjectivity as elaborated in German Idealism by Hölderlin's contemporaries.[3] He recognized as well that Hölderlin's "Notes" represent an astonishing anticipation of Heidegger's thought—one that Heidegger is not

---

[2]In "Anmerkungen zum Oedipus," *SW*2.1, 199–200. It should be noted that Heidegger qualifies his earlier use of the figure of the "eye too many" in his essay of 1951, ". . . Poetically Man Dwells . . ." (*Poetry, Language, Thought*, p. 228), but does not comment on the "strange excess" of which it would be the sign.

[3]*Hölderlin und Heidegger*, pp. 27–41.

fully prepared to recognize—and that Heidegger's reading of Hölderlin is in many ways regressive with respect to those developments in Hölderlin's late thinking that seem to offer the grounds for Heidegger's dialogue with Hölderlin. But Allemann's interpretation of this "regression" is somewhat off the mark, I would argue, as is his effort to understand it positively as being in part a calculated regression that helps to prepare a leap beyond metaphysics. Finally, Allemann proves to be too faithfully Heideggerian when he comes to interpret "In lovely blueness..." and essentially ratifies a reading of Hölderlin that he did not fully appreciate. Allemann's argument is very strong, but he fails to recognize the full complexity and even the beauty of Heidegger's reading of Hölderlin; most important, he does not recognize where Hölderlin's thinking might shake the edifice of Heidegger's project.

Thus it seems worthwhile to repeat Allemann's reading, to a certain extent, by returning to Hölderlin's "Notes" and by contrasting these first with Heidegger's lectures of 1934–35 (which illustrate Heidegger's response to the tragic dimension of Hölderlin's thought) and then with his reading of "Remembrance." The essay on "Remembrance" is the specific focus of Allemann's criticism of Heidegger, but it is also a text that will allow me to carry forward the discussion of art that I opened with my reading of "The Origin of the Work of Art." By then reading "In lovely blueness...," I will frame Heidegger's reading in the same way as Allemann but will reach quite different conclusions.

It is hardly possible to provide here anything like a complete reading of texts as dense and even obscure as Hölderlin's "Notes," but a few general observations might be made. Hölderlin posits in his "Notes" that a modern tragedy, if formally well founded, would provide what might be called a calculus of human finitude. The formal constitution of the work of art, its "poetic logic," as Hölderlin refers to it (SW5, 265), would define and manifest the development of the various human faculties in their total interaction (unlike philosophy, whose logic represents in their coherence the articulations of a single faculty). In tragedy, Hölderlin says, this play of the faculties appears in an equilibrium: "The law, the calculus, the way in which a system of sensibility, the entire person, develops under the influence of elements, and the way representation, sensibility and rationality emerge in different successions one after the other, but always following a sure rule, is in the tragic more of an equilibrium than a pure succession" (*SW*5, 196).

Tragedy manifests this equilibrium in its rhythmical structure. It is a metaphor, Hölderlin says (Hölderlin had defined it in "Über den Unterschied der Dichtarten" as "the metaphor of an intellectual intuition" [*SW*4.1, 266])—a "transport" (*meta-pherein*) presented scenically in a succession of representations and depending for its binding or determination upon what Hölderlin calls "the pure word," nothing more or less than what is termed in meter the caesura, an "antirhythmical" intrusion or suspension (*SW*5, 196). By virtue of this pure interruption, Hölderlin argues, the succession of representations gives way to the appearance of representation itself [*Vorstellung*], and the rhythm of the work, or the succession of its "calculus," is divided in such a way that it relates itself to itself (here is a "self-contrasting" similar to what I identified in my reading of "The Origin of the Work of Art") and produces the appearance of its two parts in equilibrium. The equilibrium of the work, then, is the appearance of its calculus or measure in its rhythmical succession as divided by the pure word or the antirhythmical suspension.

Hölderlin suggests that, if the work's formal law were brought to appear in this way in tragic art, then this art could be posited as exemplary and, in its technical disposition, of no lesser stature than "the *mēchanē* of the ancients." The technical precision of this art would provide it with an infallibility as well as the formal basis for its reduplication. We glimpse here Hölderlin's obsessive concern with mastering the artistic process and assuring that there can be no mistake in the "principal moment," as he writes at the end of the extraordinary sentence that opens "Über die Verfahrungsweise des poetischen Geistes."[4] But above all, we should note here Hölderlin's primary concern with his *craft* and the fact that his meditation on tragic experience cannot be dissociated from a meditation on tragic poetry.[5] This is part of what Heidegger means when he says that Hölderlin's poetic thought always turns back

---

[4]A translation of this essay by Ralph R. Read III is presented in *German Romantic Criticism* (New York: Continuum, 1982), pp. 219–37.

[5]Andrzej Warminski emphasizes this important point in his essay "Hölderlin in France," *Studies in Romanticism* 22 (Summer 1983): 172–97.

upon poetry itself. But this reflexive turn does not suspend the phenomenological claims that Hölderlin is making; rather, we should recognize that Hölderlin, like Heidegger, is defining art as a fundamental event for the human Dasein. Art, for Hölderlin, is mimetic not in the sense of an *imitation* of what is, as it is defined by the aesthetic tradition after Plato, but rather in the more inclusive sense defined by Aristotle when he writes in his *Physics*, B (II, 8, 199a), "Generally art partly completes what nature cannot bring to a finish, and partly imitates [*mimeitai*] her."[6] For Hölderlin, as for Heidegger, art is necessary to the production of something like a world, and this necessary, supplemental function of art must be understood in relation to art's material nature. "Art" is something found in works—its event does not transcend its finite determination. Hence Hölderlin's preoccupation with the rhythm of Sophocles' texts and the strange attention he paid to the letter of these texts in his translations,[7] all of which answered to Hölderlin's sense of the propriety of Sophocles' language ("Eigentliche Sprache" [*SW*5, 266]) and the *justice* of his form of representation for his time ("Sophokles hat Recht. Es ist dies Schicksal seiner Zeit und Form seines Vaterlandes" [*SW*5, 272]).

Thus it can be misleading to say that the caesura *figures* the separation between men and gods that Hölderlin describes in his "Notes." The caesura first gives form to this separation and first allows it to be. And as the caesura appears only in the work's equilibrium, it functions very much like the composed Riss as it is described in "The Origin of the Work of Art." Hölderlin describes the separation to which I am referring in the following definition of tragic art:

> The presentation of the tragic rests principally upon this, that the monstrous [*das Ungeheure*], how the God and man couple, and how without limit the power of nature and the innermost of man become

[6]Jean Beaufret discusses the Aristotelian notion of mimesis in his "Hölderlin et Sophocle," in Friedrich Hölderlin, *Remarques sur Oedipe, Remarques sur Antigone*, ed. and trans. Jean Beaufret and François Fédier (Paris: Union générale d'éditions, 1965), p. 8. Beaufret refers to this Aristotelian definition of art in order to interpret Hölderlin's concept of the production of the natural by means of the nonnatural. It also appears quite explicitly in an essay such as "Grund zum Empedokles" (see, for example, *SW*4.1, 152).

[7]See the notes that accompany Lacoue-Labarthe's translation of Hölderlin's *Antigonä* in Friedrich Hölderlin, *L'Antigone de Sophocle* (Paris: Christian Bourgois, 1978).

one in fury, is conceived in that the limitless becoming-one is purified through limitless separation. [*SW*5, 201]

Hölderlin understands this separation primarily in temporal terms inasmuch as he seeks to represent it in a modern fashion (*SW*5, 268). Thus in the "Notes to Antigone," the God Zeus is named "the father of time," and in the "Notes to Oedipus," the cathartic event of separation is described as a veering of time:

> In such a moment man forgets himself and the God and turns about, indeed, in a pious fashion, like a traitor. At the extreme limit of suffering there remains in fact nothing more than the conditions of time or of space.
>
> At this limit man forgets himself because he is entirely within the moment; the God, because he is nothing but time; and both are unfaithful: time, because in such a moment it veers categorically, and in it beginning and end cannot rhyme whatsoever; man, because in this moment he must follow the categorical turning; and in this, what follows absolutely cannot resemble the initial situation. [*SW*5, 202]

Holding firm in this moment, man "stands there most openly in his character [*Karakter*]" (*SW*5, 266)—a description that we should probably understand in a literal or formal sense, since man stands forth in this way as a *sign*. (This assertion will form the center of Heidegger's reading of "Remembrance," a point missed by Allemann). Communication between the gods and men is preserved in this way, Hölderlin says, but beginning and end no longer accord. Countering in this way one of the fundamental propositions of Aristotle's description of tragedy in his *Poetics*, Hölderlin describes what I have termed the irreversible nature of Oedipus's tragic destiny. The tragic event marks a revolution of time—a revolution that preserves the past (men and gods communicate in their infidelity so that "the memory of those of the heavens should not fade" [*SW*5, 202]), but in a radically altered form. Man, following the "categorical veering" of the gods, can no longer return to his initial situation. There is no self-recovery in the tragic experience, as Hölderlin underscores when he writes that man "forgets himself." Defining the impossibility of self-appropriation in terms of this irreversible temporality, Hölderlin returns in a most severe manner to the Kantian notion of temporality as the fundamental condition of human subjectivity.[8]

If man thus "most openly" assumes an objective character and is able to hold or remain (*Bleiben*) in the categorical turn, this self-definition does not constitute a self-assumption or mastered self-consciousness. In the highest tragic consciousness, Hölderlin says, the soul swerves from consciousness (*SW*5, 267). Consciousness "then always compares itself with objects," as Hölderlin seeks to illustrate with the case of Niobe, and counts the simple passage of time—as Danaë—without projecting a future from its present. This "heroic hermit's life" (*SW*5, 268), a most firm dwelling (*festeste Bleiben*) before the progress of time (holding itself in this passage, but not holding it), is the highest consciousness, Hölderlin says.

Beaufret remarks that Danaë may well appear in Hölderlin's discussion of *Antigone* as a kind of figure for Oedipus who must longest endure the God's absence. But in fact, Hölderlin denies to Oedipus the same "simplicity" in his destiny. For while Oedipus manifests a "splendid harmonic form" (*SW*5, 198) at a moment of the tragic transport in which he is swept (a form that Hölderlin says "can yet stay" [*die doch bleiben kann*]), his hyperbolical drive to know exerts itself beyond itself and loses hold of itself. Could Oedipus then be the kind of exemplary tragic figure for Hölderlin that Heidegger wants him to be? To Oedipus's excessive transport there corresponds his long suffering, as present in *Oedipus at Colonus*. This is an experience of death or absence that is characteristically modern for Hölderlin in that death does not appear in corporal destruction, as is proper to Greek artistic form, but rather as a more spiritual suffering. In the contentment that Oedipus, at the beginning of *Oedipus at Colonus*, claims to have learned from time and suffering, Hölderlin may find a figure of a specifically modern dwelling that no longer shows the superlative beauty that belongs to Antigone's bearing. It may well be a figure of the contentment with which Hölderlin finally identifies, a contentment that speaks in the late poetry. But it is hardly clear that this figure

---

[8]Beaufret develops this point in "Hölderlin et Sophocle." See also Jean-Luc Nancy's "La joie d'Hyperion" (in *Les études philosophiques*, no. 2 (1983): 177–94) for a more extended discussion of Hölderlin's relation to Kant—one that is in part confirmed, I believe, by the reading of "In lovely blueness..." that I present here.

may serve the founding role that Heidegger would assign to it.

The divergence between Hölderlin's interpretation of Oedipus and Heidegger's understanding of this interpretation is most astonishing, as I have suggested, because the nature of the tragic destiny described by Hölderlin seems fundamentally related to that structure of existence described in *Being and Time*, in which the assumption of death as the extreme possibility of human existence (and with it the assumption of thrown possibility) *pushes* Dasein into the world and *binds* it in history. The relation seems most profound in that the same kind of binary structure is at work; in both cases, the event in question involves a double movement of approach and withdrawal that issues in a kind of passage that is the very movement of history and defines the conditions of historical existence. Hölderlin's notion of a temporally defined event of language (the caesura of the pure word) conditioning tragic existence would seem to define the foundation of the modern Dasein. It is true that the fate Hölderlin describes seems somehow more severe than Heidegger's own representation of the modern tragic fate, the need for binding more extreme (the backdrop for Hölderlin's readings of Sophocles' tragedies is his imminent "collapse"). But the logic at work in these readings is very close to that logic developed in *Being and Time* and in subsequent essays by Heidegger.

Indeed, in his lectures of 1934–35, Heidegger calls the task of holding the separation between the gods and man, between the earth and what Hölderlin calls "the savage world of the dead," the essence of the poetic, founding project of historical Dasein. In the fundamental tonality of mourning—which is the essence of the tragic experience—the poet occupies and founds the *Mitte des Seins*. This latter, Heidegger suggests, is to be understood in relation to the ontological difference.

But in speaking of founding this difference, Heidegger goes further than Hölderlin does in his "Notes" and in his later poetry. When Hölderlin writes "the holy be my word" (SW2.1, 118) in "As on a holiday," he does express such a desire for a saying that founds the relation between man and the divine. Heidegger interprets such a saying quite persuasively, I think, when he claims that it would articulate what is a properly *poetic* experience of the opening of the Open as Heidegger defines it in "The Origin of the Work of Art" (and as he defines it essentially in the lectures of

1934–35, which do not yet focus on the holy in an effort to name the gathering separation of men and gods). According to Heidegger, the holy must be understood in relation to the truth of Being.[9] Thus, when Heidegger, in his essay "As on a holiday," develops Hölderlin's notion of the holy in relation to his use of the word "nature" (which Heidegger locates initially close to the original Greek understanding of physis), he articulates this term with a series of notions that each names some aspect of the opening of the Open by which a law is posed for the discernment (from the Latin *discernere*, to separate and distinguish) of what is, and first for the distinction of men and gods: "The holy originarily decides beforehand concerning men and concerning the gods, whether they are and who they are and how they are and when they are" (*EHD*, 76). "Intimacy," then, names the gathering of what is in the firm statute posed by the "rigorous mediacy" of the holy (itself immediate); "spirit" (the name for nature as it inspires) is the unifying unity of the Auseinandersetzung by which everything is brought into the well-defined limits of its presence (*EHD*, 60). Both of these terms figure importantly in the essays under consideration here.

But in Hölderlin's "Notes," nothing indicates that the caesura, which marks the separation between men and gods, is anything more than a trace of a relation to an ungraspable alterity. To be sure, it *is* a sign of the holy (though it is nothing more than a rhythmical break); for Hölderlin, there *is* an opening to the divine presence that gives a law for the human Dasein. But the origin of the injunction (to "count time" or to "dwell") remains veiled. Thus Hölderlin asserts that Sophocles' authentic speech describes human understanding "as it advances under the unthinkable" (*SW*5,

[9]Karsten Harries's simple statement (in "Heidegger's Conception of the Holy," *Personalist* 47, no. 2 [Spring 1966]: 179) that the holy is the truth of Being is quite correct, I believe (though it passes somewhat quickly over the source of the difference that prompts Heidegger to distinguish between the tasks of the poet and the thinker). Thus, Heidegger can state in his *Letter on Humanism* that he reads the notion of *Heimat* in Hölderlin's "Homecoming" in his essay of 1943 in terms of the proximity to Being that is "there" of Dasein (*W*, 337/217). In this essay, in fact, Heidegger speaks not of a proximity to Being but of a proximity to the origin, and he defines this latter concept in relation to the notion of the holy. Heidegger is not imprecise here, for Heidegger's later elaboration of the fourfold entails precisely such an understanding of the holy as part of the "intense intimacy" of the infinite belonging of gods, mortals, earth, and sky. Below, I discuss further Heidegger's interpretation of the holy.

266). Hölderlin's certitude that there is such a law given and that a trace of the holy does offer itself will not falter in the poetry he writes after he names this law in his "Notes," but his own ability to grasp and to assume its injunction comes increasingly into question.

One might want to argue that Heidegger is describing in his reading of Hölderlin nothing more than Hölderlin's certitude (which for Heidegger always emerges in a questioning) concerning the fact that his poetic saying is a saying of the holy, even if it says no more than a trace of the holy. Heidegger's words in the opening pages of his essay "What Are Poets For?" (an essay devoted largely to Rilke but opening with an extended reference to Hölderlin) concerning the "near obliteration" (*H*, 251/95) of the traces of the holy in this destitute time between the flight of the gods and their return might suggest such an interpretation. But when Heidegger brings forth the "unsaid" of Hölderlin's poetry by reading it in terms of the history of Being and when he thereby ascribes to him a founding of the holy, he projects upon Hölderlin's desire for a poetic saying in a way that not only misrepresents the ever-increasing rigor with which Hölderlin defines the absence of God and the poet's stance in the history defined by this absence but also forecloses any understanding of the *questioning* that accompanies Hölderlin's search for the conditions of a measure for human existence.

To begin to describe how Heidegger "accomplishes" Hölderlin's poetic saying by projecting it in terms of his own thought of the history of Being and to suggest how Heidegger's reading diverges from the "poetic logic" of the "Notes," I would like to turn briefly to Heidegger's lectures of 1934–35. Since Heidegger refers to the "Notes" in his readings of both "Germania" and "Der Rhein" (poems that predate the "Notes") and since his argument in his readings of Hölderlin's later poetry will not invalidate the claims I want to describe here, I believe it is not inappropriate to introduce the contrast I want to establish by focusing on these lectures. There is a very clear development in Heidegger's reading of Hölderlin; Heidegger's increasing focus on the notion of the holy in Hölderlin's poetry and his attention to the implications of Hölderlin's notion of the "vaterländische Umkehr" (*SW*5, 271) certainly transform his reading. But the effort to define the founding character of Hölderlin's poetic saying also gives to Heidegger's reading of Hölderlin a remarkable continuity, as we see in Heidegger's consistent claim for the possibility of the founding of a poetic self. With this brief consideration of the 1934–35 lectures on Hölderlin, I particularly wish to introduce this last component of Heidegger's argument.

The contrast between the logic of the "Notes" and what Heidegger seeks in Hölderlin's *Stromdichtungen* appears most immediately when Heidegger describes the course of the Rhine, as it is presented in the poem to which the river gives its name, in terms that recall aspects of the destiny of Oedipus. The Rhine's destiny, Heidegger says, is the destiny of a "halfgod"—its being is the Mitte (the center or middle region) that defines or determines the being of both gods and men. To think the halfgod, as the poet does in "Der Rhein," is, as Heidegger states, to step into the founding differentiation (*Unterschied*) between gods and men and to bring this differentiation into question. "This thinking founds and breaks open the entire domain of being" (*HH*, 167).

The stream's destiny is a tragic one in that it is founded in conflict. The being of the stream first comes to *be* in the movement of revolt by which the stream turns back upon and assumes its origin. The revolt is a tragic "fault," but it is one that issues from the stream's original determination. At its origins, the stream manifests an "excess of will" (*HH*, 230)—a "blindness" in its original surge that derives from an origin that is uncanny and over-determining, and itself of a conflictual nature (the stream's origin is a reciprocal, differential relation of the earth and the gods). But the stream's original, excessive *Stromwillen* is broken with the irruption in it of a counterwill. The stream's counterwill brings it into necessity or distress (*Not*) and first makes it possible for the stream to encounter its destiny. By virtue of this *Gegenwille*, the stream's assumption of its destiny is a manifestation of freedom. The stream suffers its fate in an active sense; it carries out its fate not in the manner of a preordained lot but as a destiny that it creates. The stream's revolt—its entry into distress and its turn in a creative counterdecision—belongs to the "mystery" of Being (*Geheimniss*), and we may observe that it is the same mystery as that to which I pointed in Chapter 1 as I questioned the impetus for the passage from the experience of Unheimlichkeit to the decision that Heidegger terms "resolution."

In his reading of Hölderlin's Stromdichtung, Heidegger is describing the same event as that which forms the center of the existential analytic. We recognize, too, that the figure of destiny described here is that of Oedipus. Heidegger points to this fact when he writes:

> Now we sense to what extent these half-gods are the blindest—because they will to see, as no being ordinarily sees, because they have an eye too many: an eye for the origin. Such a vision is no unconstrained looking or retrospection, but rather the accomplishment of an original binding. This hostility of its essence, grounded in the origin itself, that urges to boldness only in order to will the preservation of the origin—that is the fault. [*HH*, 267]

Inasmuch as this tragic destiny entails a manifestation of freedom in an active assumption of destiny, we might suspect that the Oedipus that figures here owes as much to Schelling as it does to Hölderlin. As in a dialectical model, the tragic conflict here issues in, indeed produces, a unity (though this unity is to be thought not in terms of a synthesis but rather in terms of the unity in conflict described in "The Origin of the Work of Art"):

> In that which springs purely from its origin must the origin, as well as the having-arisen [*Entsprungensein*], unfold in the serenity of their determining powers. However, insofar as these, according to their essence, enter into conflict against themselves, they must unfold as more pure in highest hostility. But because hostility as supreme bliss constitutes the unity of Being, this unity must also gain, and better, retain the highest purity. [*HH*, 241]

As in the "Notes to Oedipus," in which tragic destiny entails a "turning about," we see in this description of the stream's course a "revolt." But the revolt allows an appropriation and founding of the origin's conflictual nature—a preservation and accomplishment of the conflict. Here, beginning and end accord as the stream comes into its own and achieves its destiny. I hardly need to emphasize that this description of the tragic conflict does not correspond with Hölderlin's description of the categorical veering that he finds in Sophocles' *Oedipus*. In Hölderlin's "Notes," we remember, the tragic "turn" marked a temporal caesura by virtue of which "beginning and end cannot rhyme whatsoever" and "what follows absolutely cannot resemble the initial situation." A "purifying separation" in the tragic conflict does in fact produce a lawful "equilibrium," but nothing in Hölderlin's "Notes" would allow us to describe this separation in terms of a gathering unity, as Heidegger does when he defines the reconciliation (Austrag, "settlement") of the tragic conflict as "intimacy" (*Innigkeit*).

We know from Hölderlin's own note to "Der Rhein" that he had sought to present in the final strophe of the poem a "total metaphor" reconciling the movement of the poem in a dialectical fashion.[10] It would thus seem that Heidegger is not unjustified in reading it in terms of a movement of reconciliaton and in seeking to find in the poem the "essential simplicity" of a "gesagte Innigkeit." The gathering and unifying movement of Being that Heidegger describes is certainly suggested in the great poems of the Hamburg period (consider, for example, the magnificent opening section of "Homecoming," which suits so well Heidegger's descriptions of the gathered nature of conflict). But insofar as Heidegger extends this understanding of Being to Hölderlin's later thought on tragedy, including the "Notes," he turns aside from the more radical thought of tragic "separation." This is the avoidance of Hölderlin's later thinking that Allemann sought to document in his lengthy study.

One more example of this avoidance may help to establish the point. As I have noted, Heidegger asserts that the poem, as it brings into speech and thereby founds the original relatedness of Being and Nonbeing that belongs to the origin, "stands before us as a 'holy chaos'" (*HH*, 259)—it is the birth of Dionysus, Heidegger suggests.[11] But as a "spoken intimacy," it is also the achievement

---

[10]Allemann cites this note and analyzes it in *Hölderlin und Heidegger,* pp. 141–42.

[11]Heidegger's identification of Dionysus as the essence of the halfgod is quite appropriate inasmuch as "Der Rhein" begins and ends with a reference to him. The poem's act of founding, Heidegger says, reaches into the *Grundbereich* designated with his name. But Heidegger's description of Dionysus is particularly worthy of notice, since it would seem to strain the notion of unity (in its "highest purity" as *Innigkeit*) that guides his interpretation: "He is the yes of the most savage, inexhaustible life in its creative urge, and he is the no of the most terrible death through annihilation. He is the bliss of enchanting captivation and the dread of a confused horror. He is the one while he is the other, that is, he is, while at the same time he is not; while he is not, he is. Being means for the Greeks, however, 'presence' [*Anwesenheit*]. Becoming present, this halfgod absents himself [*west dieser Halbgott ab*], and in becoming absent he presences. The emblem of the presencing absenting

of an essential simplicity. Again, it is the accomplishment of unity in and as conflict. This paradoxical essence of the poem derives from the "ambiguous" essence of language itself. Language is ambiguous or "double-edged," Heidegger says, because it is essentially dangerous. It is *the* danger, the most dangerous, in that it bears in it the opening of what is and thus creates the possibility of the "menace of being as such through nonbeing" (*HH*, 62). Through language, man stands exposed (*augesetzt*) in the "proximity and distance of the essence of things" (*HH*, 76); language opens to the "overwhelming" while it preserves a distance from it.

Heidegger's description of this double movement and the danger born in it recalls, of course, the definition of tragedy offered by Hölderlin in the "Notes," in which the presence of the tragic resides in a movement of unification and separation and in the presence of the God "in the figure of death." In fact, Heidegger illustrates this ambiguous essence of language with his only citations from the "Notes." From the "Notes to Oedipus," Heidegger draws Hölderlin's sentences on the essence of speech, which is said to bear the "powerful relations" (or *Grundstellungen*, to be compared with the notion of "fundamental metaphysical position") in which Oedipus stands in relation to the totality of what is. Oedipus's speech itself is said to bear the character of the Being that it opens to man as it "bears and conducts the confrontation with the overpowering power" (*HH*, 66). But while language participates in that character of the Being that it opens, it also guards man from the God: "Man turns against the God in it, guards himself against him" (*HH*, 66). Thus, Heidegger cites Hölderlin's words in the "Notes to Antigone" in which he says that the soul, in the highest moment of consciousness (in *Antigone*, a "sacred delirium"), confronts the God with a rash and even blasphemous word in order to preserve "the holy, living possibility of the spirit" (*HH*, 67). Language would thus be a kind of gapping or spacing by which there

---

and the absenting presencing is the mask. This is the preeminent symbol of Dionysus, that is, understood in a Greek and metaphysical fashion: the original relatedness to one another of Being and Not-being (presence and absence)" (*HH*, 189). This description, of course, recalls Nietzsche; indeed, Heidegger adds: "We know that the last, and at the same time futural, preparatory Western interpretation of Being by Nietzsche also names Dionysus" (*HH*, 191). Heidegger thus names with "Dionysus" the proximity of Nietzsche and Hölderlin as tragic thinkers.

is an opening to an overpowering relation of Being and Nonbeing that both preserves (*wahren*) this relation and preserves man from it (hence the protecting nature of truth, or *Wahrheit*).

The tragic "revolt" would thus be essentially a turn in language. But whereas in Hölderlin's "Notes" the language of tragedy is said to mark an irreversible temporality, in Heidegger's argument language, as the ground for a people's historical Dasein, founds a repetitive history that takes form in an increasing intensification and unfolding of essence.[12] In Hölderlin's description, the language of tragedy bears the presence of the God "in the figure of death"; correspondingly, in Heidegger's, it opens a proximity experienced as *Nichtigkeit*. In Heidegger's interpretation, however, this difference is recovered as the source of an ever more profound unity in the poet's creative preservation of the opening of Being.

For Heidegger, this unity manifests itself perhaps first of all in the unity of the poet's own being (a notion that finds an echo in Hölderlin's statements in his "Notes" concerning the accomplishment in tragedy of an equilibrium of faculties). For the poet's stance in relation to the intimacy of conflict drawn out in the poem is also defined as intimacy. His understanding of the "mystery" of Being preserves its character as a mystery—it is a "standing in" and "holding" of the mystery that Heidegger describes as "not just any enigma, the mystery is intimacy [*Innigkeit*], this latter, however, Being itself, the hostility of the conflicting powers, in which antagonism decision occurs regarding the gods and earth, men and everything that is made. Poetry, as the institution of Being, is the grounding manifestation of intimacy" (*HH*, 250–51). The poet stands in and founds by his saying this Auseinandersetzung, in which the being of the halfgod as the Mitte des Seins comes to define the relations of gods, men, and earth. The stream, whose essence is to create paths and borders for the history of a people

[12]Heidegger writes, for example: "All that is great is singular, but this singular has its own manner of constancy, that is, historically transformed and altered recurrence. Singular here does not mean present at one time and then gone at another, but rather: having been, and therefore in the constant possibility of a transformed development of essence, and consequently inexhaustibly disclosed in appropriation always anew, and becoming more powerful. . . . The great has greatness because, and insofar as, it has always a greater above it. This ability-to-have-beyond-itself of the greater is the mystery of the great" (*HH*, 144–46). Its being, that is to say, *consists in* repetition.

and whose course is the establishment of a land *as* a land and as a home, comes to be in the poet's saying. The destiny of the stream is in its essence the destiny of poetry, and to the destiny of the stream belongs the poet himself: "To these halfgods belong the creators themselves, to these latter, the poets. The Being of the poet is grounded in 'Nature' (Being as such), which originally says itself in poetry" (*HH*, 259).

In "Hölderlin and the Essence of Poetry," an essay that appears to be based largely upon the work presented in the 1934–35 lectures, Heidegger will take up this argument for the founded character of the poet's dwelling in the intimacy of Being and assert most clearly that this founding of a poetic self is a representative act for a people ("the poet holds out in the void of darkness, and by thus remaining true to the law of his own being, he brings about truth as a representative of his people and therefore can bring truth truly home to it" [*EHD*, 45]). In this essay, as I have noted, Heidegger asserts that Hölderlin's poetry distinguishes itself for the purposes of a meditation on the essence of poetry, inasmuch as Hölderlin's poetic determination (Bestimmung) is to poetize this essence. Hölderlin, he adds, is thus the poet of poetry. He approaches this assertion through five leitmotifs, the second of which is: "Therefore, man was given language, the most perilous of all blessings . . . that he bear witness to what he is." Explicating this phrase, Heidegger argues that for man to bear witness to what he is, he must show *who* he is: "Who is man? He is the one who must bear witness to what he is. To bear witness means to give evidence, but it also means to answer for the evidence that is being given. Man is *who* he *is*, precisely in the testimony he gives of his own existence. This testimony does not refer to an incidental expression of human nature coming after the fact; rather it contributes to the constitution of the human Dasein" (*EHD*, 36).

To show *who* is to posit a historically defined identity that is not accounted for with the properly philosophical question "*what is* man?" The question "what is man?" can be answered authentically only in a testimony that is an Auseinandersetzung of men, the gods, and things, as Heidegger explains in the course of the essay. (Both the lectures of 1934–35 and "Hölderlin and the Essence of Poetry" follow the argument of *An Introduction to Metaphysics*, as I presented it above.) As an Auseinandersetzung, this question of

191

man's identity is *constitutive* for man's essence, as Heidegger asserts in the passage I have just quoted. But Heidegger adds here that the testimony given in such a "performative" questioning authenticates or authorizes the answer inasmuch as the identity posed answers for the testimony given. Hölderlin's poetry, Heidegger suggests, is "guaranteed" as authentic inasmuch as Hölderlin posits *himself* in the act of reflecting on the essence of poetry. Thus, even though poetry is essentially endangered by the essence of language itself inasmuch as language can never overcome the ambiguous simplicity of its appearance (no word can ever guarantee its own authenticity, the second aspect of the danger to which Heidegger refers in the 1934–35 lectures), Hölderlin's poetry seems to offer itself as authentic by virture of the fact that Hölderlin offers *himself* in his speaking.[13]

But this in itself is a most dangerous act, Heidegger suggests, since it entails stripping from poetry its normally harmless appearance, thereby removing from it its protection against everyday life from which it is excluded. For this latter description of the isolation and veiling that protects this "most dangerous work," Heidegger refers somewhat ominously to Hölderlin's tragedy, "The Death of Empedocles," just as in a most astonishing way he quotes from this text Panthea's ecstatic description of Empedocles (assuming her words as his own to describe the poet) in order to illustrate the founded character of the poet's being.[14] It would appear, though

[13]David Halliburton provides a useful discussion of Heidegger's complex and ambiguous notion of the referent of Hölderlin "himself" in *Poetic Thinking*, pp. 86–91. Halliburton identifies too rapidly, in my view, the poet of "Remembrance" with the future poets to whom the poet's remembrance turns (for the nature of the poet's solitude must not be neglected), but he points out appropriately that the "me" of "Remembrance" is the poet *of* "Remembrance"—the one whose essence is realized in and by the poem.

[14]In "Hölderlin and the Essence of Poetry," Heidegger quotes the lines "To be him, that / Is life. And we others are but the dream of it" (*EHD*, 45); in the 1934–35 lectures, these lines appear in their full context to define the essence of the poet (*HH*, 215–16). Of particular interest is Delia's response (in the published lectures, Heidegger writes "Rhea" instead of "Delia"):

> I cannot find fault with what you say, dear friend
> Yet my soul is strangely grieved by it.
> And I would like to be as you
> And again would not want to. Are all of
> You then like this on this island? We too

suggested only by the rhetorical structure of Heidegger's argument, that the poet's gesture of self-identification, which forces us to decide whether we will take poetry seriously as the ground of our historical being (*EHD*, 34), is analogous to—and just as volatile as—Empedocles' act of presenting himself to the Agrigentine people as a semidivine, exemplary figure. If Heidegger only hints at this analogy in "Hölderlin and the Essence of Poetry," his reiteration of the phrase "the first born are sacrificed" in his lectures of 1934–35 and later in the essay "Remembrance," as I will note,[15]

> Have our joy in great men, and one
> Is now the sun of the Athenians,
> Sophocles!...
>
> . . . . .
>
> But our pleasure is untroubled
> And the good heart never loses itself so
> In painful, rapt homage.
> [*HH*, 215–16]

Delia's response ends as follows: "You sacrifice yourself—I believe he is / Too great to leave you peace / The unlimited you love without limit." In the commentary that follows his citation of these lines, Heidegger does not take Empedocles as the exemplary poet but rather takes Sophocles—despite the fact that Heidegger states elsewhere in the lectures that Hölderlin sought to fashion (*dichten*) in Empedocles the figure of the poet.

[15]The phrase "the first born are sacrificed" occurs twice in the interpretation of "Germanien." In both cases, the "sacrifice" is said to be the result of a kind of "historical struggle" that takes place in and through language. The first born (the poets) are "sacrificed" in that their original saying is lost in the mediation of everyday, "inauthentic" usage: "The highest pleasure of the first founding saying is at the same time the deepest pain of loss; the first born are sacrificed. The original language that grounds Being stands under the fate of necessary downfall: the flattening out in debased idle talk" (*HH*, 63). The second instance of the use of the phrase comes in relation to the poet's struggle to transform the "fundamental tonality" of a people (*HH*, 146), and as in the first, "sacrifice" seems a curiously strong word. Heidegger summarizes the position of the poet in relation to the "struggle for Being" when he writes, "The poet experiences poetically a creative downfall of the hitherto existing truth of Being, that is, in the dissolution he is captivated and carried away by the youthful and the new powers" (*HH*, 150)—words that recall the "thrusting down of the familiar" in "The Origin of the Work of Art" (*H*, 54/66), where the work is said to embody the struggle between the old gods and the new and where this struggle, again, is essentially one of and in language. In the lectures on Hölderlin, Heidegger remarks in this respect that a change in the experience of the essence of speech must come about if Dasein is to be brought back into the "original domain" of Being (*HH*, 64). In these descriptions of the "battle over Being," Heidegger may well be referring to Hölderlin's essay "Das Werden im Vergehen," in which Hölderlin describes the creative aspect of "authentically tragic language" through which "the *possible* enters into reality" (*SW*4.1, 283), and to

confirms that his tragic rhetoric is overdetermined by a dimension of tragic experience that is more or less effaced in the philosophical elaborations of German Idealism but powerfully present in Sophocles and increasingly constraining, as Lacoue-Labarthe has argued,[16] in Hölderlin's successive elaborations of his *Empedocles*. Heidegger, in other words, sets up Hölderlin as a *pharmakos* when he sets him up as exemplary—and Hölderlin's madness serves to warrant this sacralizing interpretation. The gesture, I would argue, is no more benign that Plato's own similar response to the poets. And we might surmise that it is motivated by a response to the same perceived danger, namely, the destabilizing character of mimesis as it appears in the plasticity of the poet's self-presentation: his capacity to move between voices and roles, and the *apparent* lack of propriety of poetic discourse.[17] Something in Hölderlin's poetry provokes in Heidegger what Girard calls mimetic violence.

In accounting for a response such as Heidegger's to Hölderlin's *text*, we must presume that the provoking element belongs somehow to the very structure of the linguistic act by which Hölderlin posits an identity in his written work (or posits the failure to achieve an identity). As the poet *of the poet*, Hölderlin somehow brings forth in poetry—which takes its essence from language itself—an abyssal dimension that threatens, perhaps even as it makes possible, the constitution of identity. Heidegger has pointed to this dimension of poetic language in "The Origin of the Work of Art," I believe, by referring to the concealment that occurs in poetry. The event of truth in art is originary, as we have seen in Heidegger's essay, and thus the work of art must necessarily play a determinant role in the constitution of its "preserver's" very identity. Though the preserver's response cannot be simply passive, the work of art opens the possibility of its own reception. The ambiguity of the work's "strange beauty" (residing in the double concealment that I described in Chapter 4) might then be understood as the

Hölderlin's designation of Empedocles as a sacrificial victim in "Grund zum Empedokles" (*SW*4.1, 156).

[16]"La césure du spéculatif," pp. 213–14.

[17]For a discussion of Plato's own recourse to this ritual mechanism, see Derrida's "La pharmacie de Platon," in *La dissémination* (Paris: Editions du Seuil, 1972), pp. 69–197, translated by Barbara Johnson in *Dissemination* (Chicago: University of Chicago Press, 1981), pp. 61–172. See also Lacoue-Labarthe's "Typographie."

source of a fundamental distress. The work will both prompt self-definition and call it constantly into question.

But Heidegger's description of the fascinating or unsettling nature of the work remains quite indirect in "The Origin of the Work of Art"; I would argue, in contrast, that Heidegger is attempting to describe formally what he finds so arresting in Hölderlin's language and what it means for a poetic act to be exemplary, when he attempts to define how Hölderlin's poetry works reflexively as it poetizes the essence of poetry and thus of the poet. He does this most explicitly in his reading of "Remembrance," and so I would like to turn now to this reading and follow Heidegger's argumentation somewhat more closely than I have thus far. The claims Heidegger makes for the act of poetic founding are essentially the same as those of his readings of the mid-1930s, and thus I will be able to reinforce a contrast that I have sought to establish between Hölderlin's understanding of what it means to dwell in the nearness of Being in the time of God's absence, and Heidegger's understanding of this poetic act. This analysis of Heidegger's reading of "Remembrance" will also allow me to demonstrate the persistence of Heidegger's most fundamental claims for poetry and for the relation it founds between Being and human being, beyond the period of Heidegger's writing that is distinguished (as I have tried to demonstrate) by its tragic tones. The concern with selfhood and with the grounding of the human Dasein remains a priority for Heidegger beyond the period of his description of an essentially tragic self-affirmation—and it remains no less a problem.

The reflexive nature of "Remembrance," Heidegger asserts, is already marked in the title of the poem.[18] The title does not indicate that the poem contains a description of something remembered—it is not a poetic account, for example, of the poet's trip to Bordeaux but rather a poetic saying of the essence of remembrance (*Andenken*) itself. The poetic truth of this essence is said poetically in this poem, meaning that this essence is first founded in the poem. The essence of remembrance thus founded, Heidegger says, is "the essence of the poetic thinking of the future

---

[18]The full text of the poem, with Michael Hamburger's translation, appears below in Appendix 1.

poets [of Germany]" (*EHD*, 84). The poem "Remembrance" poses in an initial or originary fashion the essence of remembrance.

But if the poem works in this originary way, it is because this poem's own mode of poetic saying is remembrance. "Remembrance," as Heidegger defines it, is letting what has been unfold initially as what is to come. ("Initially," because what has been exists in no simple past. It is not found, Heidegger says, nor is it made; rather, it is projected or predicted in a manner that remains an opening or "letting happen.") The poem "Remembrance," of itself, turns upon or turns to remembrance in this fashion, letting a poetic destiny that has been given—and a fitting (*Geschicklich*) mode of saying—unfold in a way that is historical not simply because this letting-happen answers to a history (of Being) but also because this answering is an active transformation that initially poses or trans-poses this destiny.

We should recognize in this performance the structure of the hermeneutic circle. "Remembrance" is a speech act that opens the conditions of its own performance; it poses them initially with the act of defining the nature of remembrance (late in his essay, Heidegger says that we recognize poetry in such an event of the constitution of a new genre [*EHD*, 138]). It *enacts* a mode of poetic saying, both posing the law or rule for such a saying and being itself such a saying. It is a speech act that takes form and founds itself in a reflection upon its own performance. Whether or not speech act theory can account for such a proposition, this event is nevertheless fully characteristic of Heidegger's writing (or at least we can say that Heidegger's writing works constantly toward such an event; *Being and Time*, as I have suggested, would be such a project that describes itself). The riddle of Heidegger's extraordinary preference for Hölderlin may lie in large measure in Heidegger's fascination before Hölderlin's repeated enactment of such a reflexive mode of enunciation.

The self-reflexive nature of "Remembrance" is understood by Heidegger in terms of a complex structure of repetition that is signaled with the opening words of the poem. These words, he says, break a concealed silence: the silence of the decision to will that the wind should be as that wind that has opened the time-space [*Zeit-Raum*] out of which the poet may will the destiny that comes to him and out of which he may name this will, thereby posing a time and place for this founding act. "The north-easterly blows . . . go now" is an enunciation that corresponds precisely to the performative utterance that is made manifest or is "spoken" by the work of art as it projects its createdness, as Heidegger describes it in "The Origin of the Work of Art." The act of creation is created into the work, as we have seen, and the work brings forth, literally, the phrase "dass es sei" ("that it be"). Heidegger isolates the famous lines from "As on a holiday"—"But now day breaks. I waited and saw it come, / And what I saw, the holy be my word" (*das Heilige sei mein Wort*)—as a similar performative enunciation; in fact, Heidegger designates these lines as the initial lines with which Hölderlin assumes his poetic destiny. So, just as Heidegger implies in "The Origin of the Work of Art" that the work brings forth the artist's creative act, his offering "that it be" (that truth should be offered a site for its appearance), Heidegger argues in "Remembrance" that the poet's will (his assumption of his destiny) is brought forth in the poem and situated in the space it opens: "The poem does not express the poet's experiences, but rather takes the poet into the domain, opened as a poem, of his essence" (*EHD*, 151). The poem thus brings forth and founds (marking its time and place) a relation in which the poet already stands and which is the source of his poetic act. I have said that Heidegger's fascination for Hölderlin may be explained in relation to the structure of Hölderlin's poetic saying. I might add now that Heidegger finds in Hölderlin's poetry a mode of saying that realizes what Heidegger terms the "step back," or that circling by which a saying would point beyond itself in such a way as to become a sign of the relation (the opening to Being) that makes it possible and that must escape any representational mode of description.[19]

The wind gives its movement to the entire poem, we might say, since it is a figure that embraces all poles of the journey that the poem commemorates. The wind promises an experience of the

---

[19]Karsten Harries addresses the problem of language's pointing beyond what he calls its "ontic" aspect in "Heidegger and Hölderlin: The Limits of Language." Harries focuses upon Heidegger's privileging of the individual word's isolated meaning over its grammatical determination. But with Heidegger's emphasis on *aber* in his reading of "Remembrance" (to which I will turn), as well as his emphasis upon the poem's movement, we see that rhythm, syntax, and tone must also be accounted for in defining the distinctive reflexive character of poetic saying.

heavenly fire of the foreign land (the appearance of the holy) by favoring the voyage south; in so doing, it clears the northern sky, bringing forth the essential properties of this sky of the homeland. At the same time, it salutes those already in the south, calling upon them to return. Promising the foreign land and calling back to the homeland, the wind also figures the poet's own act of poetic remembrance. As it goes forth, Heidegger says, it remains.

Heidegger's interpretation works toward an understanding of precisely such a remaining (Bleiben) and thus turns upon an interpretation of the last line from "Remembrance"—virtually a leitmotif for his meditation on poetry—"But the poets found what remains" (*Was bleibet aber, stiften die Dichter*, translated by Hamburger as "But what is lasting the poets provide"). Heidegger will define "what remains" in terms of the poet's own poetic dwelling in his homeland near the origin. The act of remembrance, he argues, founds the poet's dwelling or remaining in proximity to the origin in that it consists in an appropriation of what is proper to the poet in his homeland through a constant recalling of the experience of the holy in a foreign element. The poet has already received his proper capacity for poetic exposition when he begins the act of remembrance; he has already undertaken the journey to the foreign land and experienced the holy fire, and he has already been given the free use of his proper mode of exposition that must now be learned—that is, appropriated in such a way that it is founded for the coming poets (let us recall Hölderlin's concern with such a founding in the opening paragraphs of his "Notes to Oedipus"). The repetition marked with the opening of the poem thus signals, we might say, that the poet's proper capacity has been released to him in his previous journey between the home and the foreign land; the act of remembrance, however, represents the acquisition of this capacity and its historical definition.

Heidegger defines the relation between the foreign (*das Fremde*) and the proper (*das Eigene*) in the terms of Hölderlin's letter to Böhlendorff of December 4, 1801, in which Hölderlin states that nothing is more difficult to learn than the free use of the proper (also what is "natural" or "national"). Heidegger draws from Hölderlin's remarks what he terms Hölderlin's "law of history": what is proper or natural for a people can be appropriated only when it is founded historically in an encounter with what is foreign for that people. This law, Heidegger argues, led the poet into a kind of exile. The natural for the German people, Hölderlin says, is clarity of exposition (*Klarheit der Darstellung*). Heidegger interprets this trait as the ability to grasp a destiny through the capacity for setting up frameworks, classifying, articulating, and disposing— these terms all pointing to Heidegger's later meditation on the essence of modern *Technik*. The German foreign, on the other hand, is defined by Hölderlin as "beautiful passion" and corresponds, in the chiasmic structure of terms that Hölderlin posits in defining the relation between the Germans and the Greeks, to the "holy pathos" of the Greeks and their relation to the "heavenly fire" that secures for them, as Heidegger puts it, "the approach and nearness of the gods" (*EHD*, 87). This Greek natural corresponds to the German foreign, then, just as the Greek foreign— what they mastered through their art or culture—corresponds to what is natural for the modern German.

Heidegger appropriates these definitions of the foreign and the proper for his reading of "Remembrance" in a fairly abstract manner. He does not pose the question of the relation between the modern proper (clarity of exposition) and a foreign that it might encounter in Greece (the Greek proper corresponding to the modern foreign) in terms of a relation between modern and Greek *art*, as Hölderlin does by positing his "law of history" in relation to the question of the ancients and the moderns. Were he to have done so, he would have had to recognize that access to the modern proper through an artistic encounter with the Greek proper is a more problematic task than the one he describes—in brief, he would have had to recognize the necessity of translation.[20]

[20]Lacoue-Labarthe has opened this question in an exemplary manner in his essays "La césure du spéculatif" and "Hölderlin et les grecs," *Poétique* 40 (1979): 465–74. Andrzej Warminski, in "Hölderlin in France," also provides a cogent discussion of Hölderlin's notion of the relation between Greece and Hesperia. See also here his analysis of Peter Szondi's reading ("Überwindung des Klassizismus," in *Hölderlin-Studien* [Frankfurt am Main: Insel Verlag, 1967], pp. 85–104) of Hölderlin's letter to Böhlendorff of December 4, 1801. I might add that while Heidegger fails to take up the problem of the relation between modern and Greek art in this fairly schematic presentation of the relation between the "natural" or "proper" and the "foreign" in "Remembrance," he is nevertheless quite attentive elsewhere to the distinctive character of Hölderlin's position on the question of the ancients and the moderns. One may consult on this point the remark on "Remembrance" that appears in the *Letter on Humanism* (*W*, 339/219).

Hölderlin signals the problematic nature of the relation between Greek and modern art (and signals his break from a Winckelmannian classicism) when he says in his letter to Böhlendorff that, "aside from that which has to be the highest for the Greeks and for us, namely the living relation and the skill, we ought not to have anything in *common* with them" (*SW*6.1, 426). The Greeks are "indispensable," but they cannot be imitated: first, as Hölderlin suggests in his letter, because their art is the product of a specific destiny and corresponds in its distinctive character to the modern natural—we cannot deduce from it, Hölderlin says, laws for modern art or culture. But Hölderlin's "eye too many" also makes him see in Greek art what might be termed an *excessive* mastery or appropriation of what is foreign for the Greeks: the clarity of exposition provided by the "junonian sobriety" of the West. In the very splendor of Greek culture, Hölderlin finds the sign of a Greek failure to appropriate what is proper or natural to them: the "holy pathos." Hölderlin sought to correct just such a failure in his translations of Sophocles, as he indicated to his editor.[21]

In other words, translation for Hölderlin was a means of repeating, by a kind of après-coup, as Lacoue-Labarthe puts it, what never happened in Greek art.[22] Such a notion of translation, of course, cannot be understood in terms of a model of adequation, or in terms of a process of recovery of meaning. For the "unsaid" that Hölderlin seeks to bring forth in the process of translation cannot be defined as a *signified* of any kind: it has no place (even as a veiled or reserved meaning) before its repetition.

While Heidegger's definition of "remembrance" might be made to accomodate itself to such a project (as I want to show), he bypasses the question of the modern relation to Greek art in his discussion of the relation between the proper and the foreign and focuses instead on Hölderlin's description of his trip to France in the letter to Böhlendorff written after his catastrophic journey. In that letter, Hölderlin says he was "struck by Apollo," a figure for an experience of the heavenly fire. But it should be noted that Heidegger does not rest his interpretation upon biographical data in this way; rather, he is interpreting the poet's voyage as itself a

---

[21]See the letter to Friedrich Wilmans of September 18, 1803 (*SW*6.1, 434).
[22]"La césure du spéculatif," p. 204.

figure of a law that defines the course of Hölderlin's poetic experience. In this way, Heidegger can suggest that the foreign encountered by Hölderlin is not the proper of Greece but is rather a more initial, more oriental source. Hölderlin repeats more originally, it seems, the Greek beginning. But we might assume that only by sidestepping Hölderlin's *reading* of the Greeks (and particularly as it takes shape in a project of translation) is Heidegger able to present this original encounter as a *domestication* of the foreign.

"Domestication" may be too strong, but the economy that Heidegger describes in defining the relation between the proper and the foreign is sufficiently closed to have prompted Beda Allemann to argue that this relation is thought by Heidegger in the dialectical terms of the metaphysics of subjectivity. Allemann finds evidence for his argument in Heidegger's interpretation of lines from a late revision of "Bread and Wine":

> For Spirit is not at home
> In the beginning, not at the source. It is consumed by the homeland
> Colony spirit loves, and bold forgetting.[23]

Allemann contests on primarily philological grounds Heidegger's assertion that these lines describe the "law of history" of the poetic spirit. His point is that one cannot import the master term of German Idealism into an interpretation of Hölderlin's late poetry without recognizing the profound displacement to which Hölderlin subjects it. Allemann's criticism does not in fact withstand an attentive reading of Heidegger's use of the term "spirit," though I believe that Allemann is correct in finding in Heidegger's presentation an argument that points to the absolute metaphysics of Hegel insofar as Heidegger describes a movement of the same to the same through *its* other in the course of his description of the "law of history."[24] I would differ from Allemann merely by suggesting

[23]Allemann cites these lines and discusses them in *Hölderlin und Heidegger*, pp. 168–73.

[24]By asserting that Heidegger understands the term "spirit" in its Idealist sense (*Hölderlin und Heidegger*, see pp. 167–69), Allemann fails to take account of Heidegger's argument in the lectures of 1934–35, in which Heidegger identifies the spirit in question with Dionysus, and fails to consider how Heidegger is in the process of reworking the term in his reading of "As on a holiday." (A similar argument might be made concerning Heidegger's use of the term "real," which Allemann hastens to

that Heidegger situates this dialectical moment within a movement of repetition that exceeds it (thereby opening up the speculative economy and permanently suspending it), rather than somewhat forcibly imposing it upon Hölderlin's poetry in order to bring forth all the more visibly Hölderlin's "leap beyond metaphysics."

It seems odd, in fact, that Allemann does not attend a bit more closely to Heidegger's use of the term "spirit" in order to substantiate his thesis. Even if we recognized a more properly Heideggerian definition of this term (following Heidegger's argument in "Homecoming"), the movement Heidegger describes in accounting for spirit's "inspiration" of the poet and the relation of the poetic spirit to its origin follow a strictly controlled economy. Poetic spirit, Heidegger says, desires immediate access to its home as a proximity to the origin, but the home closes to any immediate appropriation and with this movement directs the spirit to a foreign that allows spirit to remain oriented to its home. The poetic spirit is given the foreign as a *colony* of the homeland, Heidegger says, and goes to meet the "heavenly fire" in the foreign land (with the repose, the circumspection, and the constancy that already belong to being at home but are not yet appropriated as such) already sheltered by the homeland, as it recognizes upon its return (*EHD,* 95). This recognition, following the chiasmic structure of the apparently closed economy Heidegger describes, turns into a knowledge that, without the experience of the heavenly fire, the gift of the poet's proper capacity for poetic exposition would never have been given to him as his own.

This is, we might say, a most happy Oedipal scenario—though I use the term this time in a more psychoanalytical sense. Spirit is directed away from its motherland (*Mutterland* [*EHD,* 93]) so that it will not consume its forces in its desire for immediate access to the origin. But it is directed to the foreign land and the fire of the

---

identify as a kind of Idealist marker; a more attentive reading would interpret this term in relation to Heidegger's interrogation of it throughout "The Origin of the Work of Art.") Of course, Allemann will recognize that the "formal parallelism" he defines between Heidegger's interpretation of the "law of historicity" and spirit's departure from and return to self in the metaphysics of subjectivity neglects profound differences (for example, between spirit's return to self and proximity to the origin in the return to the proper). Allemann suggests that Heidegger underscores a metaphysical moment in Hölderlin only in order to show better its overcoming.

heavens (lightning, Heidegger notes, is Hölderlin's privileged sign for the heavenly father), already sheltered by the motherland so that it will not be consumed in turn by this fire. Finally, the fire orients spirit back to the motherland: "The fire has let it experience that it must be brought back out of the foreign to the homeland, so that there the proper, the capacity for clear exposition should loosen its essential powers in relation to the fire in order to bind them in what is to be exposed" (*EHD*, 94). In spirit's desire for immediate access to the origin, Heidegger may recognize the theme of a dangerously excessive desire that must be bound and thus answer to Hölderlin's need for articulation of the "vaterländische Umkehr" somewhat more faithfully than Allemann suggests.[25] But it is clear that Heidegger understands the binding of this desire in a far less severe manner than does Hölderlin in his late thinking and that he defines it more in terms of a mediation of spirit's relation to the origin than in terms of the pure differentiation or caesura that Hölderlin describes in his "Notes." "Mediation" is itself an inadequate term, because in speaking of binding the powers of exposition in what is to be exposed, Heidegger wants to describe the establishing of a proximity or nearness (as I shall demonstrate), and not an appropriation of the origin as immediate—the Hegelian schema is not ultimately applicable to Heidegger's analysis. But Heidegger seems much closer to Hegel than to Hölderlin when he defines the establishment of a proximity in terms of the *measuring* of a founding difference.

The appearance of a kind of dialectical movement in Heidegger's argument is not limited to his interpretation of the late lines from

[25]Allemann argues that the "vaterländische Umkehr" must be understood not in terms of a relation between Greece and Hesperia (or between a homeland and foreign land) but rather in terms of the relation of mortals to the absent gods and the world of the dead. Allemann insists that the turning or reversal to which Hölderlin refers entails a movement of differentiation by which the mortal desire for unification with the divine would be bound and a "sober" dwelling on the earth would be possible. Here again, I would agree in large measure with Allemann's reading (particularly as he seeks to contrast it with that of his predecessors—see his criticism of Beissner and Michel, pp. 41–45), but I believe that Allemann's effort to avoid reading the reversal in terms of the relation between Greece and Hesperia leads him to neglect important aspects of Hölderlin's meditation on history. Allemann's reading of the first and last lines of "Patmos," for example (p. 175), seems just, but he must neglect the entire central portion of the poem, just as he cannot account for the necessity Hölderlin perceived in *translating* Sophocles.

"Bread and Wine." If Heidegger was misguided by the tradition of Hölderlin criticism in his interpretation of the term "spirit" (a most unlikely hypothesis, given Heidegger's sensitivity to the language of the metaphysics of subjectivity—one that Allemann only partially retracts after offering it), he nevertheless repeats the analysis of the economy of movement that I have described late in his essay when he argues that the answer to Hölderlin's question concerning the nature of remembrance unfolds finally with the phrase "But it is the sea / That takes and gives remembrance." The sea takes the memory of the homeland, Heidegger says, and thus allows the poet the experience of the foreign that he will transform as he appropriates his proper mode of exposition in his homecoming. But the sea also gives memory as it takes. The sight of the foreign awakens remembrance of the proper, which anticipatory remembrance forgets the "merely foreign" in the foreign and transfigures it in such a way that it preserves what in the foreign is *for* the proper.

This remembrance is not pure, Heidegger says, for there is a forgetting; but Heidegger has established that there can be no pure remembrance (otherwise there would have been no need for a detour through the foreign), and it is clear that, through the economy of forgetting, nothing is lost. The poet's exile, in other words, is certainly less aggressive than a colonialism, in Heidegger's account, but perhaps not more risky than tourism, however superior Heidegger finds it to adventurism. In other accounts, as I have noted, Heidegger addresses a danger in poetic experience; but I need not pause here, I think, to reiterate that I take Hölderlin's experience of "exile" to be far more radical than Heidegger implies. Let it suffice for me to suggest that Hölderlin is referring to his voyage south (though again, as Heidegger points out, this voyage is itself a figure of the movement of poetic experience—already a kind of narrative) when he says in the second version of "Mnemosyne": "and we have almost / Lost our speech in a foreign land" (*SW*2.1, 195).

But before concluding that Heidegger simply reduces Hölderlin's law of history to a dialectical relation of same and other, we must note that what I have called a closed economy of remembrance moves between poles that are never fully appropriated in that movement. Spirit has no immediate access to the heavenly fire that it must say poetically, and it always is only in the process of appropriating what is proper to it. The more it appropriates its proper skill of clarity in exposition, the more it approaches the holy, whose advent is promised in the remembrance of what has been. Both the skill in Darstellung and the holy that is to be exposed remain always to come. This kind of open-ended movement is indeed quite characteristic of Hölderlin's thinking. And I would agree fully with Heidegger's demonstration, which I will try now to unfold, that the poet's remembrance does no more than announce this coming by reflecting upon the conditions of its enunciation. What is problematic, I want to argue, is Heidegger's assertion that this reflexive movement grounds the poet's saying and first of all his self, and that this self-grounding manifests a self-grounding unity of Being.

The fact that we must not simply reduce Heidegger's notion of poetic remembrance to the terms of the metaphysics of subjectivity is indicated by Heidegger in a most subtle way as he begins to describe the poet's actual repetition of his original encounter with the holy. This repetition takes the form of a greeting, carried by the wind, to what the poet has already encountered. The greeting, Heidegger says, lets what is greeted unfold in its essence and thereby gives it its essential place (*Wesensstätte*). It *measures* a proximity between the one who greets and the greeted, in which both of these poles of the greeting are brought back into the proper distance of their respective essences. This measuring of a proximity, of course, is to be understood in terms of Heidegger's consistent manner of describing a relation that first founds the terms of the relation (though in light of his previous discussion of the transfiguring nature of forgetting and in light of the greeting's being said to strip the greeted of its "false individuality" and give it a place to stand [*EHD*, 96], this remembrance seems distinctly appropriative). In the essays considered thus far, we have seen such a relation described as a conflict; here Heidegger tends to describe it more in terms of love (see also the passage devoted to the concept of love itself [*EHD*, 143]). But in this context, and given the psychosexual resonances of so much of Heidegger's description, this repetition of a relation that measures and articulates the relation, resembles nothing so much as a complex version of the game Freud described as "Fort/Da."

205

The greeting takes shape in a movement of figuration that is markedly specular. It moves through a landscape as it approaches a prefiguration of the advent of the holy—a landscape held open by the "gaze" of two trees that dominate it and that is defined and rendered fertile by a stream figuring (as Heidegger argues for all of Hölderlin's stream imagery) the poetic spirit. Hölderlin thus begins by saluting a figure of himself as the poet of this founding remembrance and moves through the landscape to salute the oak and white poplar, which appear as parental figures (Heidegger remarks that in saluting this "noble pair," Hölderlin thinks of the day of his departure and the beginning of his poetic destiny). The persistence of a familial configuration in Heidegger's reading (at work at several levels, as we have seen) merits emphasis and undoubtedly further attention. Heidegger may well be answering in his characteristically indirect manner the discourse of psychoanalysis. Here I shall note simply that if Hölderlin's remembrance is autobiographical in nature for Heidegger—it will terminate finally, as Heidegger reads it, with a figure that conflates the poet's birth and his marriage—this autobiography (the term, as we will see, is very problematic in this context) recounts not the history of an individual subject but that of poetic destiny. The "gaze" of the oak and white poplar issues from a play of light and shadow in which Heidegger finds also the difference of concealment and unconcealment. For Heidegger, the poet's "origin" must first be thought in these terms.

Accordingly, what first appears as a specular movement of remembrance reveals itself to be a quite different movement of poetic reflection. Heidegger introduces this point by pausing before explicating Hölderlin's greeting as it takes shape in the description of the landscape and remarking that what rises so purely before the reader's sight needs no commentary. This remark does not merely reiterate a commonplace of aesthetics; or rather, it reiterates an aesthetic commonplace in order to underscore the fact that the image Heidegger is reading must be *read* as pointing beyond its distinct quality as an *image*. Heidegger is signaling to us that the image of the landscape offers itself at first as the kind of image produced by those poets who have not yet returned from their voyage (to which the poet's thought turns late in the poem) and who gather the beauty of the earth like "painters" (*EHD*, 135). These poets still work under the domination of the Platonic concept of beauty: "They allow Being (the idea) to appear [*erscheinen*] in the aspect of the visible" (*EHD*, 135). But Heidegger's interpretation of the line that follows the salute to the "noble pair" suggests that the initial salute is already *aufgehoben*, raised to another level of reflection. The movement of reflection here, however, is not to be thought in a Hegelian fashion. What Heidegger initially describes at the end of his essay (*EHD*, 151) as a kind of climbing that retains in memory the levels of reflection that it has passed through is finally designated as a *fugue* articulated around the word "but." This word indicates transition, Heidegger says, and thus marks a movement in Hölderlin's poetry; but it also marks a kind of interruption and a retention (a moment of catching breath). "Aber" is not a negation or a simple qualification but, rather, *marks the relation to an alterity*; it gives a kind of rhythmical scansion to Hölderlin's poetic thought and also sets the poem's "hidden tone" (*EHD*, 151). Thus the phrase "Still well I remember this" ("Noch denket das mir wohl"), which Heidegger lists among the linguistic forms expressing Hölderlin's "but," is said to "bind the greeted that has been to what greets in coming" (*EHD*, 99).[26]

"Still well I remember this," then, does not simply punctuate the salute; it marks the poet's awareness that he greets as one who has been given to greet what has been, that he greets as one already greeted: "It is not the poet who addresses the greeted to himself in thought, rather the greeted addresses itself to his thought" (*EHD*, 99). The image of the landscape, though initially appearing as a kind of mirror for the poet's speculation, or rather specular remembrance, now appears as a prefiguration of what approaches the poet. The phrase "noch denket das mir wohl" is transitional, Heidegger says, and obliges the poet to think of what has been as what is coming. Thus, the images that follow as Hölderlin continues to move through the landscape now appear in what I have previously termed a "strange beauty."

Heidegger remarks upon this mode of appearance when he comments the lines, "On holidays there too / The brown women walk." Heidegger first discusses the appropriateness of the appearance of women in the remembrance of the time of celebration that

---

[26]Hölderlin's use of the word "but" bears comparison with Blanchot's use of the word "pas." See Derrida's analysis of Blanchot's strategic disruption of dialectic with this term in "Pas," *Gramma* 3/4 (1976): 111–215.

prepares a marriage. He then notes that the projective or prefigurative nature of these lines appears with the term *Daselbst*:

> In order to hold the distant with its distant presencing near, the poet says this there [*daselbst*], which to the modern ear harshly borders upon juridical or commercial language.... But above all, the poet at this time so little shrinks back from what first appears as an unpoetic and strange word that he goes toward it for just that reason to listen to it. He knows that the purer the invisible is to be, the more decisively it requires that the naming word yield to the strange image. [*EHD*, 108]

The image of the women appears with the strangeness of what resides near the origin. What Hölderlin wants to show, the distant presencing of the distant, Heidegger asserts, is properly invisible (in contrast to the *eidos* brought to appearance by "painterly" poets). Nothing of the origin is shown by Hölderlin, except its nearness, which appears in the strangeness of an image that is marked by a kind of "interior distance."[27] We will see that in Heidegger's reading it is the poet himself who shows this proximity by dwelling near the origin. He shows, Heidegger says, with his *zeigendes Anblick* (showing look)—the eye too many that opens as the poet comes to dwell. But the poet's look only appears in what is seen, in the figure. The poet's reflection on his own dwelling, by which he shows or indicates an origin *beyond his seeing*, moves through the figure and beyond it—back upon the conditions of its visibility; but it does so always *through* the figure. The figure marks this movement by appearing within the distance opened by the poet's gaze; it bears this distance and thus marks the conditions of its visibility. But the movement of poetic thought (remarked with the words that convey Hölderlin's "aber") is bound by the figure and thus remains bound to a reflection upon figureability. Hölderlin in his poetry simply *reflects* the conditions of a saying of the holy, though such a reflection, Heidegger argues, is already an enunciation. I will return to this point, but I want to note with this

---

[27] I borrow this term from Blanchot. See his essay "La voix narrative," in *L'entretien infini* (Paris: Gallimard, 1969), pp. 562–63. A translation of this essay by Lydia Davis appears in Maurice Blanchot, *The Gaze of Orpheus* (New York: Station Hill Press, 1981), pp. 133–43.

description of the strangeness Heidegger finds in Hölderlin's imagery that the logic of the finitude of truth that Heidegger describes in "The Origin of the Work of Art" directs his meditation on Hölderlin.

As the poet's remembrance moves toward the women of the southern land, it moves, as I have indicated, toward a reflection on the holiday and on the marriage festival for which this holiday prepares. Heidegger interprets the marriage in question as one of men and gods, taking his lead from Hölderlin's "Der Rhein." We may also recall, of course, a more brutal description of this "coupling" in the "Notes to Oedipus." The fruit of this marriage, Heidegger argues, is what Hölderlin terms the "halfgod"; these are the streams that "must become signs" ("Der Ister," cited at *EHD*, 103) and are therefore the poets. Thus, as the poet thinks back to the preparation for the festival that is to come, he thinks toward his own birth. The birth that the poet commemorates (and thus is in the process of repeating) occurs on the day, Heidegger says, in which the poet sees come what his word must say. As I have noted, the lines from "As on a holiday," "But now day breaks / I waited and saw it come, / And what I saw, the holy be my word" are taken by Heidegger to be Hölderlin's first lines as the poet whose task is to say the holy.

As the fruit of the marriage between men and the gods, the poet is called upon to hold open the relation between them as the dissimilar (*das Ungleiche*) and to endure this inequality. Unlike either gods or men, the halfgod preserves the "between" (*Zwischen*) out of which men and gods return into their proper beings. In this *Auseinandersetzung*, destiny finds its equilibrium (*Ausgleich*), a balanced differentiation of men and gods that preserves their essential differences and in which the dwelling of the poet as Ungleiche is founded. With his founded dwelling, the poet thus opens the lingering (*die Weile*)[28] that is the measure of any authentic dwelling (including that of the poet) and the essential origin of history. Everything that is in coming has its coming in relation to the lingering as the unique that has been; to this lingering comes the holy.

---

[28]As it is translated by David A. White. See his discussion of this concept in *Heidegger and the Language of Poetry*, pp. 135–37.

We recognize in this description a summary of the paradoxical temporality of remembrance. The holy, Heidegger says, first grants with its greeting the Open that the poet is called upon to hold open in his saying. The poet's response, correspondingly (though in an anticipatory way), is a recollective prediction of the coming of the holy that first opens a time-space for its appearance and that first points to the region for man's historical dwelling (though it promises no certain salvation, Heidegger says, as in the Judeo-Christian understanding of prophecy). The prophecy takes on the character of a dream in the domain of poetry's "freien Bildens" —"free" marking again that this initial predication of a poetic dwelling upon an encounter with what is coming as what has been already presupposes the free use of the natural capacity for exposition. The poet's "dreaming" prediction thus founds the Open first granted by the holy and first gives the holy a site to which it may come. Most important, perhaps, this site is founded as the poet sets *himself* up in the "between" in his poetry. The halfgod, the poet, is the one properly greeted by the holy in its advent, and he thus becomes himself the appearance of the holy as he emerges in his essence as the Ungleiche. As the Weile founded by the poet's dwelling is the essential origin of history, the poet himself becomes as well as the founder of the history of a humanity. Of course, we shall have to ask again what appearance this Ungleiche (who resembles neither men nor things, indeed no thing that is—for which there can be, therefore, no *Gleichnis*) might have, and how someone who is like no one else can be representative in his individuality for the history of a people.

I have discussed only a small portion of Heidegger's commentary on the poet's prefigurative act of remembrance, but I would like to move now toward Heidegger's conclusion by turning to the repetition of remembrance Heidegger locates within "Remembrance" in the poet's gesture of turning his reflection back upon the conditions of his poetic enunciation. In the third strophe, Heidegger argues, the poet moves to think of his poetic vocation and of the learning of the free use of his proper capacities. This process of appropriation is the poet's actual *Heimkehr*.

In the third strophe, then, the poet turns from what he has experienced in the foreign land to what this experience has given to him to appropriate as his proper capacity for exposition. Heidegger reiterates here that the holy light experienced by the poet in the foreign land must have already accommodated the poet's word to its apparition as a word that filters the excessive brightness of the holy light. The poet's learning is thus a reiteration and appropriation of his open disposition to the holy in an ever more lucid and gathered vigilance whose measured, finite nature (*EHD*, 127) Heidegger describes as "repose." The movement of the first two strophes, we might say, repeats the determination of the poet's predictive or projective saying by the foreign ("repeats," since he is saying this determination); the following strophe folds back upon the projection itself. But this repetition is transformational in the fashion of the chiasmic reversal I have already described. (It also follows, we might note, the movement of progression and regression Hölderlin described in his note to "Der Rhein.") Thus, the poetic saying appears in the first two strophes as determined by what is to be exposed—the following strophe must now invert this movement and prepare the Darstellung as the determining condition for the appearance of what is to come. It must define the poet's exposition as belonging to a particular homeland by ordering the poet's clear exposition to what Heidegger terms the "rule of the earth" (*EHD*, 131).

The inverted repetition I am describing belongs to what Heidegger defines as a constant poetic reflection on remembrance and its poetic accomplishment. The poet's ongoing reflection upon his mode of saying is a constitutive part of the "learning" by which he founds his dwelling—constitutive for the very process of homecoming (*EHD*, 116). But the poet's reflection upon himself as the poet of this remembrance also belongs to this reflection. This reflection emerges for Heidegger in the fourth strophe in the poet's veiled question concerning the nature of the poet's task, though it begins implicitly in the third strophe with the poet's reference to the themes of dialogue and "mortal thoughts."

Mortal thoughts, Heidegger argues, are thoughts of what concerns men, inasmuch as they must dwell in what defines their home. The poet must speak of these mortal concerns in a mortal fashion, and for this, dialogue (or "converse") is "good." Heidegger explicates the notion of dialogue with reference to his argument in "Hölderlin and the Essence of Poetry"; dialogue is to be understood originally in terms of the greeting of the holy and the poet's response. But the poet acquires a "heart"—an affective disposition—for this originary exchange through the dialogue, in which he hears of "many tales," etc. This dialogue, Heidegger suggests, is itself a "remembrance" that pronounces the heart's "notion" ("opinion," as *Meinung* is translated by Hamburger, does not quite bring out the implications of a will, as Heidegger seeks to do by referring *Meinung* to *Minne*) and thus its willing of the poem of the holy, whose saying belongs to the time of the feast. The speaking of the heart's notion in dialogue prepares the poet to stand in the poetic domain that opens in the feast. At the same time, it accords to him the free and "reposed" use of his proper capacity for exposition as it prepares speech (exercises it) poetically in its give and take of mortal thoughts. The poet's thought of this dialogue is therefore a remembrance of the conditions of his appropriation of his proper capacity for exposition. Just as the poet's saying must be ordered by the "rule of the earth," it is determined by the particular history of this poet's people. The poet's capacity for exposition is released to the poet in his remembrance of the heavenly fire, but he appropriates this capacity in a remembrance that turns upon his home.

As the poet turns in the fourth strophe to inquire about the location of the interlocutors of a dialogue that is now past, we may conclude with Heidegger that the poet is meditating upon his solitude. I will turn shortly to Heidegger's understanding of this solitude, but before doing so, I should note that a reading of the lines "It is not good / To be soulless / With mortal thoughts" entirely different from the one offered by Heidegger is possible. One may hear in the German ("Nicht ist es gut, / Seellos von sterblichen / Gedanken zu seyn") what Heidegger finds, namely, that to be soulless is to be without mortal thoughts. But the line would seem to suggest more immediately that to be with mortal thoughts is to be soulless. As Hölderlin would therefore appear to be contrasting a certain experience of death with the "good" of dialogue, we may have reason to question Heidegger's understanding of the nature of the solitude to which the poet's thought turns furtively in the strophe (furtively because he does not identify himself as soulless in his solitude but merely evokes this theme after asking for the cup, in contrast to the dialogue whose interlocutors will be defined as absent in the next strophe). We must say at least that the *question* of the poet's solitude is far more problematic than Heidegger is willing to recognize.

I will pursue another aspect of this question as I turn to read "In lovely blueness . . ." and seek to establish a critical perspective on the reading I am presenting. My aim in this presentation of Heidegger's essay on "Remembrance" is not to consider the philological or critical merit of the reading but rather to identify Heidegger's essential claims concerning the poet's reflexive, founding act. But it should be clear, I believe, that the theme of death or mortality offers a critical lever for confronting Heidegger's reading of "Remembrance." However we respond finally to the question of Hölderlin's use of the notion of death (a question that requires a far more lengthy textual examination than is appropriate here), we may recognize that the relation to death of the later Hölderlin is not one of resoluteness but at best one of a questioning endurance for which, as I will try to show at the end of this chapter, no measure is given.

Turning now to Heidegger's reading of the fourth strophe in his development of the poet's reflexive turn to the question of his solitude, we may note that Heidegger understands the question concerning the "friends" as a question concerning the poet himself, inasmuch as the reference to Bellarmine and his companions points to Hyperion, whom Heidegger identifies immediately with the poet. Recalling Hyperion, the poet recollects one of the sites of his past voyage and in so doing opens the question of his current location, now that he has returned to his home. Heidegger remarks in this context that this questioning concerning the poet's proper site differs from the questioning of the philosopher insofar as the philosopher's questioning risks itself in the question-worthy and is at home in the *Unheimische*. The poet, whose task is to say the holy, seeks to say poetically the *Heimische*. His distinguishing concern, we may presume, is his testimony of his belonging to the earth, and thus the according of his mode of exposition with what Heidegger calls the "rule of the earth." Since the poet's being-at-home is the one concern of the poet's questioning, the single question of the poem, Heidegger says, is directed to the essence of remembrance itself, and what is asked about in this question is the poet himself—not the "I" of the poet's person but the essential place of the self, "whose 'proper' alone is the accomplishment of the essence of a poetic vocation" (*EHD*, 129). Such a question, as a poetic question, is properly reserved or veiled, since the poet's relation to his origin is determined essentially by a reserve issuing from the knowledge (itself determined by the origin) that the origin cannot be approached immediately. Correspondingly, the answer to the "veiling" question concerning the friends is itself veiled. The reserve that belongs to the answer is named: "Many a man / Is shy of going to the source." The answer speaks of the company of friends brought together by a common vocation; it names the coming poets to whom the poem addresses itself from its start. But only the most reserved of the reserved can first undertake the path to the source. The poet thus modestly names himself with the reference to the many, Heidegger states, because he cannot pose as an exception.

This preeminent modesty is problematic for Heidegger's argument, since it is defined socially and not simply by the poet's relation to the origin—as an avoidance of posturing, it is necessarily already a kind of posturing. As Heidegger (no less than Hölderlin) is concerned with Hölderlin's *representative* character, this question of the poet's appearance is not of merely secondary importance; it should recall to us a similar difficulty in Heidegger's remarks on the artist's lack of shame in his reading of Nietzsche. But Hölderlin's reserve does not alone define his solitude. First, he is distinguished from his friends in that he recognizes the necessity, as Hölderlin puts it, that the modes of representation be transformed with the "vaterländische Umkehr" (*SW5*, 271). His friends are still "painting," in the sense already described, and their dialogue can no longer be his own—he must discover a new genre. If the poet now thinks of those afar, out of his solitude, it is in order better to interpret this solitude; he thinks of the coming poets' voyage as a remembrance of his own, in order that the standing (or existing, *bestehende*) law of "becoming-at-home" should be well interpreted. Interpreting this law, he also affirms his solidarity with those who are coming. The poet thus thinks his solitude only in relation to a community that has helped to prepare his saying and whose future he is in turn founding. "So speaks now," Heidegger writes, "the collected courage of the *solitary man*, who experiences his isolation as the essential accomplishment of a friendship, which demands from poetic men a first who will be offered [*geopfert*] for the learning of the free use of the proper" (*EHD*, 141). Near the end of his essay, Heidegger reiterates the point that one is offered (sacrificed) in the founding of a poetic domain (and of the history of a people): "Destiny has sent the poet into the essence of this poetic domain and has designated him in the offering of the first born" (*EHD*, 150). The thematics of sacrifice that I pointed to in "Hölderlin and the Essence of Poetry" continue to overdetermine Heidegger's *isolation* of Hölderlin.

Heidegger comments at some length upon the lines of the final strophe, in which the poet thinks of those who have embarked for the east in search of what will reveal itself in the most distant distance to be their elder's provenance. He underscores in this discussion a point that has been made but that is worth emphasizing in relation to the question of what Heidegger means by a homeland. The origin sought by the poets is not German and not Greek; it exists in relation to, but is not identical with, the historically defined, "natural" home of a people.[29] The return to the provenance of the elders is a return to the domain founded by the *Stromgeist* of the Indus—a domain therefore grounded poetically, and thus historically. But let us move here to Heidegger's actual discussion of this notion as he finds it expressed in Hölderlin's line "But the poets found what remains."

The meaning of "remaining," Heidegger says, unfolds in the poet's veiled question concerning the remembrance and thus his questioning of his own situation as one who has returned. "Remaining," as it is defined in this questioning, is a dwelling in the poet's proper determination. Though it is a "repose," it is also an ongoing movement into proximity to the origin. But as a founding, this going is a making-fast that takes its firmness from the origin's own self-grounding. This self-grounding is figured, Heidegger says, with the movement of the stream as it flows from its source to the sea and then back to its source. (Heidegger describes this movement at the very outset of this essay when he refers to Hölderlin's lines concerning the Danube's apparent movement of reversal near its source.) The origin grounds itself as it makes itself fast in its return upon itself; flowing back, it shelters itself in its ground. To dwell near the origin is to follow this movement, as the poet does in his act of remembrance (moving between the foreign land and the homeland) and in his ever more

[29]See Michael Murray's very sound and useful discussion of the problem of nationalism and Heidegger's interpretation of the notion of *Heimat* in "Heidegger's Hermeneutic Reading of Hölderlin."

firm appropriation of his proper capacity for poetic exposition. He repeats the movement in such a way that the essence of the origin, its "intimacy" (in which is reserved a relation of earth and sky and whose withdrawal first prompted the poet to seek the heavenly fire that gave him in turn a knowledge of the earth of his homeland) is unfolded in its essential elements—that is to say, in a "firm character" that brings forth in its clear outline the "rule of the earth" while responding to a linguistic destiny and to its determination by the distant approach of the divine. Following the origin's movement by yielding to it and holding to it—retracing it—the poet shows the origin's self-grounding and finds therein the ground of his own dwelling.

What is shown, precisely speaking, is the distancing of the origin's self-grounding, sheltering movement. The more this distancing is drawn out or unfolded in the showing, the more essential the nearness of this showing to what is shown. The showing is thus an unfolding of the proximity in which the poetic dwelling comes to stand. But the showing consists *only* in the poet's dwelling in proximity to the origin, in the way the poet inhabits the distance he draws out as he follows the movement of the origin. As he follows this movement only in an act of remembrance, the showing must be understood as the *becoming founded* of this act. We must recognize here that the poetic dwelling does not found the origin—rather it is founded by the origin in its projective following of the origin's self-grounding. In this movement, it founds itself (*EHD*, 148). Thus what *shows* is the ever-increasing firmness and clarity of the poetic character as the poet appropriates ever more profoundly and firmly his proper poetic capacity. (Such, it appears, is Heidegger's interpretation of Hölderlin's statement in the second letter to Böhlendorff concerning the "highest" in art, which "maintains everything standing and for itself, so that sureness, in this sense, is the supreme function of the sign" [*SW*6.1, 433], as well as his interpretation of the final lines of "Patmos" [*SW*2.1, 172] concerning the father's concern that the letter should be maintained in its firmness.)

Neither founding nor showing, as we see, may be understood transitively, in terms of a subject/object relation. The showing approach, as Heidegger emphasizes, is a following that moves only in and through the reflexive movement of remembrance:

The poet dwells near the origin insofar as he shows the distance that draws near with the coming of the holy. The poet can then first perceive what comes, and so be the poet and the one showing, when he first remembers the heavenly fire and brings what he has thus experienced back into the necessity of an exposition that remembers in its turn the appropriation of the poet's proper capacity. For only inasmuch as he is open for divinity and for humanity by virtue of his remembrance of what has been in his voyage and what is to be learned from the place of his home does he have the showing look for the Open, in which alone gods may come as guests and men may build a shelter in which the true is and to which they may hold firmly. [*EHD*, 148]

The poet's "showing look," his "eye for the origin" (Heidegger's interpretation of the "eye too many"), opens with the founding of the poetic saying that marks itself *as* a relation to the origin. This dwelling is, finally, the manifestation of the reflexive act of remembrance as a *letting itself be founded* that points beyond itself in this founding but that shows no more than this founding. A reflexive act, remembrance founds, paradoxically, from beyond the poetic self it constitutes and situates in this act; the poet's self-reflection is an opening to an alterity.

"Self-reflection" might seem a misnomer for a process that first constitutes the self of this reflection. Heidegger would seem to be evacuating in this movement any grounding selfhood, and yet he insists that the poet's *self* shows in the reflexive act of remembrance. The poetic act of remembrance reflects what it means to "live poetically on the earth"—it reflexively grounds the poetic project in relation to which a people may subsequently build and maintain its dwelling. But it sets and reflects upon the conditions for dwelling in an exemplary act of dwelling by one being. "The poetizing *of the poet* [*Das Dichten* der Dichter]," Heidegger writes, near the end of the essay, "is now the founding of remaining" (*EHD*, 149). The poet sets himself up in an exemplary fashion (exemplary first, because he shows the conditions of this setting-up), offers himself, much as a being is said to be dedicated in "The Origin of the Work of Art" to the self-establishing of openness in the Open. To "thesis," as it is described in "The Origin of the Work of Art," corresponds the poet's "Bleiben" (as it appears in the firmness of the poetic character). Dwelling in proximity to the origin, he brings forth this nearness that (following the logic of the hermeneutic circle) first gives the possibility of such a dwelling. Standing forth in this way, the poet appears as the one who is properly greeted by the holy in its appearance at the moment of the festival.

Hölderlin thus offers to the German people a grounding figure with which to identify. Yet, even if Heidegger gives testimony of his own identification with Hölderlin (through the words of Panthea to which I referred earlier, for example), we should pause to recall Heidegger's assertion in *Being and Time* that the relation of Mitsein (even when defined historically, as in the relation to a hero chosen in an act of repetition) cannot be understood in terms of the traditional notion of identification. Indeed, if we return to "Remembrance," where Heidegger describes at much greater length the nature of the poet's self-constitution, we recognize that identification is a most problematic concept in this context, since the poet is said to emerge in his essence as the Ungleiche. With what might the German people be asked to identify if the figure with whom they are to identify resembles neither men nor gods—no thing that is? This representative figure cannot be *like* anyone or anything else, and it is a Gleichnis of the holy only if we abandon any definition of this term elaborated in the aesthetic tradition. The poet figures only his receptivity to the holy and merely announces what, in coming, appears as absent. To identify with Hölderlin would be to identify with no thing that is. No imitation of such a figure would be possible if we define imitation in terms of the reproduction of some visible aspect.

If Heidegger's preoccupation with the self-affirmation of the German people in the early and mid-1930s thus led him into at least the *rhetorical* stance of inviting the German people to identify with a *führer* (even though he insists that all following "bears resistance within itself" [SU, 21/479]), "Remembrance" (1943) brings forth clearly what in his earlier thinking had already ruled out the possibility of understanding this relation in terms of any simple model of mimetic following. Hölderlin is a most paradoxical example inasmuch as he represents (by pointing beyond himself) the unpresentable.

Is "Remembrance," despite the recurrence of the theme of sacrifice, a less violent appropriation of the figure of Hölderlin than an essay such as "Hölderlin and the Essence of Poetry," and does it offer perhaps a reading more faithful to the later developments in Hölderlin's reflection upon his role as a poet? The disappearance of the earlier tragic tones certainly mark this essay as being more in accord with the tone of Gelassenheit. And when Heidegger posits the poet as the Ungleiche and identifies the founding of the poetic self with the mere opening of an eye, he offers a description that corresponds at least to Hölderlin's *desire* for a poetic saying that would mark no more than a pure receptivity. The opening line of the second version of "Mnemosyne" refers to such purity—"A sign we are, without meaning," as does the "pure form" to which Hölderlin refers in "In lovely blueness . . ." and the late image of the heart of crystal, upon which Allemann focuses (the earlier designation of the tragic sign as "= 0" seems also to anticipate these images.[30] All of these images bespeak for Heidegger the accomplishment of what Hölderlin terms the "vaterländische Umkehr," though in a transfigured form marked by its calm.

Allemann, in strict accord with Heidegger, finds the most powerful confirmation of the "essential simplicity" of Hölderlin's late poetry in the poem, "In lovely blueness . . . ." This simplicity would be the measure, it seems, of a grounded poetic dwelling. Yet it is revealing that Allemann, in order to find testimony of this simplicity, must abandon his reading (which he opposed to Heidegger in his criticism of Heidegger's reading of "Remembrance") of the categorical turn and the danger to which it answers when he approaches this poem. Allemann misses an explicit allusion to a desire for the unbound and to the corresponding injunction ("Yet the soul . . . must remain pure") and turns instead to the image of the comet for an expression of Hölderlin's achieved simplicity— eliding Hölderlin's reference to his desire in relation to this image and asserting that the image escapes human conception. Allemann's reading of the poem is so blind to the very problematic he sought to define that we can only conclude that his interpretation has a protective function (as one must always suspect when a critic asserts that a poem escapes rational understanding and refuses to interpret it).

What exactly would Allemann be protecting in this fashion? I

---

[30]See "Die Bedeutung der Tragödien" (*SW*4.1, 274).

suggest that it is nothing other than Heidegger's own interpretation of the poet's showing and preservation of a founding differentiation—one that would gather and define a unified and stable human dwelling. There can be no question that Hölderlin sought such a measure for human existence—but it suffices to read the second and third strophes of "Mnemosyne," for example, or everything beyond the first strophe of "Patmos" or the last two sections of "In lovely blueness..." to recognize that Hölderlin doubted the possibility of defining such a measure himself and was able to pose only the *question* of such a measure.

"In lovely blueness..." begins, like several of Hölderlin's major poems, with a tableau that appears as a kind of prefiguration of a harmony or an equilibrium that will prove inaccessible in the course of the poem as the poet begins to speak in the first person and seeks to bear witness to that harmony in the way Heidegger describes in "Hölderlin and the Essence of Poetry."[31] The poem is also fully characteristic of Hölderlin in the way described by Heidegger in that it is a poem that reflects upon the meaning of poetic dwelling by addressing itself to the conditions of poetic figuration. The poem is virtually a treatise on figuration, often approaching a manifestly discursive form; but the tropological "equations" that it sets up are marked by an imbalance that is finally figured with the image of the eye too many.

The first section of the poem asserts the propriety of calling man the image of the godhead and poses the phenomenal conditions of the appearance of this capacity. Man's plasticity (*Bildsamkeit*), or his capacity to appear in his resemblance to divinity, appears against a kind of frame that is constituted by the beauty of the church

---

[31]The full text of "In lovely blueness...," translated by Michael Hamburger, appears below in Appendix 2. I will refer to the persona that says "I" in this poem as Hölderlin, though realizing the problematic character of such a designation. The most basic principles of literary criticism suggest caution in this respect. But we should also note that there is some doubt as to Hölderlin's authorship of this poem. The poem, of which no original version has survived, is taken from Wilhelm Waiblinger's novel *Phaëton* ([Stuttgart: Friedrich Franckh, 1823], pp. 153–56), in which it is attributed to a mad poet and rendered in prose (a transposition, as indicated in the novel, from the original Pindaric verse). Although Beissner refuses to recognize its authenticity, Heidegger does not hesitate to attribute it to Hölderlin and to refer to it throughout his essays on Hölderlin as one of the major supporting texts for his interpretation. I follow the majority of modern commentators in finding in this poem the seemingly unmistakable traits of Hölderlin's late poetry.

steeple. The steeple is described by Hölderlin in a way that might remind us of Heidegger's own evocation of the Greek temple in "The Origin of the Work of Art." It "blossoms" in a play of contrast of light and sound that brings forth the elements in which it emerges, including the blueness of the sky. Descending the steps of the tower (emerging from a doorway, or appearing through the windows that are "like gates in beauty"—hence my reference to a frame), a man will emerge, Hölderlin says, as a detached figure (*abgesondert so sehr die Gestalt ist*) in a kind of still life. "Still" must be understood here as an adjective (*ein stilles Leben*), but the reference to art (in *Stilleben,* a "still life") is appropriate because, in this framing of the human Gestalt, the plasticity or figurality, the capacity to be a figure, is said to issue from man. The notion of framing suggests that human figurality appears *against* natural beauty—hence, the qualifying turn as Hölderlin adds, "But purity too is beauty," and goes on to suggest that man may be an image of divinity inasmuch as he is pure. Moving "within" this diversity of natural and human beauty, Hölderlin says, "a serious mind is formed." Poetic thought, it seems, is the passage between natural beauty and the beauty of purity—to move "between" them, through the "gate" of beauty, is to live poetically.

But Hölderlin also appears to assert that purity and natural beauty are incommensurable. Man may imitate (*nachahmen*) the virtue and joy of the heavenly gods, he may be like them (*auch seyn*), and he may measure himself (*sich messen*) against the godhead (*Gottheit*) by remaining pure in kindliness. He may measure this resemblance to divinity inasmuch as God, though "unknown," is manifest like the sky: "It is the measure of man," Hölderlin states. This figure of God's manifestness appears with the blossoming of the steeple. Correspondingly, as I have noted, man's figurality appears also in relation to this natural blossoming. But man's purity, which is the basis of his resemblance to divinity, exceeds any natural appearance of purity. Hölderlin's phrasing of this incommensurability is exceedingly ambiguous (as is marked by his hesitation): "But the darkness of night with all the stars is not purer, if I could put it like that, than man, who is called the image of the godhead." The "purest" natural play of light and dark (the shades of night and the stars) is not in itself man's standard or measure. Natural beauty brings forth man's figurality (his purity), but his purity exceeds the natural image.

Heidegger's own reading of this passage in his essay ". . . Poetically Man Dwells . . ." (first presented in 1951), accounts for this incommensurability in a persuasive manner.[32] Heidegger reads the lines "Is God unknown? Is He manifest as the sky? This rather I believe" as implying that the appearance of God in the manifestness of the sky is an appearance of God as unknown. The measure provided by the godhead, he concludes, consists in precisely this appearance of a concealment. To reinforce this interpretation, Heidegger cites lines from a poetic fragment that belongs to the time of the composition of "In lovely blueness . . .":

> What is God? Unknown, yet
> Full of qualities is the
> Face of the sky. For the lightnings
> Are the wrath of a god. The more something
> Is invisible, the more it yields to what's alien.

Heidegger interprets these lines as follows: "The poet calls, in the sights of the sky, that which in its very self-disclosure causes the appearance of that which conceals itself, and indeed *as* that which conceals itself. In the familiar appearances, the poet calls the alien as that to which the invisible imparts itself in order to remain what it is—unknown" (*VA*, 194/225). He continues, "The measure taken by poetry yields, imparts itself—as the foreign element in which the invisible one preserves his presence—to what is familiar in the sights of the sky" (*VA*, 195/226). The measure of the godhead is given, therefore, in and as the holy as that foreign element (or, the "alien") by which the self-concealment, the form taken by divine presence in the modern period, comes to appear.[33] In this descrip-

---

[32]This essay is contained in the collection of essays translated by Albert Hofstadter, *Poetry, Language, Thought*, pp. 211–29.

[33]Heidegger's use here of the notion of the holy clarifies, I believe, what remains merely implicit in Heidegger's earlier use of the term. Here, the holy is defined more precisely as the condition for the reception of divine presence (the godhead), which, in turn, names the self-disclosure of the deity (*der Gott*). David White offers what is probably the most exact and helpful analysis of these terms in *Heidegger and the Language of Poetry* (pp. 115–39). He defines the holy as "the dispositional capacity in all that is other than the deity to receive the appearances of the divine presence" (p. 127). In this definition, we see a precise reference to the two related notions to which I have referred, the deity and the dimension of the deity's presence. In his *Letter on Humanism*, Heidegger refers to the distinction between these notions as

tion of the holy as alien, we find an almost explicit description of what I have referred to as the strangeness of beauty.[34] Finally, we see that if man is an image of the godhead, his own beauty must be a figure of concealment. He must figure absence. Again, we find a reference to a sign that would be " = 0."

As this figure must be incommensurable with natural appearances, Hölderlin's opening statement in the second section, though apparently contradicting the earlier statement, "It is the measure of man," in fact continues his meditation: "Is there a measure on earth? There is none." But Hölderlin adds now that the beauty of earthly beings is also potentially excessive for man. The beauty of some beings (Hölderlin may well be referring here to the human figure) threatens to sweep man beyond his essential bounds. We recognize here the theme traced by Allemann but ignored by him in his reading of the poem, as I noted above. The sweep of beauty is described by Hölderlin in glorious terms ("else on pinions the eagle reaches far as the Mighty with songs of praise and the voice of so many birds"). But the soul, Hölderlin says, must remain pure (*muss rein bleiben*): "It is the essence, the form it is." The Gestalt that man must adopt in his purity emerges now against the pull of earthly beauty.

Hölderlin thus comes to express his own incapacity to hold the pure form against an overwhelming beauty in the following line:

---

follows: "But the holy, which alone is the essential sphere of the godhead, which in turn alone affords a dimension for the gods and for God, comes to radiate only when Being itself beforehand and after extensive preparation has been illuminated and is experienced in its truth" (W, 338–39/218). Likewise, in "What Are Poets For?" Heidegger writes, "The ether, however, in which alone the gods are gods, is their godhead [*Gottheit*]. The element of this ether, that within which even the godhead itself is still present, is the holy" (H, 250/94).

[34]Heidegger defines this notion in relation to the concept of image in a way that confirms, I believe, my earlier interpretation of Heidegger's analysis of the image in "Remembrance": "The nature of the image is to let something be seen. By contrast, copies and imitations are already mere variations on the genuine image which, as a sight or spectacle, lets the invisible be seen and so imagines the invisible in something alien to it. Because poetry takes that mysterious measure, to wit, in the face of the sky, therefore it speaks in 'images.' This is why poetic images are imaginings in a distinctive sense: not mere fancies and illusions but imaginings that are visible inclusions of the alien in the sight of the familiar. The poetic saying of images gathers the brightness and sound of the heavenly appearances into one with the darkness and silence of what is alien. By such sights the god surprises us. In this strangeness, he proclaims his unfaltering nearness" (VA, 194–95/226).

"You beautiful little stream, you seem touching, as you flow so clear, clear as the eye of divinity [*Gottheit*], through the Milky Way. I know you well, but tears gush out of my eyes." The eye of divinity would seem to mark identity, since the poet has already called man the image of the godhead. The poet looks to the familiar stream of stars (taking up again the concluding image from the first section of the poem) as in a mirror for a specular reflection. But recognition brings with it a collapse of identity (though also a strangely inverted reassertion of it) as the poet's own eye begins to "stream" with tears and thus clouds over (unlike the clear flowing of the sky's stream).

The poem continues with a series of images expressing a failure to achieve the purity of form or appearance by which man would appear in his resemblance to divinity.[35] The serious spirit, Hölderlin said, must make the bridge between earthly beauty and human purity—it must bridge a difference that corresponds in some manner to the otherness or the alien quality of the holy as it exists in familiar appearances. And so, Hölderlin says, the serious spirit must praise virtue. But virtue appears in the modern world, or at least in the north, as lacking or somehow unaccomplished: "A beautiful virgin must wreathe her head with myrtle, because she is simple both in her nature and in her feelings. But myrtles are to be found in Greece." The maiden must wreathe her head, we might presume, in order to protect herself in her simplicity. But the injunction (*muss*) might also bear upon the maiden's exposure. *Because she is simple*, she must be veiled or bound in a certain fashion—marked *as* a virgin (*Jungfrau*). The lack of this properly cultural mark makes her natural simplicity appear as a nakedness. The German maiden, we might say, is excessively simple—her simplicity is volatile, it lacks measure. Even though she *is* simple,

---

[35] I pass over here the strongly marked figural transpositions by which the poet finds a "serene life" in the shapes of creation by reading these in relation to death (suggested by *Kirchhof*, churchyard or cemetery) and then juxtaposes to an expression of his suffering before the laughter of men his desire to escape the wounds of subjectivity and to be like a comet. This image, itself a transposition of the "stream" seen in the sky, is developed with two metaphors and a simile—it will be picked up again with the image of brooks, as they sweep the poet away, and reinforces the fact that the "stream" in this poem is one of figurality. Between the churchyard and the stream of images in which it figures, Hölderlin is providing a most unsettling representation of what it means to "dwell" poetically.

she transgresses in her simplicity. This figure of lack and excess is echoed, I want to argue, in the last images of the third section, in which Hölderlin compares his suffering to that of Oedipus.

Hölderlin begins this section with an image that recalls the previous address to the stream, inasmuch as it involves a kind of disrupted mirroring and a similar exchange of properties. Here the mirroring is explicit, though what is seen in the mirror is not a reflection but a painted likeness—another appearance of human Bildsamkeit, but all the more fixed or frozen. There is something vaguely grotesque about the poetic vision described here, and the association that moves by way of the term "eyes" and leads to the statement "King Oedipus has an eye too many perhaps" does indeed carry something ungeheuer with it. ("Ungeheuer" is Heidegger's own term for this poem in "Hölderlin and the Essence of Poetry" [*EHD*, 42], though unheimlich might be the more appropriate word here, for in this vision, life and death are intermingled, as Hölderlin reiterates at the end of the poem: "Life is death, and death is a kind of life.") Hölderlin continues by saying that the suffering caused by Oedipus's "eye too many" is presented (*dargestellt*) in Sophocles' drama as indescribable (unrepresentable in discursive terms; at every step in this text, Hölderlin comments upon conditions of representation). Here, the "eye too many" seems to refer to Oedipus's excessive desire to know (Oedipus interprets too infinitely, Hölderlin says in his "Notes"). Hölderlin compares it to his own excessive mourning ("the end of something sweeps me away"); both are unmeasured responses to loss or abandonment.

Among the forms of "affliction" that Hölderlin enumerates in this section (including those of Hercules and the Dioscuri), Hölderlin refers to the affliction of being "covered with freckles, to be wholly covered with many a spot!" This image would almost seem to undo any tragic pathos that Hölderlin evokes with the previous allusions, and the image that follows reiterates the insubstantiality of the afflictions in which Hölderlin claims to share: "The afflictions that Oedipus bore seem like this, as when a poor man complains that there is something he lacks." The poor man's complaint is perfectly just of course, absolutely just; but it fails—and it must fail—to express the measure of the poverty out of which it speaks. It remarks almost absurdly a boundless poverty. As a complaint, it not only bespeaks a lack of knowledge of its own limitless founda-tions (if the poor man knew his poverty, this knowledge would make it impossible for him to complain of a particular want) but also is culpable or remarks an impurity—to complain is not to express kindliness or purity in the sense of the first section of the poem (or so it would seem), and thus this comportment cannot resemble the virtue and pleasure of the heavenly and the rich. The poor man who complains does not resemble the godhead. He is not essentially poor, as Heidegger asserts the poet must be. But if he is not "properly" poor (and does not show the propriety of the essentially poor), it is because, again, his poverty is measureless or exceeds his ability to know it.

Does the image of the freckles not in fact function in the same way? Freckles caused by the sun seem almost neutral or perfectly gratuitous in relation to the concept of beauty, and yet their abundance signifies a kind of taint ("to be wholly covered with many a spot!"). The voyager has freckles to show for following the beams of the sun (a figure of the journey towards the heavenly fire). These, again, are a sign of the Bildsamkeit to which Hölderlin referred in the first section of the poem; their very abundance marks them as a sign. Yet, what they remark is the lack of a pure figure adequate to this Bildsamkeit (if the human figure is to be somehow commensurable with the absence of the divine) and perhaps even the impossibility of such an image in general, insofar as they show the illusory nature of the promise of the sun ("the allurements of its beams").

Heidegger suggests, as we have seen, that every image in Hölderlin's poetry (at least after "As on a holiday...") is an image of the poet. The clarity and firmness of the poetic character would be a sign of the founded dwelling of the poetic self (though remarking as such the relation to an alterity). This founded dwell-ing would mark in its turn the founding of a space/time for the advent of the holy and thus provide the grounding for a people's history. In "In lovely blueness...," however, Hölderlin appears to figure his own inability to achieve the purity of such a sign. If I am correct in thinking that we may read the images discussed here as part of a series that includes the "eye too many," by which Hölderlin marks his identity with Oedipus, then we may conclude that Hölderlin understands his poetry to be like the complaint of the poor man or to have the character of the virgin's nakedness or to be "covered with spots." Each of these figures, if they reflect upon the poet himself, gives a troubling aspect to a self that should appear with a purity commensurable with the absence of the divine. Hölderlin's self-reflection, he seems to say, is like a "painted likeness" whose "createdness," appearing in the obtrusive materiality of the image, is not quite subsumed by the life of the poetic spirit—death is intermingled with life in this reflection that fails to achieve even the apparent life of a mirror image or the luminosity of the "painted" image on the moon.

But the images of "In lovely blueness . . ." seem to figure more than failure or inadequacy and a certain accompanying guilt (which cannot be reduced to shame, as Heidegger defines it). Again, the freckles *are* a sign of the capacity to appear as an image of the divine, just as the poor man's complaints are just and the maiden *is* simple. The very excessiveness of each manifestation (like a strange beauty) constitutes a trace of the holy even as it marks in some way its self-refusal. Hölderlin is opening (reopening) with these images the question of his relation to the holy—with all the certitude that Heidegger attributes to him, but in a far more questioning way. The trace of the holy—or what he designates as the holy—does offer itself in Hölderlin's poetic experience and offers a promise in the absence it shows ("Near is / And difficult to grasp the God / But where danger is, there grows / Also what saves" ["Patmos," SW2.1, 165]). But although he is certain that the promise is given (brought forth in the strange beauty of the poetic character), he finds it increasingly impossible to define a history by situating himself in relation to this promise. Hölderlin may cast this relation in eschatological terms at certain points in the later poetry and thus project an end to the experience of a lack of measure that consistently remarks itself in his effort to found a space/time for the advent of the holy. But to accept this projection as Heidegger does is to fail to recognize that it takes shape in a questioning that Hölderlin does not close—perhaps not even in his final retreat ("In lovely blueness . . ." is dated after the onset of what is termed Hölderlin's "madness"). It is to refuse the possibility that in reflecting upon and seeking to bring forth the conditions of poetic representation,

Hölderlin both opens a promise and denies it—remarking the trace of an alterity that refuses itself to any appropriation. Only by beauty, Hölderlin wrote in the sketch of a preface to *Hyperion* (referring explicitly to Plato), is it possible that we should ever seek unity—ever be moved to question. But the ambiguity of a "painted likeness," or the poetic character in general, is irreducible for Hölderlin; it is marked always by an excess or a lack that points beyond itself, but it offers no ground for subsuming its appearance.

If in his "Notes" Hölderlin seemed to hold to the possibility of defining an equilibrium of human faculties in tragic art and the possibility of defining a "splendidly harmonic form," his poetic reflection on his own language and thus on his own "poetic dwelling" undercuts any attribution to Hölderlin himself of a founded and founding poetic saying. Hölderlin repeatedly answers in his poetry to an alterity that he experiences as near or imminent— he "remembers" a dimension of experience that the metaphysics of subjectivity works to repress, but he cannot achieve the firmness and purity of a poetic character that would bring forth this otherness in such a way as to found a "dwelling" in its proximity. Hölderlin assumes the finitude of his poetic language in a most authentic way, according to Heidegger's own definition of what constitutes a responsible discourse, namely, one that situates itself in its own act of saying and never closes the question of the place from which it speaks. In this way, Hölderlin reveals exactly what Heidegger himself announced in his earlier work when he said that our deepest and most authentic finitude refuses itself to the measure of our freedom.

In this respect, we may say of Hölderlin what Hölderlin says of Sophocles in the "Notes" that accompany his translations: his speech is just. It answers uncompromisingly to a time when the metaphysics of subjectivity reaches its limits. Of course, to a large extent, it is Heidegger's thought that makes possible such an assertion of the historical propriety of Hölderlin's poetic project. And insofar as the answering address of Hölderlin's text to a Heideggerian form of analysis brings into question the very notions of justice or propriety, we can measure its justice perhaps only in relation to the degree to which it brings forth the necessity of rereading Heidegger and reposing the question of measure (that is, the measuring or gathering nature of difference). No final arbitration in such a circular movement of analysis is possible, and neither is a final decision possible regarding the justice of this movement of thought. Its justice lies in its temporal character or historicity—the degree to which it opens the *question* of history.

Andenken

Der Nordost wehet,
Der liebste unter den Winden
Mir, weil er feurigen Geist
Und gute Fahrt verheisset den Schiffern.
Geh aber nun und grüsse
Die schöne Garonne,
Und die Gärten von Bourdeaux
Dort, wo am scharfen Ufer
Hingehet der Steg und in den Strom
Tief fällt der Bach, darüber aber
Hinschauet ein edel Paar
Von Eichen und Silberpappeln;

Noch denket das mir wohl und wie
Die breiten Gipfel neiget
Der Ulmwald, über die Mühl',
Im Hofe aber wächset ein Feigenbaum.
An Feiertagen gehn
Die braunen Frauen daselbst
Auf seidnen Boden,
Zur Märzenzeit,
Wenn gleich ist Nacht und Tag,
Und über langsamen Stegen,
Von goldenen Träumen schwer,

Remembrance

The north-easterly blows,
Of winds the dearest to me
Because a fiery spirit
And happy voyage it promises mariners.
But go now, go and greet
The beautiful Garonne
And the gardens of Bordeaux,
To where on the rugged bank
The path runs and into the river
Deep falls the brook, but above them
A noble pair of oaks
And white poplars looks out;

Still well I remember this, and how
The elm wood with its great leafy tops
Inclines, towards the mill,
But in the courtyard a fig-tree grows.
On holidays there too
The brown women walk
On silken ground,
In the month of March,
When night and day are equal
And over slow footpaths,
Heavy with golden dreams,

Einwiegende Lüfte ziehen.

Es reiche aber,
Des dunkeln Lichtes voll,
Mir einer den duftenden Becher,
Damit ich ruhen möge; denn süss
Wär' unter Schatten der Schlummer.
Nicht ist es gut,
Seellos von sterblichen
Gedanken zu seyn. Doch gut
Ist ein Gespräch und zu sagen
Des Herzens Meinung, zu hören viel
Von Tagen der Lieb',
Und Thaten, welche geschehen.

Wo aber sind die Freunde? Bellarmin
Mit dem Gefährten? Mancher
Trägt Scheue, an die Quelle zu gehn;
Es beginnet nemlich der Reichtum
Im Meere. Sie,
Wie Mahler, bringen zusammen
Das Schöne der Erd' und verschmähn
Den geflügelten Krieg nicht, und
Zu wohnen einsam, jahrlang, unter
Dem entlaubten Mast, wo nicht die Nacht durchglänzen
Die Feiertage der Stadt,
Und Saitenspiel und eingeborener Tanz nicht.

Nun aber sind zu Indiern
Die Männer gegangen,
Dort an der luftigen Spiz'
An Traubenbergen, wo herab
Die Dordogne kommt,
Und zusammen mit der präct'gen
Garonne meerbreit
Ausgehet der Strom. Es nehmet aber
Und giebt Gedächtniss die See,
Und die Lieb' auch heftet fleissig die Augen,
Was bleibet aber, stiften die Dichter.
                    —Friedrich Hölderlin

Lulling breezes drift.

  But someone pass me
The fragrant cup
Full of the dark light,
So that I may rest now; for sweet
It would be to drowse amid shadows.
It is not good
To be soulless
With mortal thoughts. But good
Is converse, and to speak
The heart's opinion, to hear many tales
About the days of love
And deeds that have occurred.

  But where are the friends? Where Bellarmine
And his companions? Many a man
Is shy of going to the source;
For wealth begins in
The sea. And they,
Like painters, bring together
The beautiful things of the earth
And do not disdain winged war, and
To live in solitude, for years, beneath the
Defoliate mast, where through the night do not gleam
The city's holidays
Nor music of strings, nor indigenous dancing.

  But now to Indians
Those men have gone,
There on the airy peak
On grape-covered hills, where down
The Dordogne comes
And together with the glorious
Garonne as wide as the sea
The current sweeps out. But it is the sea
That takes and gives remembrance,
And love no less keeps eyes attentively fixed,
But what is lasting the poets provide.

              —Friedrich Hölderlin
                translated by Michael Hamburger

In lieblicher Bläue . . .

In lieblicher Bläue blühet mit dem metallenen Dache der Kirchthurm. Den umschwebet Geschrei der Schwalben, den umgiebt die rührendste Bläue. Die Sonne gehet hoch darüber und färbet das Blech, im Winde aber oben stille krähet die Fahne. Wenn einer unter der Gloke dann herabgeht, jene Treppen, ein stilles Leben ist es, weil, wenn abgesondert so sehr die Gestalt ist, die Bildsamkeit herauskommt dann des Menschen. Die Fenster, daraus die Gloken tönen, sind wie Thore an Schönheit. Nemlich, weil noch der Natur nach sind die Thore, haben diese die Ähnlichkeit von Bäumen des Walds. Reinheit aber ist auch Schönheit. Innen aus Verschiedenem entsteht ein ernster Geist. So sehr einfältig aber die Bilder, so sehr heilig sind die, dass man wirklich oft fürchtet, die zu beschreiben. Die Himmlischen aber, die immer gut sind, alles zumal, wie Reiche, haben diese, Tugend und Freude. Der Mensch darf das nachahmen. Darf, wenn lauter Mühe das Leben, ein Mensch aufschauen und sagen: so will ich auch seyn? Ja. So lange die Freundlichkeit noch am Herzen, die Reine, dauert, misset nicht unglüklich der Mensch sich mit der Gottheit. Ist unbekannt Gott? Ist er offenbar wie der Himmel? dieses glaub' ich eher. Des Menschen Maass ist's. Voll Verdienst, doch dichterisch, wohnet der Mensch auf dieser Erde. Doch reiner ist nicht der Schatten der Nacht mit den Sternen, wenn ich so sagen könnte, als der Mensch, der heisset ein Bild der Gottheit.

In lovely blueness . . .

In lovely blueness with its metal roof the steeple blossoms.
  Around it the crying of swallows hovers, most moving
blueness surrounds it. The sun hangs high above it and
colours the sheets of tin, but up above in the wind silently
crows the weathercock. If now someone comes down beneath
the bell, comes down those steps, a still life it is,
because, when the figure is so detached, the man's
plasticity is brought out. The windows from which the bells
are ringing are like gates in beauty. That is, because
gates still conform to nature, these have a likeness to
trees of the wood. But purity too is beauty. Within, out
of diversity a serious mind is formed. Yet these images are
so simple, so very holy are these, that really often one is
afraid to describe them. But the Heavenly, who are always
good, all things at once, like the rich, have these, virtue
and pleasure. This men may imitate. May, when life is all
hardship, may a man look up and say: I too would like to
resemble these? Yes. As long as kindliness, which is pure,
remains in his heart not unhappily a man may compare himself
with the divinity. Is God unknown? Is He manifest as the
sky? This rather I believe. It is the measure of man. Full
of acquirements, but poetically, man dwells on this earth.
But the darkness of night with all the stars is not purer,
if I could put it like that, than man, who is called the
image of God.

Giebt es auf Erden ein Maass? Es giebt keines. Nemlich es hemmen den Donnergang nie die Welten des Schöpfers. Auch eine Blume ist schön, weil sie blühet unter der Sonne. Es findet das Aug' oft im Leben Wesen, die viel schöner noch zu nennen wären als die Blumen. O! ich weiss das wohl! Denn zu bluten an Gestalt und Herz, und ganz nicht mehr zu seyn, gefällt das Gott? Die Seele aber, wie ich glaube, muss rein bleiben, sonst reicht an das Mächtige auf Fittigen der Adler mit lobendem Gesange und der Stimme so vieler Vögel. Es ist die Wesenheit, die Gestalt ist's. Du schönes Bächlein, du scheinest rührend indem du rollest so klar, wie das Auge der Gottheit, durch die Milchstrasse. Ich kenne dich wohl, aber Thränen quillen aus dem Auge. Ein heiteres Leben seh' ich in den Gestalten mich umblühen der Schöpfung, weil ich es nicht unbillig vergleiche den einsamen Tauben auf dem Kirchhof. Das Lachen aber scheint mich zu grämen der Menschen, nemlich ich hab' ein Herz. Möcht' ich ein Komet seyn? Ich glaube. Denn sie haben die Schnelligkeit der Vögel; sie blühen an Feuer, und sind wie Kinder an Reinheit. Grösseres zu wünschen, kann nicht des Menschen Natur sich vermessen. Der Tugend Heiterkeit verdient auch gelobt zu werden vom ernsten Geiste, der zwischen den drei Säulen wehet des Gartens. Eine schöne Jungfrau muss das Haupt umkränzen mit Myrthenblumen, weil sie einfach ist ihrem Wesen nach und ihrem Gefühl. Myrthen aber giebt es in Griechenland.

Wenn einer in den Spiegel siehet, ein Mann, und siehet darinn sein Bild, wie abgemahlt; es gleicht dem Manne. Augen hat des Menschen Bild, hingegen Licht der Mond. Der König Oedipus hat ein Auge zuviel vieleicht. Diese Leiden dieses Mannes, sie scheinen unbeschreiblich, unaussprechlich, unausdrüklich. Wenn das Schauspiel ein solches darstellt, kommt's daher. Wie ist mir's aber, gedenk' ich deiner jezt? Wie Bäche reisst das Ende von Etwas mich dahin, welches sich wie Asien ausdehnet. Natürlich dieses Leiden, das hat Oedipus. Natürlich ist's darum. Hat auch Herkules gelitten? Wohl. Die Dioskuren in ihrer Freundschaft haben die nicht Leiden auch getragen? Nemlich

Is there a measure on earth? There is none. For never the
Creator's worlds constrict the progress of thunder. A
flower too is beautiful, because it blooms under the sun.
Often in life the eye discovers beings that could be called
much more beautiful still than flowers. Oh, well I know it!
For to bleed both in body and heart, and wholly to be no
more, does that please God? Yet the soul, it is my belief,
must remain pure, else on pinions the eagle reaches far as
the Mighty with songs of praise and the voice of so many
birds. It is the essence, the form it is. You beautiful
little stream, you seem touching, as you flow so clear,
clear as the eye of divinity, through the Milky Way. I know
you well, but tears gush out of my eyes. A serene life I
see blossom around me in the shapes of creation, because not
unfittingly I compare it to the solitary doves of the
churchyard. But the laughter of men seems to grieve me, for
I have a heart. Would I like to be a comet? I think so.
For they possess the swiftness of birds; they blossom with
fire and are like children in purity. To desire more than
that, human nature cannot presume. The serenity of virtue
also deserves to be praised by the serious spirit which
wafts between the garden's three columns. A beautiful
virgin must wreathe her head with myrtle, because she is
simple both in her nature and in her feelings. But myrtles
are to be found in Greece.

If someone looks into the mirror, a man, and in it sees his
image, as though it were a painted likeness; it resembles
the man. The image of man has eyes, whereas the moon has
light. King Oedipus has an eye too many perhaps. The
sufferings of this man, they seem indescribable,
unspeakable, inexpressible. If the drama represents
something like this, that is why. But what comes over me if
I think of you now? Like brooks the end of something sweeps
me away, which expands like Asia. Of course, this
affliction, Oedipus has it too. Of course, that is why.
Did Hercules suffer too? Indeed. The Dioscuri in their
friendship, did not they bear afflictions too? For to fight

237

wie Herkules mit Gott zu streiten, das ist Leiden. Und die Unsterblichkeit im Neide dieses Lebens, diese zu theilen, ist ein Leiden auch. Doch das ist auch ein Leiden, wenn mit Sommerfleken ist bedekt ein Mensch, mit manchen Fleken ganz überdekt zu seyn! Das thut die schöne Sonne: nemlich die ziehet alles auf. Die Junglinge führt die Bahn sie mit Reizen ihrer Stralen wie mit Rosen. Die Leiden scheinen so, die Oedipus getragen, als wie ein armer Mann klagt, dass ihm etwas fehle. Sohn Laios, armer Fremdling in Griechenland! Leben ist Tod, und Tod ist auch ein Leben.

—Friedrich Hölderlin

with God, like Hercules, that is an affliction. And
immortality amidst the envy of this life, to share in that,
is an affliction too. But this also is an affliction, when
a man is covered with freckles, to be wholly covered with
many a spot! The beautiful sun does that: for it rears up
all things. It leads young men along their course with the
allurements of its beams as though with roses. The
afflictions that Oedipus bore seem like this, as when a poor
man complains that there is something he lacks. Son of
Laios, poor stranger in Greece! Life is death, and death is
a kind of life.

—Friedrich Hölderlin
translated by Michael Hamburger

Index

Absence, 19, 188–89
Abyss, 81, 85–86, 100, 109, 123–24, 134, 154–55, 157, 169
Adaequatio, 87
Adequation, 82, 200
Aesthetics, 132–33, 161, 180, 206, 218
Affirmation, 47, 51, 52
Agon, 36, 38, 53
Agony, 43, 51
Alētheia, 31, 40, 81, 86–88, 101, 146, 159, 166, 169
Allegory, 156–57
Allemann, Beda, 175, 177–78, 188, 201–4, 219, 223
Amor Fati, 101, 158, 162
Anxiety (*Angst*), 36–40, 44, 48–51, 80, 122–23, 136
Anxiety of influence, 60
Appearance, 97, 99, 220–24, 228; as *Anschein*, 83, 85; as *Aufschein*, 83, 85, 159; as *Erscheinung*, 83, 149; as *Schein*, 83–86, 149
Apprehension, 118–19
Appropriation, 17, 24, 50, 78–80, 98, 105, 172
Arendt, Hannah, 61
Aristotle, 145, 180, 181
Art, 17, 20, 83–87, 103, 128–29, 131–73, 174, 179–80, 194, 199–200, 228; Greek, 199–201
Aufhebung, 40, 159, 207
Augstein, Rudolf, 111
Auseinandersetzung, 23, 27, 55–58, 81, 118–20, 125, 170, 184, 190–91, 209

Baeumler, Alfred, 61
Bataille, Georges, 126
Beaufret, Jean, 26, 180, 182
Beautiful, 161–62
Beauty, 26, 88, 157, 194, 206–7, 221, 223, 226–28
Being, 22–23, 28–29, 59, 67, 73, 74–76, 78, 80–81, 83, 87–88, 94, 102, 105, 107, 115, 119–23, 126–28, 132, 135, 140, 145, 147, 151, 153–58, 175, 186, 188–91, 193, 195, 197, 205, 207; call of, 17, 116, 152, 153; history of, 17, 21, 58, 69–70, 76, 134–35, 185, 196; and human being, 17–18, 20–21, 71, 105, 131–32, 153, 157, 167, 169–70, 172, 174, 176, 195; meaning of, 90, 101; question of, 23, 26, 58, 69, 70, 71, 90, 102, 107, 114; truth of, 29, 59, 99, 112, 115, 128, 167, 184, 193
Being-toward-death, 21, 30, 39–41, 43, 48–50, 80, 122, 125
Being-with (*Mitsein*), 29, 31–35, 37, 42, 44–46, 108
Beissner, Friedrich, 203, 220
Bildsamkeit, 220, 225–26
Birth, 31, 36, 38, 48, 50, 125, 140
Blanchot, Maurice, 34, 51, 108, 170, 171, 207, 208
Bleiben, 182, 198, 217
Bloom, Harold, 133

Böhlendorff, Casimir Ulrich, 198, 199, 200, 216

Buddeberg, Else, 175

Caesura, 179, 180, 183–84, 187, 203

Certainty, 37, 46, 77, 78–79

Certitude, 29, 74–75, 78–81, 87

Circulus Vitiosus Deus, 97, 102–3, 157

Communication, 31, 33, 43, 45, 56, 65–66, 134, 181

Community, 45, 108, 134, 137–39, 214

Concealment, 147–50, 160, 194, 222–23

Conflict, 118, 146–47, 159, 163, 171, 187–89

Conscience, 44; call of, 21, 41, 43, 48–49, 116

Createdness, 135–37, 139, 146, 155, 197, 227

Darstellung, 22, 76, 166, 168–70, 199, 211, 225; as poetic exposition, 202–5, 210, 212–13, 216–17

Dasein, 15, 17, 19, 20–24, 28–54, 55, 57–58, 71, 78–81, 85, 98, 101–2, 104–5, 107–10, 112, 116, 120–36, 154, 157, 169, 170–75, 180, 183–84, 190–91, 193, 195; Greek, 104, 119; as people, 115

Death, 30–31, 36–38, 40–41, 43–51, 97, 99, 121, 125, 127, 140, 154, 183, 189–90, 212–13, 224–25, 227

Deconstruction, 19, 129

Deinon, 120, 158

Deinotaton, 120, 124, 158

Deleuze, Gilles, 170

De Man, Paul, 19, 175

Derrida, Jacques, 19, 26, 108, 129, 143, 176, 194, 207

Descartes, René, 74–75, 78, 87

Destiny (*Geschick*), 38, 45–47, 62–63, 69, 97–98, 106, 108, 115, 125, 135, 141, 157, 158, 160, 174, 176–77, 183, 186–87, 196–97, 200, 206, 209, 215–16

Dialectic, 38, 125, 177, 187–88, 201–4, 207

Dialogue, 211–12

Dichtung, 20, 58, 77, 131, 137, 160–61. *See also* Poetry

Dikē, 120, 124, 128

Dilthey, Wilhelm, 52

Dionysian, 157, 160, 164; and Apollonian, 105, 161

Dionysus, 103, 188–89, 201

Disaster, 121–22, 124–25, 127, 131, 157, 169, 172

Discord. *See* Conflict

Distress, 17, 59, 65, 69–70, 95–96, 100, 158, 186, 195

Dostoevsky, Fedor, 168

Earth, 68, 124, 133, 140–50, 160, 171, 183–84, 190, 206, 211–13, 216–17

Eidos, 208

Empedocles, 126, 192–94

Ereignis, 17, 18

Eternal recurrence, 51, 78, 80, 83, 90, 92, 101, 152, 157, 158, 163

Eternal Return, 60, 64, 73, 77–78, 80, 83–84, 86–87, 90–91, 93–95, 97–103, 152, 157–59, 162–63

Existential analytic, 23, 28, 39, 52, 55, 68, 69, 72, 80, 91, 99, 122, 187

Eye too many, 105, 176–77, 200, 208, 217, 220, 224, 226

Factical situation, 31, 46, 52, 112

Fascination, 21, 39, 40, 44, 49, 50, 66, 80, 123, 139, 155, 170, 195–97

Fate, 45, 47–48, 50, 55, 57, 63, 85, 100, 104, 117, 183, 186

Fatum, 162

Figurality, 19, 150, 221, 224

Figure, 135, 144, 150, 160, 208, 226. *See also Gestalt*

Finitude, 16, 17, 19, 20, 21, 23, 45–46, 53, 81, 95, 101, 108–9, 111–12, 115, 123–24, 126–34, 150, 154–57, 169, 175–76, 178, 209, 228

Form, 88, 129, 132, 139, 144–45, 160, 162–64, 167–68, 180, 182, 219, 223, 228

Freedom, 35, 37–39, 41, 45–46, 48–50, 65, 74–77, 112, 122–28, 154, 163, 166, 169, 186–87, 228

Freud, Sigmund, 36, 49, 175, 205

Friend, 42–43, 49, 53

Fundamental metaphysical position, 56, 71, 87, 189

Gadamer, Hans-Georg, 25

Gasché, Rodolphe, 143, 166

Gefüge, 120, 156, 162

Gelassenheit, 20, 219

German Idealism, 22, 125, 177, 194, 201

Index

Germany, 104. *See also* People, German

Gestalt, 76, 118, 144–45, 150, 162, 166, 221, 223

Girard, René, 21, 36, 194

Granel, Gérard, 111, 112, 129, 157

Greece, 199, 203, 224; and Hesperia, 203

Guilt, 38–41, 44–45, 48–50, 79

Halliburton, David, 175, 192

Harries, Karsten, 47, 53, 109, 111, 112, 129, 175, 184, 197

Hegel, Georg Wilhelm Friedrich, 53, 75, 85, 96, 126, 132, 201, 203

Heidegger, Martin: political activity of, 110–14

—works of: "Age of the World View," 113; "Alētheia (Heraklit, Fragment 16)," 167; *Being and Time,* 17, 18, 20, 21, 23, 28–54, 55, 63, 70–72, 78–80, 89–91, 97, 98, 101, 105, 108, 110, 112, 113, 116, 122, 123, 125, 127, 132, 134, 135, 141, 153, 172, 183, 196, 218; *Habilitationsschrift,* 52, 134; "Hölderlin and the Essence of Poetry," 140, 174, 176, 191–93, 195, 211, 215, 219, 220; "Homecoming," 202; "Identity and Difference," 15, 143; *Introduction to Metaphysics,* 20, 26, 91, 104–30, 145, 153, 158, 160, 191; *Kant and the Problem of Metaphysics,* 16, 17, 22; *Letter on Humanism,* 18, 25, 71, 72, 76, 106, 113, 126, 184, 199, 222; *Nietzsche,* 20, 51, 55–103, 104, 107, 151, 157–58, 172; "Nietzsche's Word, 'God Is Dead,'" 76; *On the Way to Language,* 139; "Origin of the Work of Art," 17–20, 22, 103, 112, 120, 124, 128, 129, 131–57, 159, 160, 162, 163, 169, 174, 175, 178–80, 183, 187, 193–95, 197, 202, 209, 217, 221; "Overcoming of Metaphysics," 76; ". . . Poetically Man Dwells . . . ," 177, 222; "Rectorate 1933/34–Facts and Thoughts," 111; *Rektoratsrede,* 105–17, 123, 126, 127; "Remembrance," 195–218, 223; *Satz vom Grund,* 155; *Vom Wesen des Grundes,* 108; "What Are Poets For?," 185, 223; *What Is Called Thinking?,* 23, 76, 164; "What Is Metaphysics?," 106, 122–23, 126, 136, 139, 147, 153–54;

"Who Is Nietzsche's Zarathoustra?," 76

Hermeneutic circle, 19, 28, 29, 39–41, 68, 102, 116, 128, 133, 137, 140, 153, 157, 171–72, 196, 218

Heraclitus, 118–19, 141, 149

Hero, 46–47, 49, 53, 125, 218

Historicity, 26–27, 229; in *Being and Time,* 48, 50–52, 55, 57

Hölderlin, Friedrich, 17, 20, 21, 53, 60, 105, 120, 126, 130, 133, 135, 137, 155, 157, 160, 169, 173, 174–229; *Antigonä* (trans.), 180; "As on a Holiday," 183, 184, 196, 201, 209, 226; "Bedeutung der Tragödien," 219; "Bread and Wine," 201, 204; "Death of Empedocles," 126, 192, 194, 212; "Germanien," 174, 185, 193; "Grund zum Empedokles," 180, 194; "Homecoming," 184, 188; *Hyperion,* 228; "In lovely blueness . . . ," 176–78, 182, 213, 219–27, 234–39; "Mnemosyne," 204, 219, 220; "Notes," 177–78, 183–90, 203, 228; "Notes to Antigone," 177, 181, 189; "Notes to Oedipus," 155, 177, 181, 187, 189, 198, 209, 225; "Patmos," 68, 203, 216, 220, 227; "Remembrance," 19, 150, 161, 176, 178, 181, 192, 193, 195–219, 230–33; "Rhein," 174, 185, 188, 209, 211; "Sophocles," 126; "Über den Unterschied der Dichtarten," 179; "Über die Verfahrensweise des poetischen Geistes," 179; "Werden im Vergehen," 193

Holding-for-true, 73, 76, 77, 79–82, 93

Holy, 134, 144, 184–85, 197–98, 205–6, 208–13, 217–18, 222–23, 227

Homoiōsis, 82, 83, 87–88, 164, 166

Hyperion, 213, 228

Identification, 31, 33, 60, 218

Image, 171, 206–8, 219, 220, 221, 223, 224, 226, 227

Imagination, 77

Imitation, 180, 218, 221

Intimacy, 146, 184, 188, 190, 216

Justice, 64, 77, 84, 86, 172, 180, 228–29

Kant, Immanuel, 22, 60, 74, 77, 132, 153, 161, 182

Kehre, 21–23
Klossowski, Pierre, 168, 171, 172
Krell, David Farrell, 56, 61, 72

Lacoue-Labarthe, Philippe, 22, 37, 38, 52, 111–12, 125, 169, 180, 194, 199, 200
Language, 23, 112, 113, 118, 129, 137, 139, 143, 170–71, 176, 180, 183, 189–95, 197, 228; Greek, 120
Leibnitz, Gottfried Wilhelm von, 75
Logos, 118, 120

Mallarmé, Stéphane, 24, 127, 145
Man, question of, 21–24, 71, 89, 95, 134, 174
Marx, Werner, 26, 27
Measure, 64, 137, 140, 142, 155, 179, 203, 205, 209, 219–24, 226–28
Metaphysical tradition, 73, 75, 81, 113
Metaphysics, 22, 24, 29, 59–60, 66–69, 71, 74, 77, 78, 81, 90, 99, 101, 102, 124, 165, 178, 202; history of, 20, 76
Metaphysics of subjectivity, 16, 22, 23, 71–75, 78, 80, 86–88, 92, 96, 106, 113, 144, 166, 177, 201, 202, 204, 205, 228
Mimesis, 36, 63, 166, 168–71, 180, 194
Mimetic violence, 194
Mitsein. See Being-with
Mitte, 102, 147, 183, 190
Modern times, 59, 63, 72, 75, 81, 92, 113
Morphē, 145, 162. See also Form
Mortals, 18, 184
Mourning, 51, 183, 225
Murray, Michael, 175, 215

Nancy, Jean-Luc, 22, 37, 153, 168, 182
Napoleon, 104
Nationalism, 75, 106
National Socialism, 106, 111, 161
National Socialist Party, 61, 111, 114
Nearness. See Proximity
Nichtung, 122–24, 128, 136, 147–49, 154
Nietzsche, Friedrich, 17, 20, 21, 51–53, 55–103, 105, 116, 122, 126, 130, 132, 133, 134, 149–50, 152, 153, 156, 157–73, 189, 214; *Antichrist*, 165; *Beyond Good and Evil*, 97; *Ecce Homo*, 58, 63, 94, 132, 156, 165–70; *Gay Science*, 94, 101; *Nietzsche contra Wagner*, 165; *Thus Spake Zarathoustra*, 164; *Twilight of the Idols*,
165, 166; *Use and Abuse of History*, 52; *Wagner Case*, 165; *Will to Power*, 66, 73, 164
Nihilism, 62, 90, 96–100, 158, 159
Nothing, 80, 92, 95, 99, 122–23, 136
Nothingness, 38, 103
Nullity, 38, 44, 49, 50, 190

Oedipus, 104, 176–77, 181–83, 186–87, 189, 225, 226
Ontological difference, 57, 59, 80, 101, 129, 156, 169, 183
Origin, 24, 92, 132, 137, 152, 155, 184, 186–87, 198, 202, 206, 208, 213–17

Panthea, 192, 218
Parmenides, 143
Passion, 66, 102, 104–5, 161, 167–68, 177, 199
People, 45, 108, 129, 140–41, 190, 191, 193, 210, 212, 217; German, 105, 115–16, 161, 174, 199, 218, 226; Greek, 107, 109, 117, 146, 199, 200
Physis, 73–74, 87, 90, 117–18, 120, 121, 141, 149, 160, 184
Plato, 36, 74, 106, 158, 170, 180, 194, 228
Poetic character, 216–17, 226–28
Poetizing, 76, 77, 83
Poetry, 58, 174, 190–92, 194–96, 198. See also Dichtung
Pöggeller, Otto, 26, 175
Poiēsis, 76, 128, 169
Polemos, 118–19
Polis, 109, 112, 129
Possible, 48, 57, 94, 100, 193
Presence, 80, 87, 188, 189
Project, 19, 20, 22, 24, 39, 40, 56–57, 64, 82, 89–91, 94, 95, 99, 101, 102, 107–8, 112, 114, 116, 131, 133, 137, 142, 153–54, 157, 163, 175, 183, 196, 217, 228
Projection, 44, 45, 135, 136, 139, 211
Prometheus, 117–18
Proximity, 19, 59–60, 73, 105, 154, 167, 184, 189, 195, 199, 203, 205, 208, 216, 223
Psychoanalysis, 133, 169, 202, 206

Remaining, 215. See also Bleiben
Remembrance, 195–96, 198, 200, 204–17
Repetition, 16, 36, 39, 40, 49–52, 55, 79–81, 90, 91, 93–95, 100, 105, 116,

Index

137, 144, 152, 158, 159, 190, 196, 200,
202, 205, 210, 211; in interpretation,
23, 46–48, 56–57, 64, 70, 72, 218
Representation, 15, 16, 74–78, 80, 82, 87,
92, 113, 146, 155, 161, 179, 180
Resoluteness (*Entschlossenheit*), 21, 39–41,
44, 46–48, 72, 78–80, 117, 119, 213
Resolve, 115–17, 186
Richardson, William J., 26
Rilke, Rainer Maria, 162, 185
Riss, 124, 139, 142–48, 152, 155, 180
Rivalry, 21, 35, 36, 53, 60

Sacrifice, 126, 151, 193, 214–15, 218
Saying, 129, 137, 139, 183, 185, 191, 196–
97, 205, 208, 211, 212, 214, 217, 223,
228
Schelling, Friedrich, 75, 104, 125–26, 187
Schiller, Friedrich, 177
Schopenhauer, Arthur, 75, 97
Schürmann, Reiner, 24, 27
Science, 16, 62, 88, 105–7, 110, 111,
115–17
Self, 22, 28–32, 48–50, 75, 76, 78, 80, 98,
108, 119, 123, 168, 170, 174, 186,
191, 202, 205, 213, 217, 219, 226–27
Self-affirmation (*Selbstbehauptung*), 19–20,
78, 80, 83, 87, 105, 106, 109, 110,
114–19, 125, 127, 131, 143, 158, 170,
171, 175, 195, 218
Selfhood, 29, 108, 119, 195, 217
Shame, 167, 214, 227
Showing, 216–17, 220
Socrates, 164
Solitude, 31, 65, 97–101, 137, 139, 140,
160, 192, 212–14
Sophocles, 180, 184, 193, 194, 200, 203,
225, 228; *Antigone*, 119, 126, 189;
Oedipus at Colonus, 182; *Oedipus the
King*, 126, 187
Spirit, 53–54, 104–7, 115, 132, 184, 201–4,
206, 224, 227
State, 107, 109, 111
Stellen, 144
Strangeness, 18, 119, 125, 134, 136, 145,
146, 157, 208, 223, 227
Struggle, 45, 47, 85, 118
Style, 103, 105, 132, 160–61, 163, 168, 172
Subject, 16, 23, 28, 29, 32, 33, 52, 53,
69, 74–78, 80, 87–88, 94, 95, 109–10,
126, 144, 155, 165, 166, 169, 170

Subjectivity, 72, 74–75, 77, 87, 88, 106,
113, 133
Sublime, 132, 135, 162
Suicide, 125–28
Szondi, Peter, 38, 125, 199

Teaching, 64–68
Technē, 20, 120–22, 124, 128, 154
Technik, 22, 62, 119, 199
Thēoria, 107, 117
Thesis, 22, 128, 131, 144, 151, 170, 217
They (*das Man*), 30–31, 48, 51
Thrownness, 38–42, 44, 46, 48, 50, 123,
132
Tragedy, 86, 104, 117, 125, 126, 177–79,
188–90; and dialectic, 50
Tragic, 85, 180, 189
Tragic experience, 131, 157, 158, 179, 181,
183, 194
Transcendence, 15, 91, 107–9, 122–24, 136
Transfiguration, 83, 85, 86, 93, 151, 158,
159
Translation, 199–201, 203
Truth, 17, 56, 95–97, 115, 121, 124, 128,
132–37, 139, 140, 142, 146–47, 150–52,
156, 160, 163, 169, 171, 189; of Dasein's
existence, 31, 79–80; in modern
metaphysics, 74, 77, 81, 87–90; in
Nietzsche's thought, 73, 81, 83–86, 93,
94, 159

Uncanniness (*Unheimlichkeit*), 37, 39, 41,
50, 65, 80, 95, 103, 121, 122, 127,
224
Uncanny (*das Unheimliche*), 120; in
Freudian sense, 49, 171
Unconcealedness, 101, 135, 146, 148, 159
Unconcealment, 86–87, 117, 135, 137, 144,
148–49, 156, 160
Ungleiche, 209–10, 218–19
University, 106, 109, 111, 114, 115

Value, 73, 74, 77, 97; transvaluation of,
102
Van Gogh, Vincent, 138
Vaterländische Umkehr, 185, 203, 219
Verstellung, 149

Waiblinger, Wilhelm, 220
Warminski, Andrzej, 179, 199
White, David A., 175, 209, 222

245

Will, 69, 75, 77, 78, 85, 89, 92, 95, 97, 99, 100, 102, 115–17, 123, 132, 151, 163, 186, 196, 197, 212

Will to Power, 67, 70, 73, 75, 77–79, 83–84, 86, 87, 92, 95, 97, 99, 102, 151–52, 158–60, 162, 165–67, 170

Wilmans, Friedrich, 200

Witness, 43, 44, 140, 175, 191

Wolff, Georg, 111

Work of art, 124, 128, 131–56, 159, 194, 197

World, 30, 31, 34, 37, 47, 65, 66, 79, 89, 93, 96, 102, 105, 107, 108, 112, 113, 117, 118, 129, 133, 140–50, 160, 165, 171, 180

Writing, 143, 176

Yorck von Wartenburg, Paul Graf, 52, 54

Zarathoustra, 98, 101

Library of Congress Cataloging-in-Publication Data

Fynsk, Christopher, 1952-
   Heidegger, thought and historicity.

   Includes index.
   1. Heidegger, Martin, 1889-1976.   I. Title.
B3279.H49F96   1986   193   86-47640
ISBN 0-8014-1879-8 (alk. paper)